Computer Systems

Architecture, Networks and Commu

Computer Systems
Architecture, Networks and Communications

SEBASTIAN COOPE
Consultant and Trainer, Mobile Computing and Network Security

JOHN COWLEY
Lecturer, School of Computing, Staffordshire University

NEIL WILLIS
Dean of School of Computing, Staffordshire University

London · Boston · Burr Ridge, IL · Dubuque, IA · Madison, WI · New York
San Francisco · St Louis · Bangkok · Bogotá · Caracas · Kuala Lumpur
Lisbon · Madrid · Mexico City · Milan · Montreal · New Delhi
Santiago · Seoul · Singapore · Sydney · Taipei · Toronto

Computer Systems Architecture, Networks and Communications
Willis, Coope, Cowley
ISBN 0-07-709803-X

Published by McGraw-Hill Education
Shoppenhangers Road
Maidenhead
Berkshire
SL6 2QL
Telephone: 44 (0) 1628 502 500
Fax: 44 (0) 1628 770 224
Website: www.mcgraw-hill.co.uk

British Library Cataloguing in Publication Data
A catalogue record for this book is available from the British Library

Library of Congress Cataloging in Publication Data
The Library of Congress data for this book has been applied for from the Library of Congress

Acquisitions Editor: Conor Graham
Senior Development Editor: Caroline Howell
Editorial Assistant: Paul von Kesmark
Senior Marketing Manager: Jacqueline Harbour
Senior Production Manager: Max Elvey
Production Editor: Eleanor Hayes
New Media Developer: Douglas Greenwood

Produced for McGraw-Hill by Steven Gardiner Ltd, Cambridge
Text design by Claire Brodmann Book Designs, Lichfield, Staffs
Cover design by Kate Hybert Design
Printed and bound in Great Britain by Bell and Bain Ltd, Glasgow

The McGraw·Hill Companies

Contents

Preface

This book has been written to provide a student text that presents, in a logical and straightforward way, the ideas and concepts of computer architecture and the principles of computer communication. It is particularly suitable for students taking computing or computer science degree courses, or for those taking HNC/D courses in computing. It covers the range of computer architecture from the very building blocks that go to make up a computer – the logic gate – to collections of computers linked together – networks.

This is a new text covering a wide spectrum, but it builds on some aspects of a previous textbook of one of the authors.

No prerequisite knowledge of computers is assumed, but many of the concepts will be more easily grasped if they are related to a parallel course in low-level programming. Indeed, low-level programming might well form the practical or laboratory part of such a course in computer architecture.

The discussion is not restricted to one particular processor: in illustration of the principles, examples are drawn from a variety of computers. Clearly, however, the principles can equally well be illustrated by reference to the particular facilities available on the computer used for the student's practical work. Most chapters include problems designed to reinforce understanding of the application of the theory.

A general introduction, in Chapter 1, to all the basic concepts of computer systems gives definitions of processors, memory, file store, peripherals, communications and operating system. The following chapters then form three broad sections.

Chapter 2 deals with number systems and with the ways in which data can be represented in a computer. Chapter 3 describes the basic logic circuits that are the building blocks in the design of a computer.

In Chapters 4 to 11 the structure of a single processor system is explained in detail: memory, software, the CPU, peripherals, file storage, interrupt mechanisms, data transfer and building a small computer system.

The final chapters are concerned with networks of computers. After defining a network and discussing its possible topologies, Chapter 12 introduces the ideas of international standards, the ISO OSI reference model and the Internet. Chapters 13 to 15 then deal with the physical transmission, network types particularly point-to-point and broadcast, and communication protocols. Having identified the principal functional tasks of protocols, Chapter 15 examines, in some detail, protocols at all levels of the OSI model, with a particular emphasis on the TCP/IP protocol stack. Chapter 16 discusses the installation and management of a local area network.

Acknowledgements

The authors would like to thank Dave Hatter for his help in initiating this project, and to all students who, over the years, have helped to refine our material.

The publishers would like to thank the reviewers of the manuscript whose helpful advice contributed to the development of the book:

Saad Ali Amin, *University of Coventry*

Kevan Buckley, *University of Wolverhampton*

Craig Duffy, *University of the West of England*

Muthana Jabbar, *Middlesex University*

Aboubaker Lasebae, *Middlesex University*

Alastair Railton, *University of Coventry*

Ian Vlaeminke, *De Montfort University*

Yong Xue, *University of North London*

Finally, the author Sebastian Coope would like to acknowledge the inspiration and support given by his mother Dr Jean Coope, and dedicates his contribution to this book to her.

Basic concepts of computer systems

Modern computer systems are constructed from various different component parts interconnected to produce machines of various different characteristics. These computer systems are used for a wide variety of tasks from applications such as word processing, spreadsheet and database, to controlling a mobile phone or a passenger jet. This chapter will introduce the features that are common to all these different systems.

1.1 COMPUTERS AND COMPUTER SYSTEMS

Electronic computer systems have come a long way since their initial development in the late 1940s. Systems are now capable of storing vast amounts of information and processing that information at great speed. The Cray TE-350 is capable of performing over 3,000,000,000,000 floating point calculations per second (www.cray.com). Considerable advances have also been made in the area of miniaturisation: for example a web server has been developed at Stanford Wearables Lab that can be fitted into a matchbox (wearables.stanford.edu). Figure 1.1 shows pictures of these systems; the web server is shown standing on a computer keyboard.

These advances in computer system performance have also been matched by significant developments in software technology, which allows systems to perform more complex and diverse tasks than ever before. These new power-hungry applications have created an unceasing demand for increased system performance. The development of faster processors, quicker memory with increased storage capacity and more complex and demanding software continues unabated.

This demand for speed is particularly an issue where systems are expected to display some degree of intelligence, for example, speech and video processing and the understanding of text. One of the ultimate aims of a lot of research in this area is to develop computer systems that will communicate like a human being (i.e., understand and reproduce natural spoken language). Another area where the demand for computing power is practically limitless is scientific modelling, simulation and prediction. For example, weather-forecasting systems are required to run models using vast amounts of data to produce results within reasonable time scales.

Figure 1.1 Large and small computer systems
left Cray computer; *right* miniature web server

With all the advances in hardware performance it is important to note that software applications have not always increased in performance (efficiency) and a lot of new applications in fact run slower (for a given hardware platform) than their predecessors. This is due to a number of factors including more complex software requirements (e.g., word-processors that support embedded graphics), less emphasis on optimisation, greater memory requirements (particularly for the operating system) and introduction of new slower technologies such as interpreted languages like Java and Javascript. This means that the importance of improving hardware performance is as important as ever and will be for the foreseeable future.

1.1.1 WHAT IS A COMPUTER?

A computer is a device which given a set of instructions can be used to perform a given task or tasks. The computer reads in information (instructions or data), does some processing and generally stores or outputs some result. The computer has internal storage (for its instructions and data) and also has mechanisms to communicate with the outside world, input for reading data into the computer and output for writing data out.

1.1.2 COMPUTER SYSTEMS

A computer system is the combination of a computer plus software plus support hardware, which work together to perform a task. Computer systems can be linked together with other computer systems using a computer network. The computer network transfers data between the systems allowing them to communicate. Most computer systems nowadays provide connectivity to a network, more often than not to the Internet (see 1.3.3).

A set of computer systems connected to a network, and configured to work together on a given task is referred to as a distributed system. One of the advantages of a distributed system is that many computers can be linked together to provide a level of performance and/or storage capability that would be beyond any of the computers working alone. An example of a distributed computer system is the World Wide Web; this uses millions of computers, which work together storing and delivering data across the world using the Internet to communicate.

Computer systems can be classified as general purpose or dedicated. An example of a general-purpose computer is the PC. It can be used for a wide variety of tasks – for example, word-processing (which was used to write this book), spreadsheets and database applications. The computer system is loaded up with different software depending on the task required.

A dedicated computer system is designed for a single purpose only, with the software being loaded up at manufacture. For dedicated systems designed to control a piece of electronic equipment the software is usually stored on a chip. These are referred to as embedded systems as the computer is 'embedded' within another product (e.g., a videocassette recorder, washing machine). An example of an embedded system is the cell phone. The system needs to read the keypad, control the display, set up calls, update the phone's SIM card and many other functions. Both dedicated and general purpose computer systems are similar in their internal design but they do differ somewhat in their features and physical design (imagine carrying a desktop PC around to make your phone calls).

1.2 BASIC COMPONENTS OF A COMPUTER SYSTEM

Figure 1.2 shows a block diagram of a basic computer system. This is a highly simplified representation of the computer system displaying the most important components.

1.2.1 CENTRAL PROCESSING UNIT

The Central Processing Unit (CPU) controls the operation of the computer. It is responsible for carrying out (executing) lists of instructions (software)

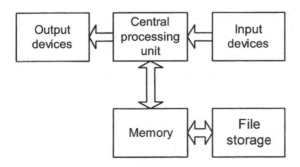

Figure 1.2 Computer system block diagram

stored in the computer's memory. The CPU can also write data to output devices, read data from input devices and store and retrieve data from the system's memory and file storage.

Modern CPUs can execute multiple instructions at the same time (concurrent processing). Another method used is to split the execution of individual instructions into more than one process allowing more than one instruction to be worked on at the same time. This technique, called pipelining, is similar to how a production line is used to work on multiple products at the same time (e.g., in a car production line). Some systems use a number of processors connected together on the same circuit board in what is termed Multi Process Architecture. Many network servers use this technique to allow them to provide data for many client computers simultaneously

In this book examples will be provided using both the Motorola PowerPC® and Intel Pentium® processors. These are two of the most commonly used processors in general purpose computing and, in the case of the Intel Pentium®, the most commonly used processor for personal computing.

1.2.2 MEMORY

The computer's memory (or primary storage) is used to store two types of information, instructions and data. The instructions are read from the memory by the CPU, which then carries them out in sequence. The list of instructions that is stored in memory for a given task is called a computer program. The program that the CPU executes processes a set of data that is stored in memory. For example with a word-processing program the data would be the document that is currently being edited.

Both the instructions and data are stored in memory cells called memory locations, see Figure 1.3. Each of the locations is referred to using a number called its address. The first address is 0, the second 1, etc. The

Address	Contents
6	94
5	23
4	170
3	85
2	0
1	101
0	45

Figure 1.3 Main memory organisation

number stored in the memory location is referred to as the location's content. In Figure 1.3 the location with address 5 contains the number 23.

Each memory location is only capable of storing numbers. If characters or other information have to be stored then this must be converted to a numeric form first. Each of the instructions that the CPU is capable of executing is allocated a number (called its opcode). This allows the computer's program to be stored in the memory. CPUs cannot distinguish between locations containing data, code or just random garbage. This means that it is crucial for memory to be loaded with the correct data and instructions before the CPU can do any useful work.

Memory can provide data to the CPU very quickly. Typically access time is measured in nanoseconds (one nanosecond = 1/1,000,000,000 seconds). The Motorola MCM63P737A, for example, provides access times as short as 2.5 nanoseconds. The faster the memory chip access time the faster the CPU can operate. One problem with fast memory is that is relatively expensive so most systems use a mixture of fast and slower memory employing a technique called caching.

1.2.3   FILE STORAGE

File (or secondary) storage provides bulk storage for the computer system. The storage capacity of file storage is typically a hundred times the capacity of the computer's memory and is also cheaper per unit of storage than memory by at least ten fold.

The programs and data are stored in file storage in logical units called files. These files are organised and grouped together to form a file system. The file system on most computer systems is controlled in such a way that users cannot access certain files that they do not have the correct permissions for. This allows the secure storage of sensitive data for multi-user systems.

File storage has much slower access times than the memory (typically at least a thousand times slower). For this reason the programs must be loaded up into memory before being executed by the processor. Since main memory is relatively expensive, the computer system is not provided with enough to store all the programs the user might want to execute. File storage is used to keep copies of data and programs not currently being used by the computer system. When required the computer loads the program into memory. File storage (unlike the memory) does not lose data when the computer system is switched off making it suitable for offline storage of programs and data.

1.2.4   PERIPHERALS

The computer system needs a way of communicating with the outside world. Peripherals are classified into three groups: input devices (e.g., keyboard or mouse), output devices (e.g., VDU or printer) and I/O devices that can do both functions (e.g., a network card or modem). Peripheral technology has advanced at a very rapid pace with headsets that allow the projection of 3D graphics (for Virtual Reality) and colour printing technology that can produce images of photographic quality.

The correct selection and connection of peripherals for the computer system is critical to its functionality. For example, a system that needs to produce photo images would require a very high-resolution colour printer. Some peripherals such as a radio transceiver or keypad would only be relevant to dedicated systems such as cellular phone. The peripherals are connected to the main system via a standard connection called an interface. The selection of an appropriate interface for each peripheral is an important design decision when constructing the system.

1.3   PUTTING IT ALL TOGETHER

So far we have discussed each of the component parts of the computer system in isolation. When designing a computer system choices have to made according to budget, purpose of the system, required processing power etc. Each component must be chosen appropriately and decisions made about component interconnection, interfacing and software. In general this involves a trade off between budget and processing power (faster computer hardware is more expensive) but a judicious choice of software and well-optimised hardware can also produce a lot of gains in system performance with no increase in cost. We will now discuss in brief some of the design decisions necessary when building a system.

1.3.1   INTERCONNECTION

The way that the system components are interconnected can affect overall performance considerably. By providing dedicated links (mesh interconnection) between each pair of components the speed of data transfer can be increased substantially. The problem with this approach is that it increases the system cost and complexity, since each component will require interface electronics to every other component. Also it will be difficult to manufacture the hardware since the number of interconnecting wires will be very great.

At the other extreme all the components can be connected to a common channel called a bus. This is cheaper than the mesh approach but slower. This slowness is due to the fact that each component has to share the bus and wait for others to finish access before they can start their transfer. Figure 1.4 shows the two configurations. In fact, a compromise between these two extremes is commonly used with systems providing multiple buses for component interconnection.

1.3.2   OPERATING SYSTEM

Most computer systems when delivered come complete with a basic set of software called the operating system. The operating system is responsible for interfacing at a low level with the system's hardware and controlling the execution of programs within the computer. Operating systems can be classified in various ways; for example, single tasking (capable of executing only one program at a time) and multitasking (capable of executing many programs simultaneously). Another distinction is between single and multi-

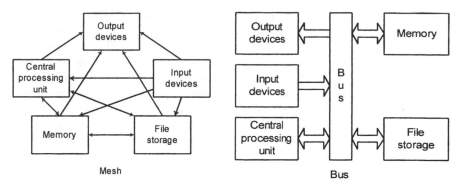

Figure 1.4 System interconnection

user operating systems (multi-user systems differentiate between different users of the system; for example stopping one user accessing or deleting another user's files).

Operating system functions include low level control of hardware, sharing memory securely between programs, scheduling the execution of different tasks (multitasking systems only) and facilitating communication across a network. The correct choice of operating system can make a great deal of difference to overall system performance in terms of the optimal use of memory, speed of execution and system reliability. A vigorous debate has been raging for some time between advocates of both the Windows and Linux operating systems. This book does not intend to add to that discussion.

Some operating systems are designed to run on particular hardware platforms while others are available for a wider range of CPUs and different configurations. The latter are termed portable. If a single operating system is required for a set of systems that will be using many different hardware platforms, finding a portable operating system will be of critical concern.

1.3.3   NETWORKS AND DISTRIBUTED SYSTEMS

These days most computer systems do not work alone but are connected to a network allowing them to communicate with others. Reliable and efficient intercommunication between systems which are using different hardware and software and may be located far apart, is a non-trivial task. A lot of work has been done in this area, particularly in producing standards which can be used to facilitate communication between heterogeneous systems. Another important development in networking is the increased performance and use of the Internet, a global network, which provides connectivity for millions of computer users.

The communication between systems is controlled by a set of rules and standards called a protocol. For two machines to communicate they must both 'talk' the same protocol. The most commonly used family of protocols is TCP/IP. This is used by the Internet and many other networks to provide the reliable transfer of data.

As explained before, in a distributed system many computers are interconnected and co-operate with each other to perform a particular task. An example of such a system would be a distributed database in which data is stored in various different locations across the network. This has a number of advantages; for example, data may be accessible quickly from many different locations and the system may still work if one or more computers fail. That given, distributed database systems are more complex to maintain and require complex protocols to ensure all copies of the data are kept up to date. Distributed systems can also have their performance affected by the speed (bandwidth) limitations of the network they are connected to. This is particularly a problem with global networks (such as the Internet) as many systems may be sharing the same long-distance connection.

1.4   SUMMARY

In this chapter we have discussed what the computer system can do, how it is constructed and have described in brief some of its component parts. We have also seen how the computer system consists of both hardware and software and how both must work together to achieve optimal performance. In Chapters 2 to 11 we will examine in detail the function of the system's component parts and how they are integrated to produce a functioning whole. Chapters 12 to 15 cover distributed systems and networking, explaining how computers are interconnected and can be made to work together.

1.5   EXERCISES

1   Find out in what ways computer system automation have been used to improve the following public services:
health provision
education
policing
emergency services
a library

2   Find out how distributed computer systems have been used to solve computationally difficult problems. (*Hint*: look for SETI on the World Wide Web.) Try and find three different applications and describe the distributed systems used.

3   What are the forces that drive the search for faster and more efficient computer hardware?

2 Number systems and data representation

2.1 NUMBER SYSTEMS

As explained in Chapter 1, modern computer systems process information internally in the form of numbers. The most commonly used number system used in everyday life is the decimal system (based on 10). The decimal number system uses the digits 0 to 9 to represent the first 10 integers and then uses place values to extend this system for greater numbers. For example the number 3567.89 is broken up into:

$3 \times 10^3 + 5 \times 10^2 + 6 \times 10^1 + 7 \times 10^0 + 8 \times 10^{-1} + 9 \times 10^{-2}$
1000s   100s 10s   1s   0.1s   0.01s

$= 3000 + 500 + 60 + 7 + 0.8 + 0.09$

Moving to the left, each place value is worth ten times the previous place value. Modern computer systems use a different number system called binary (based on 2) to represent numbers internally. The reason for this is that it simplifies the construction of electronic circuits since binary only uses two digits 0 and 1. A circuit that represents a binary digit needs only to have two valid states (for decimal it would have to have 10).

With binary numbers the place values go up by a factor of two as you move left.

$10100101_2 =$

$1 \times 2^7 + 0 \times 2^6 + 1 \times 2^5 + 0 \times 2^4 + 0 \times 2^3 + 1 \times 2^2 + 0 \times 2^1 + 1 \times 2^0$
128s   64s   32s   16s   8s   4s   2s   1s

$= 128 + 32 + 4 + 1 = 145$ decimal

In computing, the term binary digit is replaced by the abbreviation 'bit'. Note we can represent fractions in binary by putting digits after the point symbol (not decimal point but bicimal point).

$101.011_2 = 1 \times 2^2 + 0 \times 2^1 + 1 \times 2^0 + 0 \times 2^{-1} + 1 \times 2^{-2} + 1 \times 2^{-3}$
             4s   2s   1s   0.5s   0.25s   0.125s

$= 4 + 1 + 0.25 + 0.125 = 5.375$ decimal

Note this representation is called fixed point because the computer will allocate a fixed number of bits for the whole and fractional parts with the bicimal point fixed between the two.

Two other number systems commonly used in computing are octal (base 8) and hexadecimal (base 16). Both these number systems are convenient for computing since they allow binary numbers to be represented in a shorthand form. For octal 3 binary digits (or bits) represent one octal digit (range 0–7) and in hexadecimal 4 bits make up one digit (range 0–15).

In hexadecimal we have 15 possible digits. This creates a problem, since we run out of numeric digits at 9. To get round this the letters A–F are used to represent the numbers 10 to 15.

Table 2.1 shows how the numbers 0 to 15 are represented in binary, octal and hexadecimal.

Here is how the decimal number 197 is represented in binary, octal and hexadecimal.

$$\text{Binary } 1100101_2 = \quad 1 \quad\quad 1 \quad\quad 0 \quad\quad 0 \quad\quad 0 \quad\quad 1$$
$$= 1 \times 2^7 + 1 \times 2^6 + 0 \times 2^5 + 0 \times 2^4 + 0 \times 2^3 + 1 \times 2^2 +$$
$$0 \quad\quad 1$$
$$0 \times 2^1 + 1 \times 2^0$$

$$\text{Octal } 305_8 = \quad 3 \quad\quad 0 \quad\quad 5$$
$$= 3 \times 8^2 + 0 \times 8^1 + 5 \times 8^0$$

$$\text{Hexadecimal } C5_{16} = \quad C \quad\quad 5$$
$$= C \times 16^1 + 5 \times 16^0 = 12 \times 16 + 5$$

Table 2.1 Number conversion table

Decimal	Binary	Octal	Hexadecimal
0	0	0	0
1	1	1	1
2	10	2	2
3	11	3	3
4	100	4	4
5	101	5	5
6	110	6	6
7	111	7	7
8	1000	10	8
9	1001	11	9
10	1010	12	A
11	1011	13	B
12	1100	14	C
13	1101	15	D
14	1110	16	E
15	1111	17	F

Note the use of the subscript after the number to signify the base (or radix) of the number system; without this it would not be possible to distinguish between 100 decimal and 100 binary (4 in decimal).

2.2 CONVERSION BETWEEN NUMBER SYSTEMS

This section describes how to convert between various number systems by hand but, of course, many calculators are now capable of this function.

2.2.1 BETWEEN BINARY AND OCTAL

Each octal digital can be represented by three binary digits. This means we can convert from binary to octal by taking each group of 3 bits and replacing them with one octal digit, working from right to left (starting at the bicimal point). For a number containing digits after the bicimal point you process the fractional part from right to left. For example, to convert the binary number 10100010101_2 into octal:

Assemble the digits into groups of 3; *note*: you have to pad the number with an insignificant zero, to complete the left-most group.

```
Binary        010 100 010 101
Octal digits   2   4   2   5
```

Here is an example with a fractional part; *note* the number has to be padded front and back to complete the conversion:

```
Binary        1101111.0101111 = 001 101 111. 010 111 100
Octal digits                     1   5   7.   2   7   4
```

Result = 157.274

2.2.2 BETWEEN BINARY AND HEXADECIMAL

Each hexadecimal digit is represented by 4 bits and the conversion method is similar to the one used for octal except the bits are assembled into groups of four instead of three.

Let's look at the previous example again:

10100010101_2

Group the digits into groups of 4.

```
Binary 10100010101 = 0101 0001 0101
Hexadecimal digits    5    1    5     = 515₁₆
```

Here is the example with a fractional part:

```
1101111.0101111   = 0110 1111. 0101 1110
Hexadecimal digits   6    F.    5    E = 6F.5E₁₆
```

2.2.3 BETWEEN BINARY AND DECIMAL

To convert from decimal to binary keep dividing the number by two (using integer division) until you reach zero. After each division the remainder gives you the next bit in the binary number (reading from right to left).

So, starting with 178:

Dividend	Remainder after division by two	
178	is even so 0	0
89	is odd so 1	10
44	is even so 0	010
22	is even so 0	0010
11	is odd so 1	10010
5	is odd so 1	110010
2	is even so 0	0110010
1	is odd so 1	10110010
0	Finish	

Therefore $178_{10} = 10110010_2$.

To convert the fractional part of the number you keep multiplying by two; if the result is odd you add a one to the right side of the binary fraction; if the result is even you add a zero. You stop conversion when there is no fractional part left.

Example 42.6875_{10}

First convert left-hand side (integer part) using the previous method

$42 = 101010_2$

Now, starting with 101010 as the integer part, keep multiplying by two to get the fractional bits.

Multiplicand		Binary number so far
42.6875		101010.
85.375	is odd so add a 1	101010.1
170.75	is even so add a 0	101010.10
341.5	is odd so add a 1	101010.101
683	is odd so add a 1	101010.1011

So $42.6875_{10} = 101010.1011_2$.

Note that some numbers that can be represented easily in decimal produce a recurring fraction when converted to binary (for example, try converting 0.2 to binary). To convert from binary to decimal just add up the powers of two that correspond to bits set to one in the binary number (see the example in section 2.1).

Further examples

Convert 100 to binary and then to hexadecimal, convert the hexadecimal value back to decimal to confirm the result.

Dividend	Remainder after division by two	
100	is even so 0	0
50	is even so 0	00
25	is odd so 1	100
12	is even so 0	0100
6	is even so 0	00100
3	is odd so 1	100100
1	is odd so 1	1100100
0	Finish	

Therefore $100_{10} = 1100100_2$.

Now convert to hexadecimal

Binary 1100100   = 0110 0100
Hexadecimal digits   6   4

Therefore $100_{10} = 64_{16}$.

Converting back to decimal

$64^{16} = 6 \times 16^1 + 4 \times 16^0 = 6 \times 16 + 4 = 96 + 4 = 100$

Convert decimal 3.1415 to 8 binary places and calculate the error incurred in this process.

$3 = 11_2$

Multiplicand		Binary number
3.1415		11.
6.283	is even so add a 0	11.0
12.566	is even so add a 0	11.00
25.132	is odd so add a 1	11.001
50.264	is even so add a 0	11.0010
100.528	is even so add a 0	11.00100
201.056	is odd so add a 1	11.001001
402.112	is even so add a 0	11.0010010
804.224	is even so add a 0	11.00100100

$3.1415_{10} = 11.00100100_2$

$11.001001_2 = 1 \times 2^1 + 1 \times 2^0 + 1 \times 2^{-3} + 1 \times 2^{-6}$

$= 2 + 1 + 1/8 + 1/64 \qquad = 3.140625$

Error $= 3.1415 - 3.140625 = 0.000875$ or 0.02%

2.3 THE REPRESENTATION OF NUMERICAL INFORMATION

2.3.1 INTEGERS

To store a number inside the computer it must first be converted to binary and then written into a memory location. What we looked at in previous examples was the representation of whole numbers (0, 1 , 2 .. etc.) and fractions. For example, to represent the decimal number 19 in an 8-bit memory location we would store the number 00010011.

Many applications require the representation of both negative and positive values. For example if you were storing an individual's bank balance they might be in debt to the bank. These values are referred to as signed and in this section we will look at the two most commonly used techniques used to represent signed numbers, sign and magnitude and two's complement.

Sign and magnitude

Using this representation the most significant bit of the number (called the sign bit) represents the sign (zero for positive or one for negative). The rest of the bits are used to store the absolute value (or magnitude) of the number.

Here are a few examples using 16-bit representation.

Decimal	Binary
−4	1000000000000100
+100	0000000001100100
−20	1000000000010100
−100	1000000001100100

Note that zero has two representations (+0 and −0). This may cause confusion in a system that did not take this into account since −0 is not binary equivalent to +0.

Two's complement

In two's complement, as in sign and magnitude, the most significant bit also represents the sign. For positive numbers in two's complement, the representation is identical to signed magnitude. Negative numbers, however, are stored as the two's complement of the equivalent positive value. To get the two's complement of a number reverse (complement) all the bits (replacing 1 with 0 and vice-versa) and add one.

In the following example we calculate −20 in 8-bit two's complement.

```
+20          = 00010100
Complement = 11101011
                    1 +
−20          = 11101100
```

More examples

Represent −100 in 8-bit two's complement.

```
+100         = 01100100
Complement = 10011011
                    1 +
−100         = 10011100
```

Two's complement has a couple of advantages over signed magnitude. Firstly, there is only one representation of zero and, secondly, negative numbers can be added directly to positive numbers giving a correct result (this is not possible with signed magnitude).

Table 2.2   Integer ranges

Storage size	Min value	Max value
8 bit unsigned	0	255
8 bit signed	−128	+127
16 bit unsigned	0	65535
16 bit signed	−32767	+32768
32 bit signed	−2147483648	2147483647

Example −20 + 30

    −20 = 11101100
          00011110 +
          00001010 = 10

The carry into the ninth bit is lost since we are dealing with 8-bit numbers. The range of numbers that can be stored is dependent on the number of bits available and whether the number is signed or unsigned.

For unsigned integers the range is 0 to $2^N - 1$ and for signed integers the range is -2^{N-1} to $+2^{N-1} - 1$. Table 2.2 gives the storage range for some different sizes of memory storage.

When adding numbers together the computer program has to be aware of the possibility of overflow. This occurs if the result cannot be stored in the space available. For example, when adding the unsigned 8-bit numbers 200 and 100 the result is 300, this cannot be stored in an 8 bit unsigned representation (see Table 2.2), therefore resulting in overflow. The setting of the carry flag after addition indicates the unsigned overflow condition.

For signed arithmetic the rules are different; overflow is deemed to have occurred if two numbers of the same sign are added together giving a result of a different sign. For example, add −20,000 to −30,000 in signed 16-bit arithmetic.

    −20,000 = 1011000111100000
    −30,000 = 1000101011010000 +
              0011110010110000 = +15536

Since we have added two negative numbers together the result should be negative, since it is positive we can tell that a signed overflow has occurred.

Fractional accuracy

The number of bits in the fractional part of the number determines the accuracy obtainable. The maximum error that will be obtained when storing the number will be $\pm 1/(2^{N+1})$, where N is the number of bits in the fraction. So, if you use 10 bits to store the number the error will be a maximum of $\pm 1/2048$.

Bytes and nibbles

A byte is defined as 8 bits and is used as the basic unit to measure computer-storage capacity. A nibble is defined as 4 bits and is equivalent to one hexadecimal digit.

2.3.2   FLOATING POINT NUMBERS

When storing real numbers in the computer (numbers that include fractions not just integers) the most common representation used is called floating point. This not only allows for fractions but also gives the computer scope to store very large or very small numbers: for example, the mass of a hydrogen atom = 1.660×10^{-24} grams or the distance to the moon = 385,000,000 metres.

When representing a number in floating-point, the decimal point is allowed to move or 'float' to the left or right, any movement of the point is compensated by multiplying the number by an appropriate exponent, look at the following examples.

Real number	Floating point number
1.66×10^{-24}	1.66×10^{-24}
385,000,000	$3.85 \times 10^{+8}$
200	2×10^2
-200	-2×10^2
-0.001	1×10^{-3}

The general representation for a floating-point number is as follows:

$$m \times r^e$$

Where m is known as the mantissa, r the radix and e the exponent, both m and e are signed values (i.e., can be positive or negative). For the previous decimal examples the radix is equal to 10 and the point was made to float to a position where there is only 1 digit to the left of the mantissa.

Within computer systems the radix for floating point numbers is fixed as two. When the numbers are stored the bicimal point is always adjusted so that the most significant bit of the mantissa is always one (normalised form). The bicimal point is assumed to be located directly after this most significant bit.

Real number	Floating point (normalised form)	Mantissa	Exponent
10001010.111	1.0001010111×2^7	1.0001010111	7
1110111	1.110111×2^6	1.110111	6
0.000101	1.01×2^{-4}	1.01	-4
-1011	-1.011×2^3	-1.011	3
1000	1×2^3	1.0	3

So, for the first example only, 10001010111 and 7 will need to be stored. Note that the first digit of all the mantissas is 1. This means that we don't need to store this digit (assuming its value) and only store 00001010111.

When the mantissa is read in the processor automatically adds in the missing 1.

The exponent part is commonly stored in a format called excess form. In this a bias value of $2^N - 1$ is added to the signed number before it is stored. For example, the value -50 in 8 bits would have the value 127 added and stored as 77. This means that all exponent values are stored as positive numbers, which helps to simplify the handling of the number by the processor. An exponent value of 0 is used for special cases, as we will see when we describe IEEE 754.

Floating point arithmetic

Addition/subtraction: to add or subtract two floating point numbers one of the number's mantissa has to be adjusted so that the exponents are equal. To do this the point of the number with the lower exponent is moved to the left and the exponent increased until the two exponents are equal. For example, add the following numbers:

$N1 = 1.0011 \times 2^{23}$ $N2 = 1.1111 \times 2^{27}$

First adjust N1's point to the left by 4 places, so that its exponent equals 27.

$N1 = 0.0001011 \times 2^{27}$

Now we can just add the mantissas together:

```
  1.1111000
  0.0001011 +
 10.0000011
```

So the answer is 10.0000011×2^{27}.

We now normalise the answer before storing it back.

Answer $= 1.00000011 \times 2^{28}$

If the smaller number is a lot smaller then the process of adjustment can result in loss of precision. For example, if we were adding the following numbers (assuming the mantissa is stored in 8 bits):

1.11×2^{28} to 1.1111×2^{18}

Adjusting the second number

$1.1111 \times 2^{18} = 0.00000000011111 \times 2^{28}$

Adding the mantissas the result is

$1.11000000011111 \times 2^{28}$

Since only 8 bits are available to store the mantissa the result will be

1.11×2^{28} (since the lowest bits are lost)

For subtraction the process is similar to addition.

So if $N1 = 1.001 \times 2^{-1}$ $N2 = 1.11 \times 2^{-4}$

If we want to take N2 from N1 we must adjust N2's point by 3 places left to get an exponent of -1.

So N2 = 0.00111×2^{-1}

The mantissas can now be subtracted.

```
1.00100
0.00111 −
0.11101
```

Therefore the answer is 0.11101×2^{-1} or 1.1101×2^{-2} after normalisation.

Multiplication/division: no adjustment of the numbers is necessary before multiplication or division. For multiplication just multiply the mantissas and add the exponents. So:

$(m1 \times r^{e1}) \times (m2 \times r^{e2}) = m1 \times m2 \times r^{(e1 + e2)}$

For example, multiply 1.11×220 by $1.0011 \times 2 - 10$

Mantissa of result $= 1.11 \times 1.0011 = 10.000101$
Exponent of result $= 20 + -10 \quad = 10$

Therefore the answer is $10.000101 \times 2^{10} = 1.0000101 \times 2^{11}$ (Normalised).

If the absolute value of the numbers is large enough then multiplication can result in overflow since the exponent of the result may be too large to store.

On the other hand, if two very small numbers are multiplied then the exponent may be too negative to store resulting in underflow.

Overflow example (assuming exponent stores in 8 bits two's complement).

Range of exponent is -128 to $+127$

So if we multiply

N1 = 1.11×2^{20} by N2 = 1.001×2^{111}

The result of N1 $\times$ N2 = 1.11111×2^{131} (Normalised)
The exponent is positive and too large to store resulting in overflow.
Underflow example:

N1 = 1.1×2^{-100} N2 = 1.11×2^{-96}

Result = $10.101 \times 2^{-196} = 1.0101 \times 2^{-195}$ (Normalised)

The exponent is negative and too large to store resulting in underflow.
For subdivision the mantissas are divided and the exponents subtracted.

$(m1 \times r^{e1}) / (m2 \times r^{e2}) = (m1 / m2) \times r^{(e1 - e2)}$

For example,

Divide N1 = 1.1×2^{8} by N2 = $1.0011 = 2^{25}$
Mantissa of result is $1.1 / 1.0011 = 1.01000011$
Exponent of result is $8 - 25 = -17$
Therefore the result is $1.01000011 \times 2^{-17}$

If the dividend is a lot smaller than the divisor then the result may under-flow. On the other hand if the size of dividend is much greater than the divisor then the answer may overflow.

Division overflow example: (8 bit two's complement exponent)
$N1 = 1.111 \times 2^{60}$ $N2 = 1.1 \times 2^{-80}$

Mantissa of result is 1.111 / 1.1 = 1.01
Exponent of result is $60 - (-80) = 140$

Answer is 1.01×2^{140}
Exponent is too large to store in 8 bits.

2.3.3   IEEE 754

This standard, which was produced in 1985 by the Institute for Electrical and Electronic Engineers (IEEE), is used in most processors that perform floating-point arithmetic and is also used as the floating-point standard for the Java programming language.

The standard defines two levels of precision: single 32 bits with an 8 bit exponent and 24 bit mantissa and double with 11 bit exponent and a 53 bit mantissa.

Mantissa

For both formats the normalised mantissa is stored in sign and magnitude format and the exponent is stored in excess form (see Figure 2.1). *Note* that even though we have 24 and 53 bits precision for the mantissas we are only storing 23 and 52 bits. This is because we are throwing away the normalised bit which is guaranteed to be one.

Exponent

The exponent is stored with bias value 127 for single precision and 1023 for double precision. Exponent values of all zeros and all ones are reserved for special cases. This gives us an exponent range of -126 to $+127$ for single precision and -1022 to 1023 for double precision.

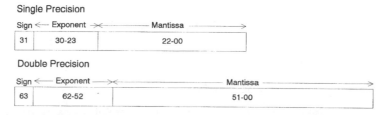

Figure 2.1   IEEE 754

2.3.4 SPECIAL NUMBERS

Zero

The number zero has a special representation which consists of both an exponent of all zeros and a mantissa of all zeros (since the mantissa is sign and magnitude, there are two zeros, positive and negative).

Infinity

In IEEE 754 a result of infinity is represented by an exponent of all ones and a mantissa of all zeros. There are two values for infinity: positive infinity and negative infinity.

2.3.5 DENORMALISED NUMBERS

To store very small numbers a format is allowed where the exponent is all zeros. In this case the number represented is $(-1)^{sign} \times 0.mantissa \times 2^{-126}$ for single precision and $(-1)^{sign} \times 0.mantissa \times 2^{-1022}$ for double precision.

Range (single precision)

Since the exponent has a range of -126 to $+127$, the largest magnitude that can be stored is $1.11111111111111111111111_2 \times 2^{127}$.

Using the denormalised number format the smallest non-zero magnitude that can be represented is $0.00000000000000000000001_2 \times 2^{-126} = 2^{-149}$.

This gives us overall range in decimal of:

$$\sim\pm1.401 \times 10^{-45} \text{ to } \sim\pm3.40310^{+38}$$

Range (double precision)

The largest magnitude that can be stored is

$$1.1111111111111111111111111111111111111111111111111111_2 \times 2^{1023}$$

Using the denormalised number format the smallest non-zero magnitude that can be represented is

$$0.0000000000000000000000000000000000000000000000000001_2 \times 2^{-1022}$$
$$= 2^{-1074}$$

This gives us overall range in decimal of:

$$\sim\pm4.94 \times 10^{-324} \text{ to } \sim\pm1.79 \times 10^{+308}$$

Underflow and overflow

The floating point unit in a processor will signal underflow if it tries to return a single precision positive value less than $+1.401 \times 10^{-45}$ ($+4.94 \times 10^{-324}$

for double precision) or a non-zero negative value greater than -1.401×10^{-45} (-4.94×10^{-324} for double precision). This indicates that a loss of precision has occurred since a non-zero number cannot be distinguished from zero.

Underflow can occur, for example, by subtracting two numbers that are very close in value but not equal or by dividing a very small number by a large number.

Overflow is signalled if a number greater than $+3.403 \times 10^{+38}$ ($1.79 \times 10^{+308}$ double precision) less than $-3.403 \times 10^{+38}$ ($-1.79 \times 10^{+308}$ double precision) is produced in the single precision result. In this case, the result can be returned as $+$ or $-$ infinity, depending on the direction of the overflow.

2.4 CHARACTER CODES AND GRAPHICS

When using computer systems we not only need to deal with numeric data but also information in other forms. In the next two sections we look at how computer systems handle both characters and graphics.

2.4.1 CHARACTER CODES

Each character is represented by a different number or code and the number of different characters that can be represented is 2^N where N is the number of bits in the code. Character code systems can be used for both information storage and transmission (e.g., over a network).

American Standard Code for Information Interchange ASCII code

In the early days of computer systems different computer manufacturers used different coding schemes (e.g., IBM's proprietary EBCDIC). This caused problems when systems tried to communicate or share data since one machine's representation of the letter 'A', for example, would not be compatible with another machine's representation.

For this reason the American National Standards Institute developed the ASCII code, giving manufacturers one coding scheme they could all work to. ASCII is the most widespread and commonly used scheme in use today. For example, ASCII is the code used by PCs to transmit key presses from the keyboard to the main system.

Standard ASCII uses 7 bits to represent each character, which gives you 128 different codes: see Table 2.3. There is also a version called extended ASCII, which uses 8 bits to represent 256 codes. The first 128 characters in extended ASCII are the same as ASCII.

ASCII was originally developed as a transmission code and, for this reason, a number of the codes (called control codes) have special meanings which are only relevant in data communications. Here is a description of some of the most commonly used control codes:

Table 2.3 ASCII character set

Code	Character	Code	Character	Code	Character	Code	Character
0	NULL	32	SP	64	@	96	
1	SOH	33	!	65	A	97	a
2	STX	34	'	66	B	98	b
3	ETX	35	#	67	C	99	c
4	EOT	36	$	68	D	100	d
5	ENQ	37	%	69	E	101	e
6	ACK	38	&	70	F	102	f
7	BELL	39	'	71	G	103	g
8	BKSP	40	(	72	H	104	h
9	HT	41	)	73	I	105	i
10	LF	42	*	74	J	106	j
11	VT	43	+	75	K	107	k
12	FF	44	'	76	L	108	l
13	CR	45	−	77	M	109	m
14	SO	46	.	78	N	110	n
15	SI	47	/	79	O	111	o
16	DLE	48	0	80	P	112	p
17	DC1	49	1	81	Q	113	q
18	DC2	50	2	82	R	114	r
19	DC3	51	3	83	S	115	s
20	DC4	52	4	84	T	116	t
21	NAK	53	5	85	U	117	u
22	SYNC	54	6	86	V	118	v
23	ETB	55	7	87	W	119	w
24	S0	56	8	88	X	120	x
25	S1	57	9	89	Y	121	y
26	S2	58	:	90	Z	122	z
27	ESC	59	;	91	[	123	{
28	S4	60	<	92	\	124		
29	S5	61	=	93	]	125	}
30	S6	62	>	94	↑	126	~
31	S7	63	?	95	↓	127	DEL

SOH (start of header)	Indicates the start of a transmission header.
STX (start of text)	Indicates the end of the header and the start of a block of data.
ETX (end of text)	Indicates the end of a block of data.
ACK (acknowledgement)	Used to acknowledge that a message has been received correctly.
NACK (negative acknowledgement)	Used to indicate that a block of data was received in error.

These control codes are used in communication protocols such as HDLC, which is described in Chapter 15.

Table 2.4   UNICODE scripts

Min value	Max value	Name	Languages
0000	007F	Latin	European
0370	03FF	Greek	Greek
0590	05FF	Hebrew	Hebrew
0600	06FF	Arabic	Arabic
0A80	0AFF	Gujarati	Gujarati
0E00	0E7F	Thai	Thai
13A0	13FF	Cherokee	Cherokee
1780	17FF	Khmer	Kham
F900	FAFF	Han	Chinese, Japanese, Korean

UNICODE

The limitations of ASCII become only too apparent when we try and communicate in languages other than English that do not use the Roman alphabet (e.g., Russian, Thai, Chinese or Greek). Also, some languages use the Roman character set with special character additions, such as the German umlaut. None of these cases can be represented in ASCII.

To get round these problems a new coding system called UNICODE was developed in 1991. The UNICODE standard is controlled and developed by a non-profit-making organisation called the UNICODE consortium. Members include companies such as Apple, Sun, Xerox, IBM, Microsoft and Novell.

UNICODE uses 16 bits (allowing for 65,536 different characters). The first 128 characters of UNICODE are the same as ASCII, allowing for backward compatibility. Table 2.4 shows some of the available character sets in UNICODE. UNICODE is the character code for the Java programming language and is also now widely supported in operating systems (such as Windows and Linux) and application software such as MS Office. For more information on UNICODE including all the script charts you should try www.unicode.org.

2.4.2   GRAPHICS

To represent graphics in the computer system, pictures are broken up into small dots called picture cells or pixels. For a black and white image each pixel can be represented by a bit (e.g., with 1 representing white and 0 representing black). For greyscale images more than 1 bit is used per pixel. For example, using 8 bits per pixel, 256 levels of greyscale would be available.

Colour

For colour graphics the situation is more complex. The most common method of internal representation is to use three colour components: red, green and blue (referred to as RGB), although there are other schemes. These three primary colours are mixed together to produce the full chromatic

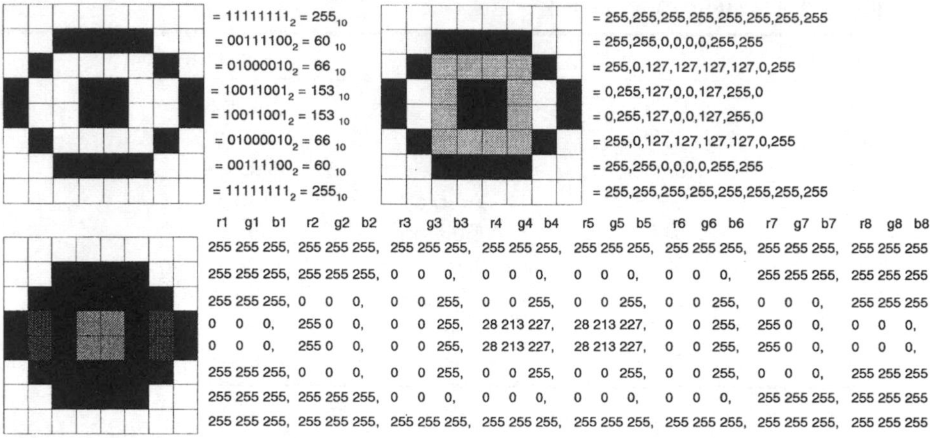
= $11111111_2 = 255_{10}$
= $00111100_2 = 60_{10}$
= $01000010_2 = 66_{10}$
= $10011001_2 = 153_{10}$
= $10011001_2 = 153_{10}$
= $01000010_2 = 66_{10}$
= $00111100_2 = 60_{10}$
= $11111111_2 = 255_{10}$
= 255,255,255,255,255,255,255,255
= 255,255,0,0,0,0,255,255
= 255,0,127,127,127,127,0,255
= 0,255,127,0,0,127,255,0
= 0,255,127,0,0,127,255,0
= 255,0,127,127,127,127,0,255
= 255,255,0,0,0,0,255,255
= 255,255,255,255,255,255,255,255
r1 g1 b1 r2 g2 b2 r3 g3 b3 r4 g4 b4 r5 g5 b5 r6 g6 b6 r7 g7 b7 r8 g8 b8
255 255 255, 255 255 255, 255 255 255, 255 255 255, 255 255 255, 255 255 255, 255 255 255, 255 255 255
255 255 255, 255 255 255, 0 0 0, 0 0 0, 0 0 0, 0 0 0, 255 255 255, 255 255 255
255 255 255, 0 0 0, 0 0 255, 0 0 255, 0 0 255, 0 0 255, 0 0 0, 255 255 255
0 0 0, 255 0 0, 0 0 255, 28 213 227, 28 213 227, 0 0 255, 255 0 0, 0 0 0,
0 0 0, 255 0 0, 0 0 255, 28 213 227, 28 213 227, 0 0 255, 255 0 0, 0 0 0,
255 255 255, 0 0 0, 0 0 255, 0 0 255, 0 0 255, 0 0 255, 0 0 0, 255 255 255
255 255 255, 255 255 255, 0 0 0, 0 0 0, 0 0 0, 0 0 0, 255 255 255, 255 255 255
255 255 255, 255 255 255, 255 255 255, 255 255 255, 255 255 255, 255 255 255, 255 255 255, 255 255 255

Figure 2.2 Graphical representation *top left* monochrome; *top right* greyscale; *bottom* colour

range. For example, if we have red = 255, blue = 255 and green = 0, this will produce the colour violet. Figure 2.2 shows more examples. If we use 8 bits to represent each colour the total number of colours available will be 256 × 256 × 256 = 16,777,216 (approximately 16 million). This format is referred to as true colour and is supported widely by video card manufacturers.

Figure 2.2 shows how a simple picture of an eye can be represented in the computer, in black and white, greyscale and true colour.

2.5 SUMMARY

In this chapter we have examined how computer systems process, represent and store numeric and non-numeric information. We have seen how all this information at the lowest level is represented in binary form, using just two symbols, 1 and 0. This subject of data representation will be examined in further detail in Chapter 5, section 5.4, where we will see how a computer program's instructions are encoded.

2.6 EXERCISES

1 Convert the following decimal numbers to the equivalent binary numbers:

a 14	e 21	i 256
b 13	f 19	j 0.4375
c 15	g 63	k 512.5
d 6	h 103	l 131.5625

2 Convert the following binary numbers to equivalent decimal numbers:
   a 1101   d 1011   g 0.1011
   b 1001   e 11011   h 111011.1011
   c 10111   f 10101   i 11.01010111

3 Perform the following additions and check by converting the binary numbers to decimal and adding:
   a 1001.1 + 1011.11   c 0.1011 + 0.1101
   b 100101 + 100101   d 1011.01 + 1001.11

4 Perform the following subtractions in binary and check by converting the numbers to decimal and subtracting:
   a 1111 − 1000   d 1101 + 1011
   b 1011.1 − 111.1   e 1111.01 − 1011.1
   c 111.11 − 111.1   f 1101.1 − 1110.01

5 Convert the following hexadecimal numbers to decimal:
   a B6C7   b 64AC   c A492   d D2763

6 Convert the following octal numbers to decimal
   a 14   d 124
   b 105   e 123
   c 156   f 15.5

7 Convert the following binary numbers to octal:
   a 101101   c 101101110   e 10110111
   b 110110.011   d 11.1011011

8 Convert the following octal numbers to binary:
   a 56   c 43   e 231.2
   b 231.4   d 454.45   f 32.234

9 Convert the decimal numbers to octal:
   a 15   c 9   e 19
   b 0.54   d 0.625   f 2.125

10 Convert the following hexadecimal numbers to binary:
   a CD   b 649   c A13   d AA   e ABCDE

11 Convert the following binary numbers to hexadecimal:
   a 10110111   c 1011111   e 101011.1011001
   b 10011100   d 0.01111110

12 To convert a decimal number X, whose value lies between 0 and 32767, into a 15-bit binary number, the following algorithm can be used:
   a Is X >=16384? If so, set the most significant bit to 1 and subtract 16384 from X. Otherwise, set the most significant bit to zero and omit the subtraction step.
   b Repeat step a using one half of the previous test constant to determine the next significant bit.
   c Repeat until 15 bits have been obtained.
   Write and test a program to implement the above algorithm.

13 Find the two's complement of the following binary numbers:
   00110101 and 01000000

14 Add the binary number 0101000 to each of the two's complement number computed in exercise 13. Verify the results by converting all the binary numbers to decimal and reworking the calculations in decimal.

15 Perform the following subtractions using two's complement arithmetic:
   a   00110110 − 00011101   c   01001001 − 01101000
   b   00011111 − 11101010   d   00001110 − 00001111

16 Consider the following addition exercises for three bit binary numbers in two's complement. For each sum, determine whether overflow has occurred:

000	000	111	100	100
001+	111+	110+	111+	1001
—	—	—	—	—
—	—	—	—	—

17 a   Describe one of the methods commonly used for representing signed integers in digital computers. What are the maximum and minimum values that can be represented by your method?
   b   Express the contents of the 32 bit word containing hexadecimal 30424450 as:
      ESCII characters
      integer decimal number
   How is a computer able to distinguish between the two?

18 Calculate the exponent and mantissa values using both low and high precision IEEE 754 format or declare if an overflow or underflow occurs.
   a   123456789
   b $12 \times 10 - 9$
   c $1.2 \times 10 - 100$
   d $356 \times 10 + 100$

19 Find out and describe what the IEEE 754 NaN (Not a Number) is and when it will be produced as a result.

20 a   Represent each of the following decimal values 26, − 37, 19909 in a fixed point format assuming 16 bits has been allocated to the integer part.
   b   A number has to be stored to 20 decimal points of accuracy, i.e., an error not exceeding $\pm 0.5 \times 10^{-20}$, how many bits will be required for the fractional part of this number.
   c   What is meant by the term 'floating point number'? Explain how a floating point number is represented by a fixed point mantissa and an exponent, indicating particularly the effect on range and accuracy of your representation.

21 The following data is to be stored in a computer system, for each case decide if you are going to use fixed or floating point representations and how many bits will be required. (For the floating point just state double or single.) For each case state any assumptions you have to make.
   a   weight of person measured in grams
   b   height of a person measured in centimetres
   c   distance between stars in the universe measured in metres
   d   time a historical event occurs measured in seconds.

22 Convert the following message into numbers using the ASCII coding system in Table 2.3. 'Hello how are you'. Do not forget the spaces.

23 Here is an example of some ASCII codes stored in memory (values are in decimal).
65 83 67 73 73 32 109 101 115 115 97 103 101 32 104 101 114 101
Decode the hidden text.

24 Can you think of a simple method to convert a lowercase ASCII message to an uppercase message and vice versa?

3 Digital logic and integrated circuits

In Chapter 2 we saw that computers store and process data in the form of binary numbers. The electronic circuits that make up the computer have to be able to store and transmit two different states, one and zero. Within most computer systems this is done by assigning a different voltage level for each value, typically +5 volts for a one and 0 volts for a zero. Since circuits do not work with 100 per cent accuracy some degree of tolerance is allowed when determining the value, for example, a value greater than 4.5 volts and less than 5.5 volts would be read as a one and between 0 and 1 volt would be a zero.

This chapter describes the function of the fundamental electronic circuits that make up the computer system and how these can be wired together to perform computations.

3.1 LOGIC GATES AND BOOLEAN ALGEBRA

Logic gates are the fundamental building blocks of all computer systems. They manipulate binary data using the rules of binary logic, also known as Boolean algebra. For each operation in binary logic there is a corresponding logic gate that performs the function electronically. The behaviour of a particular logic gate or circuit can be described by means of a truth table (see Table 3.1). A truth table lists the output values of the circuit against all the possible different input values.

Table 3.1 Truth tables

A	B	$A \oplus B$	A	B	$\bar{A} \cdot B$	$A \cdot \bar{B}$	$\bar{A} \cdot B + A \cdot \bar{B}$
0	0	0	0	0	0	0	0
0	1	1	0	1	1	0	1
1	0	1	1	0	0	1	1
1	1	0	1	1	0	0	0

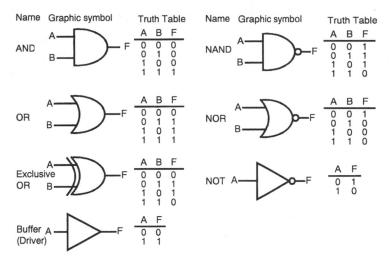

Figure 3.1 Logic gate operations

The four basic logic operations available are AND, OR, EXCLUSIVE OR and NOT. The Boolean algebra symbols for the fundamental logic operations are defined as follows.

$$A \text{ AND } B = A \cdot B \qquad A \text{ OR } B = A + B$$
$$A \text{ XOR } B = A \oplus B \qquad \text{NOT } A = \bar{A}$$

These are illustrated in Figure 3.1, including their electronic symbols and truth tables. If we look at the figure we can see that the AND gate only produces a logic 1 on its output when both its input values are logic 1. Binary AND can also be thought of as binary multiply since the following is true: $0 \times 0 = 0$, $1 \times 0 = 0$, $0 \times 1 = 0$ and $1 \times 1 = 1$, following the same rule as logical AND.

The OR gate will produce a logic 1 if either of its inputs are 1. The EXCLUSIVE OR gate produces a one when one or the other inputs are logic 1 but not both. *Note* all the gates we have considered so far have had only two inputs; in fact versions of each are available with multiple inputs.

Since Boolean algebra is associative, the rules for multiple input gates can be worked out by combining the results of two input expressions, so, for example, we get:

$$A \cdot B \cdot C \cdot D = A \cdot (B \cdot (C \cdot D)) = (A \cdot B) \cdot (C \cdot D)$$
(Associative rule for AND)
$$A + B + C + D = A + (B + (C + D)) = (A + B) + (C + D)$$
(Associative rule for OR)
$$A \oplus B \oplus C \oplus D = A \oplus (B \oplus (C \oplus D)) = (A \oplus B) \oplus (C \oplus D)$$
(Associative rule for EXCLUSIVE OR)

3.1.1 UNARY OPERATORS (1 INPUT VALUE)

The NOT operation reverses the value of the bit producing a 1 if its input is 0 and a 0 if its input is 1. The buffer (or driver) does not change the binary value but is used to increase the capacity of the output to be connected to other inputs. This allows 1 output to drive many inputs; this is useful, for example, when connecting a processor up to a computer system with many memory chips.

Finally the operation NAND defined as AND followed by NOT and NOR is OR followed by NOT therefore:

$$A \ NAND \ B = \overline{A \bullet B}$$
$$A \ NOR \ B = \overline{A + B}$$

3.1.2 TRUTH TABLE EQUIVALENCE

Two expressions are said to be truth table equivalent if their output is the same for a given set of inputs (i.e., their truth tables are the same).

For example, the following expressions are truth table equivalent:

$$A \oplus B = \overline{A} \bullet B + A \bullet \overline{B}$$

One can use truth table equivalence to find a circuit with the same logical operation but better characteristics; for example, one with reduced delay.

The following expressions are found to be equivalent in Boolean algebra (prove it yourself by drawing their truth tables).

$$A \bullet 0 = 0 \qquad A \bullet 1 = A$$
$$A + 0 = A \qquad A + 1 = 1$$
$$A \oplus 0 = A \qquad A \oplus 1 = \overline{A}$$
$$A + \overline{A} = 1 \qquad A \bullet \overline{A} = 0$$

Boolean operators are commutative, i.e.

$$A \bullet B = B \bullet A \qquad A + B = B + A \qquad A \oplus B = B \oplus A$$

and also distributive:

$$A \bullet B + A \bullet C + A \bullet D = A \bullet (B + C + D)$$

The following truths are also provable:

$$A + \overline{A} \bullet B = A + B$$
$$A \bullet (\overline{A} + B) = A \bullet B$$
$$\overline{A} \bullet \overline{B} = \overline{A + B}$$
$$\overline{A} + \overline{B} = \overline{A \bullet B}$$

We can use these rules to help simplify complex Boolean expressions. For example:

$$A \bullet B \bullet C + A \bullet \overline{B} \bullet C + \overline{A} \bullet B \bullet C = A \bullet B \bullet (\overline{C} + C) + \overline{A} \bullet B \bullet C$$
$$= A \bullet B + A.\overline{B} \bullet C = A \bullet (B + \overline{B} \bullet C) = A \bullet (B + C)$$

There are more examples given in the exercises at the end of the chapter.

3.2 COMBINATIONAL LOGIC

By combining a number of logic gates complex circuits can be built which will do functions such as arithmetic, comparison and instruction decoding. In fact a microprocessor is just a very large grouping of combinational circuits, which contains millions of gates.

Here are some examples of combinational logic circuits.

3.2.1 HALF ADDER

This adds two binary bits, producing a sum and a carry. The half adder is used as a building block when producing circuits that can add multiple bit numbers.

First let us look at what the truth table should be for adding two binary digits, X and Y, i.e., the result of X + Y: see Table 3.2.

Note also that the S column is identical to the Exclusive OR truth table and the C column is identical to AND truth table. From this we get:

$$S = X \oplus Y$$
$$C = X \bullet Y$$

The circuit is show in Figure 3.2.

3.2.2 FULL ADDER

When you add two binary numbers together, for each bit position there are three digits to sum. Two of these digits are from the added numbers and the third is the carry in from the previous position. Look at the following example (X + Y). Table 3.3 shows each individual sum.

```
X   0111
Y   1110+
    10101
```

Table 3.2 Truth table for adding two binary digits

X	Y	S	C
0	0	0	0
0	1	1	0
1	0	1	0
1	1	0	1

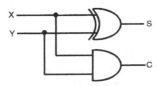

Figure 3.2 Half adder circuit

Table 3.3 Binary addition with carry

X	Y	Carry in	Sum	Carry out
1	0	0	1	0
1	1	0	0	1
1	1	1	1	1
0	1	1	0	1

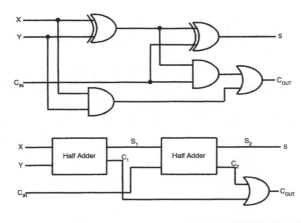

X	Y	Carry In	Sum	Carry Out
0	0	0	0	0
0	1	0	1	0
1	0	0	1	0
1	1	0	0	1
0	0	1	1	0
0	1	1	0	1
1	0	1	0	1
1	1	1	1	1

Figure 3.3 Full adder logic circuit and truth table

The Boolean expressions for the full adder are as follows:

$Cout = (X \bullet Y) + (X \oplus Y) \bullet Cin$
$S = X \oplus Y \oplus Cin$

Figure 3.3 shows the logic diagram and truth table for the full adder. Note the adder can be made up of two half adders plus an extra OR gate.

By using a number of full adders connected (see Figure 3.4) we can add multiple bit numbers. *Note* that the carry out of each full adder is connected to the carry in of its more significant neighbour.

When analysing the performance of this circuit, we will want to know how long it will take to add the two numbers. To do this, one calculates the longest path (measured in logic gates) across the circuit from any input to any output. This number can then be multiplied by the gate propagation delay to give the delay for the whole circuit. (In fact, since different gates may display different delay characteristics the calculation is more complex but this approach will suffice for illustrative purposes.)

For example, the full adder has a longest path of 3 gates (from X or Y to Cout); therefore, if each gate's propagation delay is 10ns, the whole circuit will take 30ns to add two bits.

If we want to add two 4 bit numbers using the circuit in Figure 3.4, it will take $4 \times 30ns = 120ns$. This is because each full adder needs to wait for the carry in from its immediate neighbour.

Note this means that the time it takes to add the numbers is directly proportional to their size in bits ($N \times$ full adder delay). Some adders get round this problem by generating the carries separately using another circuit. This is called carry look ahead generation and significantly improves the performance of the computation. Figure 3.5 shows how two 4 bit numbers can be added this way.

How much faster is the circuit in Figure 3.5 than the equivalent conventional multiple bit adder?

Longest delay time = 3 (for full adder) + 2 (carry generation) = 5 gates. So the total delay will be $5 \times 10ns = 50$ nanoseconds, i.e., more than twice as fast as the other addition circuit. The difference would be even greater if we were adding two 8-bit numbers.

3.2.3 DECODERS

A decoder translates from a binary number on its input lines to select just one of its output lines. A decoder with N input lines has 2^N output lines. Figure 3.6 shows the truth table and logic diagram for a 3-bit decoder. *Note* the use of the circle on the input to the AND gates, this signifies a NOT gate.

Decoders are used in memory systems when an address is used to select a particular memory chip. Another use of a decoder might be when interpreting machine code instructions; each different instruction will be enabling a different output on the decoder and therefore a different function in the microprocessor.

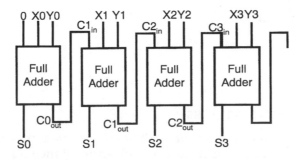

Figure 3.4 Circuit to add multiple bit numbers

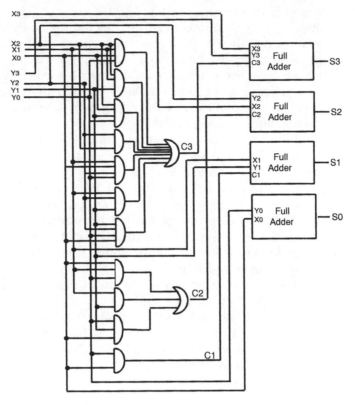

Figure 3.5 Carry look ahead generation

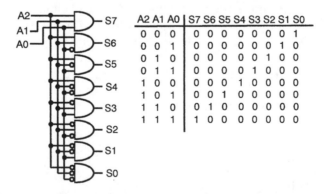

A2	A1	A0	S7	S6	S5	S4	S3	S2	S1	S0
0	0	0	0	0	0	0	0	0	0	1
0	0	1	0	0	0	0	0	0	1	0
0	1	0	0	0	0	0	0	1	0	0
0	1	1	0	0	0	0	1	0	0	0
1	0	0	0	0	0	1	0	0	0	0
1	0	1	0	0	1	0	0	0	0	0
1	1	0	0	1	0	0	0	0	0	0
1	1	1	1	0	0	0	0	0	0	0

Figure 3.6 3 bit decoder

3.2.4 SEQUENTIAL DEVICES

The logic circuits shown up until now (combinational circuits) produce a set of output values which are a direct function of their input values. Sequential devices behave differently in that the output is dependent on the input and

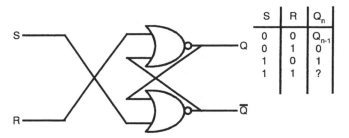

S	R	Q_n
0	0	Q_{n-1}
0	1	0
1	0	1
1	1	?

Figure 3.7 R-S flip-flop

the current internal state of the device. An example of a sequential device is a memory cell, when the cell is activated for a read operation its output will depend on what has been written into the cell previously.

The simplest example of a sequential device is the flip-flop, which has two different states and is capable of storing one bit of data.

R-S flip-flop

The R-S flip-flop has two inputs, R and S and and two outputs, Q and $\bar{Q}$ which represent the internal state of the flip-flop. Figure 3.7 illustrates how the flip-flop can be made up of two NOR gates with the outputs feeding back to the inputs.

The expressions for the output of an R-S flip-flop are as follows:

$$Q_n = \overline{\overline{Q_{n-1}} + R} \qquad \overline{Q_n} = \overline{Q_{n-1} + S}$$

Where Q_{n-1} is the last value of Q and Q_n is the current value. *Note* if R and S are zero these expressions can be simplified to:

$$Q_n = Q_{n-1} \qquad \overline{Q_n} = \overline{Q_{n-1}}$$

i.e., the output does not change.

If S = 1 and R = 0 the expressions simplify to:

$$Q_n = 1 \qquad \overline{Q_n} = 0$$

Conversely if S = 0 and R = 1 then

$$Q_n = 0 \qquad \overline{Q_n} = 1$$

Note that S sets the output to 1 and R resets the output to zero. If both S and R are set to 1, the output is invalid since Q and $\bar{Q}$ will not be the complement of each other.

Clocked R-S flip-flops

In computer systems it is useful to be able to synchronise the activities of various components so that they can function in a co-operative manner. The clocked R-S flip-flop as shown in Figure 3.8, allows the timing of the change of state of the flip-flop to be controlled by a clock pulse.

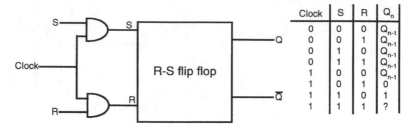

Clock	S	R	Q_n
0	0	0	Q_{n-1}
0	0	1	Q_{n-1}
0	1	0	Q_{n-1}
0	1	1	Q_{n-1}
1	0	0	Q_{n-1}
1	0	1	0
1	1	0	1
1	1	1	?

Figure 3.8 Clocked R-S flip-flop

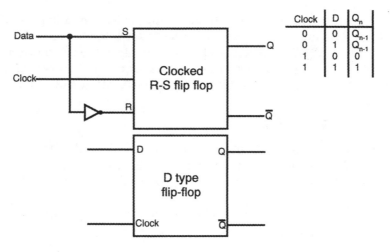

Clock	D	Q_n
0	0	Q_{n-1}
0	1	Q_{n-1}
1	0	0
1	1	1

Figure 3.9 D type flip-flop

Note that the output can change state only when the clock is set to logical one. The output actually changes state when the clock goes from zero to one. This is called a positive transition clock trigger.

D type flip-flip

The D type is set or reset using a single input D. This simplifies the operation of the flip-flop and gets rid of the problem of the illegal state that is possible with the R-S flip-flop (when R = S = 1). Figure 3.9 shows the circuit symbol and truth table for a D type flip-flop and how it can be constructed from a clocked R-S flip-flop.

Note: $R = \bar{D}$ $S = D$

Another name commonly used for this device is the transparent latch. *Note* that when the clock is logical one the device is transparent because Q = D; when the clock returns to zero the current value of D is fixed or latched onto the output.

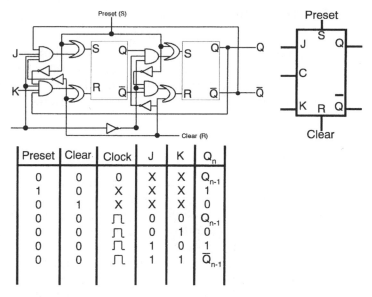

Preset	Clear	Clock	J	K	Q_n
0	0	0	X	X	Q_{n-1}
1	0	X	X	X	1
0	1	X	X	X	0
0	0	⊓	0	0	Q_{n-1}
0	0	⊓	0	1	0
0	0	⊓	1	0	1
0	0	⊓	1	1	$\bar{Q}_{n-1}$

Figure 3.10 J-K flip-flop

J-K flip-flop

The J-K flip-flop solves the problem of the undefined state of the R-S flip-flop by having the output invert if both inputs are set to one. So, if J = K = 1 the output will change from 1 to 0 or from 0 to 1 each time the clock is pulsed. Figure 3.10 shows the symbol for the J-K flip-flop and how it can be built from two R-S flip-flops.

Note that the clock has to pulse from 0 to 1 and back again for the flip-flop to change the state of its output lines, the clock pulse is indicated by in the truth table. The left hand flip-flop is called the master and controls the output of the other (slave) flip-flop. The J-K flip-flop is not transparent; when the clock is logical 1 (unlike the D type latch) the output does not follow the input.

Commonly the J-K flip-flop is fitted with two more inputs, S (or preset), which sets the flip-flop to one and R (or clear), which clears the flip-flop (see figure 3.10). *Note* the use of X in the truth table, this indicates the input value is not significant, when R = 1 and S = 0 then flip-flop will clear regardless of the other inputs and we give them the value X.

Common Sequential Circuits

In the previous section we looked at a number of flip-flops or bistable devices, each with different characteristics but each able to store 1 bit of information. By connecting a number of these flip-flops together we can produce a number of useful circuits. In this section we will examine some of the more common applications.

Parallel register

Since a flip-flop can store a single bit, using multiple flip-flops allows us to store a group of bits representing a binary number. Figure 3.11 shows how eight D-type latches can be connected to store an 8-bit binary number.

When the clock is pulsed the number on the inputs is stored in the register and presented on the outputs. The parallel register is useful for the temporary storage of numeric data.

Shift register

A shift register allows a number to be moved one place to the left or right whenever the clock is pulsed. Figure 3.12 shows how a shift register can be constructed from J-K flip-flops. The data output of each flip-flop is fed into its right-hand neighbour. Every time the clock is pulsed the data will move from left to right across the register.

The data can be entered into the shift register in parallel from the top by enabling the write line. For example, if we load the register with the number $0110_2 = 6_{10}$ and pulse the clock once, the bits will all be shifted to the right one place to give $0011_2 = 3$, assuming the Serial in line is set to zero. *Note*

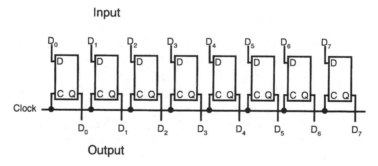

Figure 3.11 8-bit register

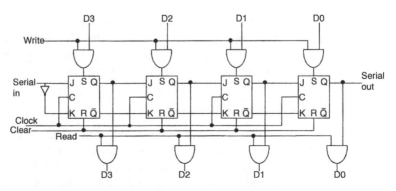

Figure 3.12 Shift register

Figure 3.13   Serial data transmission

Figure 3.14   Transistor

this has the effect of dividing the number by two; to multiply a number by two you must shift it the other way (from right to left). The answer is read out of the register via the output lines by enabling the Read line.

Another application for shift registers is in data communications, to convert numbers from parallel to serial format. Many communication links between machines use just one wire and the number has to be sent bit by bit as a serial stream, at the other end the bits are converted back into parallel form suitable for handling by the computer.

So if we started with the number 1011_2 and pulsed the clock four times the following output sequence would appear from 'Serial out': 1, 1, 0, 1. This output can be sent across a line to another computer and fed into the 'Serial in' line of another shift register, which converts the data back to a parallel. Figure 3.13 illustrates how this can be done using two 8 bit shift registers.

Note we have glossed over how the clocks of the two shift registers are kept in synchrony. This is an important issue and will be covered in detail in the later chapters on data communications.

3.3   INTEGRATED CIRCUITS

In all our discussions up to now we have talked about the logical function of integrated circuits but not how they are implemented using electronic components. All logic gates use transistors which operate as switching devices. Figure 3.14 shows the electronic symbol for a transistor; *note* it has three connections: collector, emitter and base.

The voltage presented at the base controls the flow of electrical current from the collector to the emitter. If the voltage at the base is less than a certain threshold value, the transistor will be switched off (in the cut off state) and no current will flow from collector to emitter. As the base voltage

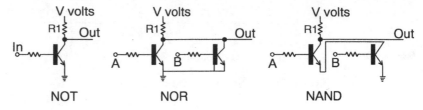

Figure 3.15   Implementation of logic gates

is increased above the threshold value, the collector emitter current increases as the resistance between the collector and emitter falls.

To summarise:

base voltage low, collector emitter current low, transistor switched off

base voltage high, collector emitter current high, transistor switched on

We will now examine the three transistor circuits for NOT, NOR and NAND gates shown in Figure 3.15.

In the first case we have the NOT gate. If the input is a low voltage then the transistor will be switched off. This means that no voltage will be dropped across R1 and V volts will be presented to the output. If the base voltage is high then emitter collector resistance will drop to a very low value, V volts will be dropped across R1 and the output will be connected effectively to ground (the output is connected to ground via the collector emitter path). This will give a low voltage (close to zero) at the output.

In summary:

In = low
high collector emitter resistance   Output = V volts
In = high
low collector emitter resistance   Output = 0 volts

For the NOR gate we have two NOT gates connected in parallel. If both base voltages are low then neither transistor will conduct and the output will be V volts. If either of A or B provide a high voltage to the base then at least one of the transistors will provide a low collector emitter resistance and therefore give a low voltage at the output.

In summary:

A and B = low
high collector emitter resistance   Output = V volts
A or B = high
low collector emitter resistance for either transistor R1 drops V volts
                              Output = 0 volts

For the NAND gate the transistors are connected in series. This means that both transistors must be switched on for the resistance from Out to ground to be low. So if either A or B provide a low base voltage the path from the Output to ground will be of high resistance and the Output will be high.

Table 3.4   Evolution of integrated circuits

Scale of integration	Year	Number of transistors	Example
SSI	1950s	Less than 100	AND gate
MSI	1960s	100–1000	Parallel adder
LSI	1970s	1000–100,000	8/16 bit processors
VLSI	1980s	100,000–10,000,000	32 bit processors 4M memory chips
ULSI	1990s	10,000,000–100,000,000	64 bit processors 256M memory chips
SLSI	2000s	>100,000,000	1G memory chip

If both A and B are switched on then the Output will be connected to ground and the Output will be low.

In summary:

A or B low voltage
High emitter collector resistance   Output = V volts
A and B high voltage
Low collector emitter resistance for both transistors
R1 drops V volts   Output = 0 volts

Integrated circuits (also known as chips) consist of a number of electronic components, which are fabricated on to a crystal of silicon. The chip is housed within a metal or plastic package that provides the chip protection and allows for connection to the circuit within. Building circuits within chips has a number of advantages including reduced size, lower power consumption, higher operating speed and reduction in production costs (for volume production).

Chips can be classified in terms of their complexity, generally measured in terms of transistor count. Small-scale integration (SSI) refers to chips that contain less than 100 transistors. These chips provide simple logic functions, e.g., flip-flops, drivers and counters. Medium-scale integrated chips contain typically 100 to 1000 transistors and can provide a whole function on a single chip – an example might be a parallel adder. Large-scale integrate circuits are more complex still, containing between 1000 and 100,000 transistors. These can provide complex functions such as information processing, e.g., CPUs or input/output chips. Beyond LSI there is VLSI (Very Large Scale Integration), ULSI (Ultra Large Scale Integration) and Super Large Scale Integration. Modern processors and high-density memory use these technologies extensively. Table 3.4 shows how chip density has developed since the 1950s.

Examples of current integration levels are the Pentium® III processor with 9.5 million transistors and Sun's ULTRASPARC® III with 29 million.

Integrated circuits are classified into families based on the technology of their construction and operation. The families use different fabrication techniques and different ways of constructing logic gates from the electronic components. The three most common families are:

TTL   Transistor Transistor logic
ECL   Emitter Coupled Logic
MOS   Metal-oxide semiconductor.

For each family there are defined a number of variants or series, with different power requirements and propagation delay. Table 3.5 compares the characteristics of the most common series for TTL, ECL and CMOS families. *Note* that, in general, the faster the gate the higher its power consumption requirements.

TTL

The TTL logic family uses a conventional bipolar transistor described earlier in the chapter, although the construction of a typical TTL gate is more complex than shown. There are a number of different versions or series of the TTL gate, based on power consumption and speed.

ECL

The ECL logic family, like the TTL family, uses bipolar transistors but with gates constructed differently. With ECL circuits the transistor is not switched on fully (does not reach a saturated state). This means that it takes less time to switch the transistor off and the circuit can change state very quickly. ECL gates are very quick but consume a lot of electrical power. ECL technology

Table 3.5 Comparison of IC families

Family	Series	Propagation delay (ns)	Power requirements (Mw)
TTL	Standard	22	15
TTL	Advanced	3	26
	Schottky	15	3
TTL	Low-Power		
	Schottky		1
ECL	ECLinPS Plus™	0.175	300
CMOS	Advanced	9	0.04
CMOS	Advanced high speed	3.5	0.04

used to be very popular with supercomputer and mainframe manufacturers such as Cray, Fujitsu and IBM. These systems were so power hungry that they required water-cooling. For this reason and others ECL has now been largely replaced by CMOS.

MOS

MOS or MOSFET technology uses a transistor (called a field effect transistor) which requires very low power requirements and can be packed very densely on a chip; for these reasons it is ideal for producing chips with high levels of integration. Practically all microprocessors and other chips within the computer (including memory) are manufactured using CMOS technology.

TTL is only generally required when high line driving currents are needed; ECL could find a use in very high speed line drivers, such as a Gigabit rate communications device.

IC packaging

Small and medium scale integrated circuits are most commonly mounted in a dual in-line (DIP) package. This is a block of plastic or ceramic that the chip is mounted on, providing both protection to the delicate and tiny piece of silicon and connection to the circuit within. The chip itself can be soldered directly onto the board or pushed into a socket. For this smaller scale logic a system of standardised numbering has been developed to distinguish between different types of package. For instance the 7402 DIP package contains 4×2 input NAND gates, the 7408 contains 4×2 input AND gates.

Memory chips for computer systems are often mounted in a small piece of circuit board that has an edge connector that can be clipped onto the computer's motherboard. This type of packaging is called DIMM or Dual Inline Memory Module. The advantage of a DIMM over regular types of packaging is that the chip can be fitted or removed with no special skills or tools. This allows, for example, a home user to upgrade their PC memory by clipping in another DIMM.

For microprocessors, because of the large number of connections involved, the pins are laid out on a square grid. Since a great deal of force is required to push this many pins into a socket, these type of chips are usually mounted into a zero insertion force (ZIF) socket. The socket is provided with a lever arm, with the arm in the up position; the chip can be added or removed easily. With the arm in the down position the chip is locked into place. Figure 3.16 shows all three types of packaging.

Integrated circuit specifications

All semiconductor manufacturers publish details on the technical specifications of the chips that they manufacture. As well as the technical specification, application notes are provided which give developers important information on how the chips can be used in practice. All this data is now commonly provided on the web; the information in this

Figure 3.16   IC packages   DIP (*lower left*) DIMM (*top*) and CPU (*right*)

chapter on logic gate performance was obtained from the Texas Instruments (www.ti.com) and OnSemi (Motorola subsidiary) websites (onsemi.com).

Logic circuit emulation

Rather than build complex circuits in hardware and then test them it is possible to use logic circuit emulation software to look at the behaviour of a circuit before it is constructed. This allows complex designs to be perfected before the expensive process of hardware prototyping is begun.

One type of emulation software is referred to as SPICE (Simulation Program with Integrated Circuit Emphasis); these systems commonly are connected to a database containing exact details and specification of different manufacturers' components.

3.4   SUMMARY

Since chips make up the internal components of the computer system, the correct design and manufacture of these components is crucial in the production of a fast and reliable computer system. We have looked at the basic logic gates and how these gates can be used to build up more complex circuits that can perform arithmetic and control functions within the computer system. At the end of the chapter there are a number of exercises that can be carried out using the logic circuit emulation software such as MMLogic available free from Softronix (http://www.softronix.com/logic. html). The reader is encouraged to try out these exercises since the most effective way to understand digital logic is to see it working in practice.

3.5   EXERCISES

The following exercises can be carried out using a logic trainer system which allows you to build and test circuits from a range of logic components. Alternately you can use a logic software emulation package such as MMLogic.

1   By connecting switches to the inputs and a lamp (or LED) to the output, produce the truth tables for each of the logic gates AND, OR, EXCLUSIVE OR and NOT.

2   Determine what logic state is assumed by an unconnected input on the above gates.

3   Many of the logic functions can be developed using simple NAND gates. By producing the truth tables, show that the circuits in Figure 3.17 are functionally equivalent.

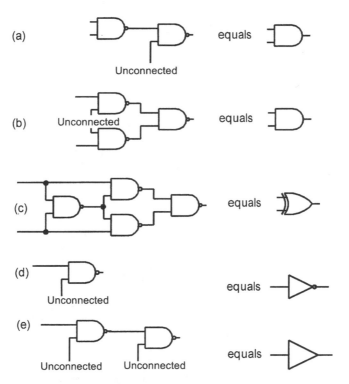

Figure 3.17   Logic gate equivalence

4   On an automatic plant alarm system, the following events occur as a result of fault detection:
   i   Fault signal arrives – red lamp on, buzzer on, operator acknowledges that the alarm is received by operating the acknowledge switch.
   ii   Acknowledge switch on – red lamp off, buzzer off, yellow lamp on.
   When the fault is corrected:
   iii   Fault signal clears – yellow lamp off, green lamp on, buzzer on.
   iv   Acknowledge switch returned to normal – buzzer off, green lamp on

From the above it can be determined that the system will consist of two inputs (alarm and acknowledge) and four outputs (red, yellow and green lamps and buzzer). Produce a truth table to describe the system. Implement the system practically (using logic gates) and test for correct operation.

5   Build the circuit in Figure 3.18 for a half-adder and, by changing the switch, produce its truth table. Check it against Figure 3.2.

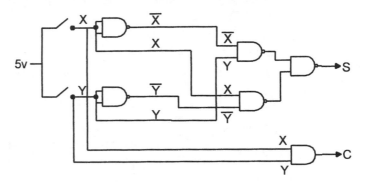

Figure 3.18   Half adder circuit

6   Connect a full adder as shown in Figure 3.3 and verify its truth table.
7   Build the 3 input decoder shown in Figure 3.6 and verify its truth table.
8   Construct the circuit shown in Figure 3.19 and produce the truth table by experiment.

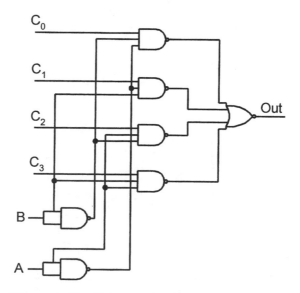

Figure 3.19   Selector circuit

9   Sketch a circuit which realises an eight input multiplexer from two four input multiplexers in IC form and NAND gates. Produce its truth table.

10 Verify the truth tables of the R-S, the J-K and D type flip-flops.

11 The block diagram of a J-K flip-flop is shown in Figure 3.10; using this device connect up the shift register circuit shown in Figure 3.12, excluding preset/clear sections. By applying a series of different states to the serial input and clocking the register, show how this series eventually becomes available from the four flip-flop outputs.

12 Find out what type of technology is used to fabricate the Pentium 4 processor.

13 Describe the different ways that ICs are packaged.

14 Why can a computer work faster if more logic gates can be integrated onto the chip? (Think of the carry look ahead example.)

15 What is the significance of propagation delay when designing a logic circuit for a computer system?

Memory

Computer memory is used to store the program's instructions that are currently being executed by the CPU and also provides storage for the program's working data. This chapter will describe the main types of memory technology and explain how these can be interconnected in such a way as to optimise the transfer of information to and from the micro-processor. *Note* that modern memory systems not only provide fast storage for programs and data but also provide protection functions; for example stopping one program's code or instructions being accessed (or modified) by another program.

4.1 TYPES OF MEMORY

Memory is split into two basic types. The first is Read Only Memory, or ROM, in which the data is stored permanently when the chip is manufactured and no modification of the information is possible. The other type of memory, Random Access Memory, or RAM, allows the data to be modified (or written to) at any time. A ROM chip remembers its data when the power is switched off (non-volatile) and, for this reason, is used to store the program that starts a computer system on power up. Many other systems for which storing the program on disk would be impractical (for example a mobile phone or washing machine) store their software in ROM chips. RAM, on the other hand, loses its data on power down (volatile memory). The code and data for a program are loaded up from the file storage into RAM before being executed by the processor. In the section on memory technologies we will examine various types of ROM and RAM.

4.2 BUILDING BLOCKS OF MEMORY

All computer memory stores information in the form of bits. Each bit is stored in a memory cell that can be made up of a flip-flop, a single transistor or, for ROM, a fixed wire (connected to logical 1 or 0). Each memory cell has a data line (bi-directional for RAM, input only for ROM); read/write line

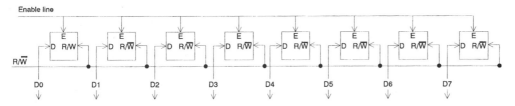

Figure 4.1   Single byte memory cell

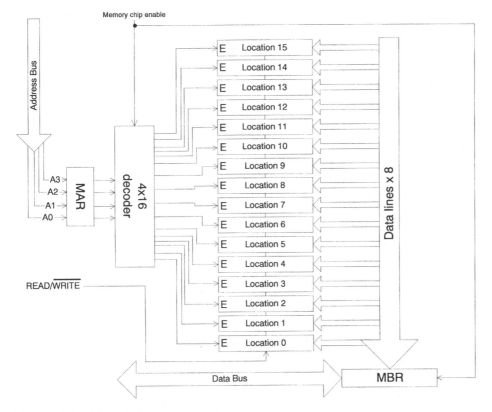

Figure 4.2   16 × 8 bit memory chip

and an enable line. By adding multiple memory cells in a row, so they are enabled as one, multiple bit numbers can be stored. Figure 4.1 shows the block structure of an 8-bit memory storage device. *Note* how the enable and read/write lines are wired together to make sure all the cells work in synchrony.

When more than one memory location is stored inside a chip there is a need to distinguish between them and enable each one individually. To do this each memory location is allocated a unique number (called an address), starting at zero and finishing at N-1, where N is the total number of memory locations. Figure 4.2 shows a diagram of a 16 byte memory chip (admittedly, not of great practical use). *Note* how the decoder (described in Chapter 3) is used to enable a different memory location depending on the 4-bit number input on the address lines.

The memory access address is stored on a latch called the memory address register or MAR, this allows the chip to keep the address stable even if it changes on the external address bus. Before a read from memory or write to memory, the address must be presented on the address bus and the address latched (i.e., stored in the MAR).

Read from memory (getting data out of the chip) is non-destructive, i.e., the data read out of a memory location is still left in there after the read and not modified. When the memory chip performs a read it stores the result in the Memory Buffer Register or MBR. The Memory Buffer Register is connected to the data bus that transfers the signal to other components in the computer system (commonly the CPU).

Write to memory is destructive (the old data that was in the memory location is replaced by the new data). The data to be written is stored in the MBR at the same time as the address of the memory location to be written at stored in the MAR, the write line is then activated and the data written to memory.

The processes of reading and writing data are called bus read cycle and bus write cycle respectively. These operations do not occur instantaneously but after a short delay. Making this delay as short as possible is a critical factor in improving the performance of the computer system. *Note* also that there is a memory chip enable line which allows the whole chip to be enabled or disabled; this is important since there may be many devices attached to address and data bus, only one of which should be enabled at once.

Data is transferred between the memory and the CPU over the data bus. The number of CPU data lines determines the size of the data bus; the wider the data bus the faster the CPU can transfer data to/from memory. This is because a 32 bit wide data bus can read in 4 bytes at a time whereas a 64 bit data can read up to 8 bytes for each bus cycle.

Early microprocessors commonly had 8- or 16-bit data buses, whereas nowadays typical data bus widths are 64-bits for a general purpose CPU such as the Pentium III or Motorola Power PC. The width of the data bus specifies the word size of the memory system: for example, a 32-bit data bus defines a 32-bit memory word size. The memory word size defines the largest unit of information that can be transferred in one bus cycle (read or write) between the processor and the memory.

The size of the address bus determines the total number of possible different addresses that can be generated. For an N bit address bus 2^N locations are addressable. The Pentium III, for example, has a 33-bit address bus which can address a total of $2^{33} = 8,589,934,592$ locations. Since each location refers to 8 bytes of data the total amount of addressable information is $8 \times 8,589,934,592 = 64$ Gigabytes. The address lines on the Pentium III are labelled A3–A35; that defines effectively a 36-bit number (with the least three significant bits set to zero): see Figure 4.3. The processor internally addresses the memory byte by byte, so the first byte is at address 0, the second at address 1, etc. If, for example, the processor needs to access a byte

A35-A3	0 0 0

Figure 4.3 Pentium III physical address

of data located at address 67, this, in binary, is 1000011; now, since the lowest three bits of the physical address are zero, the address sent to memory will be 1000000 or 64. This will retrieve the 8 bytes of data located at addresses 64, 65, 66, 67, 68, 69, 70 and 71. *Note* that reading a byte of data in this instance will take the same time as reading 8 bytes of data since a total of 8 bytes are always transferred.

4.3 DEDICATED REGISTERS

Dedicated registers are storage locations that are not accessed via the system address and data bus but are located within a piece of hardware: for example, an I/O chip, or the central processing unit itself. Transfers from one dedicated register to another within the processor are extremely quick. The processor's dedicated registers are also used, for example, to store temporary program variables, results of calculations and pointers such as the address of the next instruction to be executed. Each processor register is referred to by name (e.g., D0, D1, D2 for the Motorola 68030 and EAX, EBX, IP for the Pentium).

4.4 CONTENT ADDRESSABLE OR ASSOCIATIVE MEMORY

So far, when talking about memory, we have assumed that we know the address of the memory location that we want to read from (or write to). In some cases this is not known beforehand: see Figure 4.4. This shows a block of memory containing the names and telephone numbers of employees in an organisation. If we want to find the telephone number of any given individual we will have to search through the list item by item until we find the name we want. If we want Smith's telephone number and we start searching from the lowest address first we will have to look at five names before we get the one we want.

With a content addressable memory, this type of searching is not required. The memory chip itself does all the comparisons for you (in parallel) and returns the appropriate data field. Figure 4.5 shows the operation of a content addressable memory chip. The data is split into two; the first associative field is used to look up the data contained within the second conventional field. *Note* that instead of sending an address to the chip we put the look up data value into the interrogative register. For our example this is the name SMITH (represented as ASCII). The chip then compares (in parallel) this value with all the values in the associative fields

Address

50	J	O	N	E	S	7	8	4	2	1
40	S	M	I	T	H	5	7	3	2	1
30	B	R	O	W	N	6	7	3	4	5
20	W	H	I	T	E	9	7	8	2	7
10	D	A	K	E	R	4	2	9	2	5
0	P	R	I	C	E	8	7	9	2	6

Figure 4.4   Associative memory operation

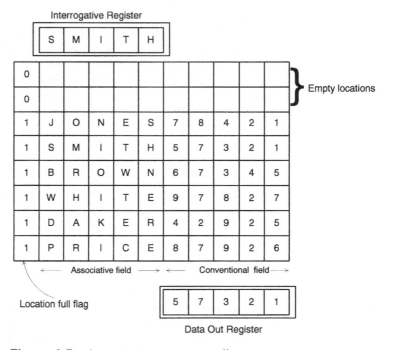

Figure 4.5   Associative memory cell

in the memory, then returns the value in the conventional field; in this case the telephone number 57321.

Figure 4.6 illustrates how an 8-bit wide content addressable memory cell might be built and wired to the interrogative and data out registers. Note how the XOR gates are used to perform comparison between the search data and the actual value in the associative field. Since the XOR gates produce a

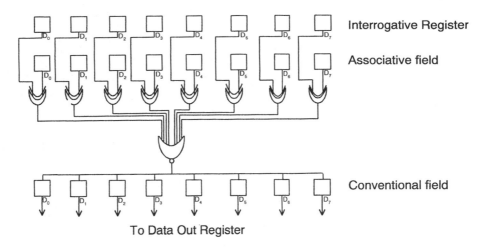

Interrogative Register

Associative field

Conventional field

To Data Out Register

Figure 4.6　Cache memory operation

zero if both the inputs to the gate are equal, the outputs of these gates are fed into a multiple input NOR gate. This will produce a one on the output only if all its inputs are zero, i.e., all the XOR gates are signalling equality. The output of the NOR gate is used to enable the output of the conventional field register which is connected to the data out register.

When writing to an associate memory, if the associative field does not exist in the memory, an empty location must be found to store the new associative and conventional data. This is done by looking for a store with a location full flag set to zero. If the associative field value already exists then only an update of the conventional field is required. Work out what the result would be of writing to the telephone number associative memory, first with SMITH, 12345 and then WOOD, 98123. Sketch a diagram of the resultant contents of the storage.

Associative memory allows data to be looked up extremely quickly but this does come at a price in terms of the complexity of the memory chip and very high cost per memory cell. For this reason associative memory is only used where extremely high performance is crucial but storage requirements are relatively small, for example, processor cache and memory management.

4.5　CACHE MEMORY

When a processor fetches instructions from a memory cell there is a certain delay (called the memory access time) before the data is returned along the data bus. This delay can have the effect of slowing the processor down since it cannot carry on with executing the program until the data (or instruction) has been fetched from memory. In practice we want memory access times to be as short as possible to allow the processor to operate at maximum speed.

Certain types of RAM, called static RAM or SRAM, exhibit very low access times but they do have the drawback of being very expensive and providing relatively low storage density. To build a computer with all SRAM storage would be prohibitively expensive and bulky. Another type of memory called Dynamic RAM or DRAM provides cheap high-density storage but is much slower than SRAM. If we used DRAM for all the computer's memory this would cripple the processor's performance, making it wait a long time for its instructions and data.

The solution to this dilemma is to use a small amount of fast SRAM storage (called the cache) that is connected to the processor directly. The rest of the storage, i.e., the main memory (consisting of DRAM) is connected to the cache. The cache contains copies of recent reads from main memory. When the processor makes a request to read a particular memory cell the cache first checks to see if it has a copy of the data. If the cache contains a copy of the requested data (a cache hit) it sends back this copy to the processor with minimum delay. If the contents of address location is not stored in the cache (cache miss) the data is read from main memory, and at the same time copied into the cache.

Since the data in the cache is a copy of the data in main memory it needs to be marked with the main memory address to which it corresponds. This extra addressing information is stored in a location in the cache called the tag field. We can see from Figure 4.7 that reads from addresses 1052 and 1053 result in cache hits (since the address value is contained in the tag fields) but the read from address 6000 is a cache miss and the main memory has to be accessed. After the read from 6000 has been completed a copy of the location's contents, 99 with the tag value, 6000 will be stored in the cache.

The first time a location is read from memory it has to be read from the slower DRAM; if this memory location is read again soon afterwards the read will be from the cache and require no main memory access, allowing the processor to operate at full speed. If the processor rarely repeats a read on the same memory location then the cache will have little effect since most reads will be from main memory. Fortunately, since programs commonly contain loops and will often operate on the same set of data repeatedly, cache hits rates greater than 95 per cent are not unusual, resulting in a considerable performance boost for the processor.

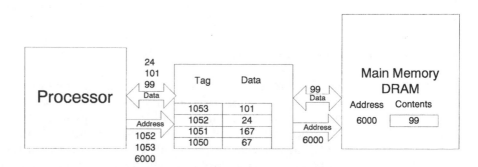

Figure 4.7   Direct mapped cache operation

4.5.1   MEMORY WRITES AND CACHE MEMORY

When writing data from the processor to memory, two possible strategies are possible. The first and simplest is called 'write through': in this all writes to the cache are immediately written to the main memory at the same time. Another approach is just to write the data to the cache but delay the write to main memory as long as possible. The data is only committed to main memory when the cache is full or the location required by another read/write operation. The first approach is slower but results in a simpler implementation of the cache.

4.5.2   FULLY ASSOCIATIVE CACHE

In the example given in Figure 4.7 we didn't explain how the cache memory looks up the tag value to find the corresponding data. One approach would be to build the cache as an associative memory with the tag values (corresponding to the full address values) stored in the associative fields. This type of construction provides a very efficient cache but is very expensive. In practice, because of the great expense, no processors on the market at the moment use a fully associative cache.

4.5.3   DIRECT MAPPED CACHE

With this technique the location of the tag field in the cache is calculated by taking the N least significant bits of the address value (where N is the number of bits for the cache address).

To see how this is done we will consider an example of a main memory containing 64 Megabytes of RAM using a cache of 64 Kilobytes.

If we assume the processor has a 64 bit data path then each transfer between the memory and the processor will be $64/8 = 8$ bytes (i.e., a 64 bit word size). For 64 Megabytes of storage we will need an address space of 64M/8 or 8M different locations with each location storing an 8-byte word.

Therefore the number of main memory address lines required will be 23 since

$$2^{23} = 8M.$$

The number of cache memory address lines will be 13 since

$$2^{13} = 4K \times 8 = 64 \text{ Kilobytes.}$$

For our example we represent the address as a byte address since this is the way they are stored within the microprocessor and therefore interpreted by the computer program. To convert from an 8 byte per location physical address to a byte address you need to multiply the address values by 8. The main memory address is now represented as 26 bits (since $2^{26} = 64$ Megabytes) and the cache address 16 bits (since $2^{16} = 64$ Kilobytes)

The address location in the cache memory is calculated by taking the sixteen least significant bits of the (byte) address value. The value stored in the tag field in the cache is the remaining ten most significant bits of the address.

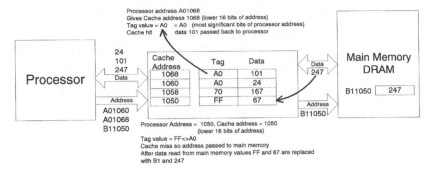

Figure 4.8 Direct mapped cache operation

When the processor generates a 26-bit address, the sixteen least significant bits of this address are used to look up the tag value, which is then compared to the ten top bits of the address. If the tag value equals the address value a cache hit is signalled. Figure 4.8 illustrates this process; *note* for this example the addresses are displayed in hexadecimal. This simplifies the calculation since the sixteen least significant bits of a hexadecimal number can be derived by taking the four least significant hex digits (4 bits = 1 hex digit).

We can see from the diagram, three memory reads from locations A01060, A01068 (both cache hits) and B11050, a cache miss. *Note* that the data value stored in the cache at location 1050 corresponds to main memory address FF1050 since the tag value is FF. When the data is read from main memory address location B11050 the tag value at cache location 1050 is replaced with B1 and the data value is replaced with 247.

The directly mapped cache is relatively simple to manufacture but does have one drawback. Imagine, for our previous example, manipulating two strings of data, each 20 bytes long that happen to be located at addresses 64K apart. String 1 might be located at address B110A0, for example and string 2 might be located at B210A0. *Notice* the cache address for each of these strings is the same 10A0. If we load up string 1 into the cache and then load up string 2 it will be placed on top of string 1's data erasing it from the cache, subsequent access to string 1 will require reads from main memory, slowing the processor down. The fully associative cache does not have this problem but is a lot more expensive and complex to implement.

4.5.4 SET ASSOCIATIVE MAPPED CACHE

This type of cache is a compromise between a direct mapped and a fully associative cache. The set associative mapped cache consists of N direct mapped caches that operate in parallel. When a direct cache address is generated all the N caches are searched in parallel for the tag value. If any one of the caches returns a hit then the value can be read from the cache. When writing data into the cache it can be written into any one of the caches that has a free location. This provides a cheaper alternative to using

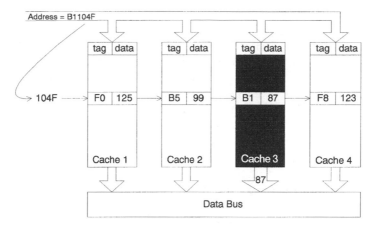

Figure 4.9 Set associative cache

a fully associative cache but with better performance than a simple direct mapped cache since data with same cache offset address can be stored in the different caches.

Figure 4.9 shows a four-way 256 Kilobyte set associative cache (each cache containing 64K). We can see that the address B1104F finds a hit in cache 3 so the data 87 is driven onto the data bus and sent back to the microprocessor. When writing data into the cache memory there are four cache locations that can store the data, reducing the chance of one cache write erasing another cache item (the problem we had with the single set direct mapped cache).

4.5.5 CACHE LEVELS

Sometimes systems are built with more than one cache. The cache closest to the processor is called the level 1 cache, the next the level 2, etc. The level 1 cache will be faster than the level 2 cache but smaller in capacity. The processor will always look for the data in the level 1 cache first; if it is not there (a level 1 cache miss) the level 2 cache will be interrogated and if the level 2 does not contain the data it will be fetched from the main memory. If the motherboard also contains a cache then this will be level 3 and interrogated before the main dynamic RAM access.

4.5.6 CACHE MEMORY IN PRACTICE

Practically all high performance processors come with level 1 cache memory built onto the chip. The Pentium III processor is provided with two level 1 caches (one for code and one for data), which are each 16 Kilobytes and four-way set associative. Two options are provided for the level 2 cache, either an on chip 256 Kilobyte or a discrete 512 Kilobyte cache, both of which are four-way set associative.

4.6 VIRTUAL MEMORY

With a virtual memory system, the main memory and part of the secondary storage is treated as one large addressable memory space, called virtual for the reason that it is larger than the actual main RAM memory available on the system. This allows programs and data that are a lot larger than the RAM capacity of the machine to be loaded into memory.

With a virtual memory model (see Figure 4.10) two types of addresses now exist, logical addresses as seen by the programmer and handled internally by the processor and physical addresses that are used to access the hardware. The logical addresses are translated into physical addresses by the memory management unit and are then used to locate the data in the main memory. The data is stored in chunks of a given size and is loaded up from secondary storage into main memory on demand.

There are two options for the organisation of virtual memory. The first of these, paged virtual memory, uses chunks of a fixed size. This simplifies the loading and unloading of data from the disk and is easiest to implement in hardware. Segmented virtual memory, on the other hand, uses variable size chunks and provides a model of memory that fits in better with the program's view of the machine. A program is commonly split into a number of different modules (for example, main program code, common library code, network library code and data) each of which can be stored in different segments, each with a different segment size.

4.6.1 PAGING

As stated, paged virtual memory splits the virtual address space up into chunks or pages of equal size. The physical memory is divided up into page frames of the same size, each page frame having the capacity to store one page. *Note* a page can be resident either in main memory or on the

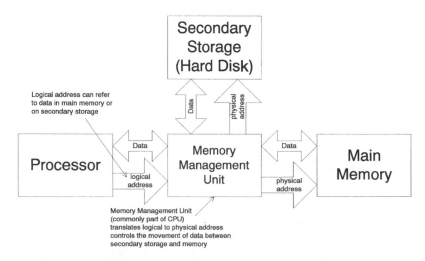

Figure 4.10 Virtual memory

secondary storage (in nearly all cases the hard disk). The area on the hard disk that stores these pages is called the swap space.

A program will occupy a number of pages depending on its size. When the program is initialised the pages may reside currently on the hard disk; as the program runs its pages are loaded up into RAM for execution by the processor. If at any point the program makes a reference to a page that is not in RAM, this generates what is called a page fault; the page is fetched from the secondary storage and the execution continues.

At some point, however, the main memory will become full and it will be necessary for one of the pages to be stored (or swapped) back onto secondary storage before the new page can be loaded up. The decision on which page should be swapped back to the secondary storage can be based on a number of factors. Possible prime candidates for swapping might be:

1   A page that has been accessed the least number of times.
2   A page that has been accessed least recently.
3   A page that has not been modified since the last time it was loaded.

The idea of choices 1 or 2 is to swap a page that is not going to be accessed again soon (and therefore require loading up again). The idea of swapping 3 is that it will not be necessary to write the page back to secondary storage, therefore speeding up the whole process.

To facilitate the process of locating and loading pages, the virtual memory system uses a table (called the page table) to store information about each page in the system. Each entry in this table will contain, typically:

1   The physical base address of the page.
2   A flag indicating if the page is resident (stored in main memory).
3   A flag indicating if the page has been written to since being loaded into memory.
4   Permission flags for data (read/write/execute).

The information in this table is used by the virtual memory system to translate a logical address into a physical address. The logical address is split into two parts, page number and offset. The page number is used to look up the entry for that page in the page table, the physical base address of the page is read out then added to the offset to calculate the final physical address. The size of each page is always a power of two (i.e., page size $= 2^N$). This simplifies the offset and page calculation. The offset can be obtained by just taking the N least significant bits. To get the page number, take the address and shift it right by N places. Figure 4.11 shows how this could be done with a 4K page size and a 32 bit address. Since $2^{12} = 4K$, the twelve least significant bits of the address define the offset and the top twenty bits define the page number.

Since the page tables are large they have to be stored in main memory. This means that each memory access will require two memory cycles: the first to look up the page table entry and the second to fetch the data from the location. This process would be very slow if this is what the processor did

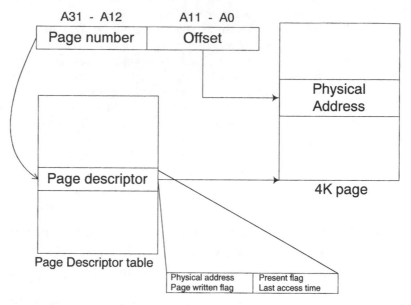

Figure 4.11 Page address translation

for every memory access. In fact most processors keep a copy of the most recent page descriptor values on board in an area of fast, fully associative memory called the translation lookahead buffer. For most page table translations the page table entry will be fetched from this buffer and not main memory.

4.6.2 SEGMENTED MEMORY

With segmented virtual memory each chunk of data is not the same size but defines a segment that can be of varying size. The segment is defined by two parameters, a physical base address and a length. For example, you might have a segment with a length of 32 Kilobytes and base address 0A0000. The first physical address in this segment would be 0A0000 and the last would be 0A7FFF (see Figure 4.12).

The translation from logical address to physical address follows a similar scheme to the one used in paged memory. This logical address is first split into segment number and offset; the segment number is then used to look up the segment descriptor in the segment descriptor table. The segment descriptor has the physical base address of the segment which is added to the offset to produce the final physical address (see Figure 4.13). As in the case of paged virtual memory, the segment can be present (currently in main memory) or stored on the secondary storage. If the segment is not present it will have to be loaded up before the program can continue. Handling virtual memory as segments is problematic because when they are swapped back to secondary storage a big enough space has to be found to store the segment. This may result in a problem called fragmentation where there are many

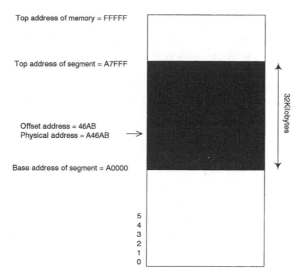

Figure 4.12   Memory segment

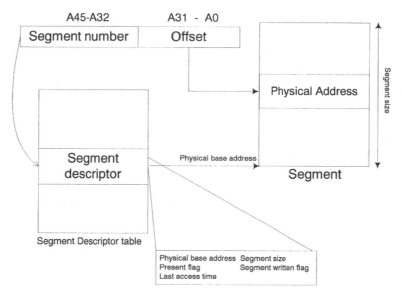

Figure 4.13   Segment descriptor tables

small areas of free memory on the hard disk but none large enough to store the whole segment.

4.6.3   SEGMENTATION IN THE PENTIUM PROCESSOR

For the Pentium the logical address consists of a 14-bit segment index number and a 32-bit offset. This provides a very large logical address space

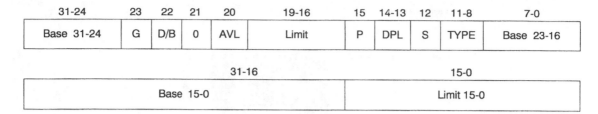

31-24	23	22	21	20	19-16	15	14-13	12	11-8	7-0
Base 31-24	G	D/B	0	AVL	Limit	P	DPL	S	TYPE	Base 23-16

31-16	15-0
Base 15-0	Limit 15-0

Figure 4.14 Pentium segment descriptor

of 2^{46} or 64 Terabytes. However, since the number of physical address lines is less than 46, the actual physical address space is more limited: 64 Gigabytes on the Pentium III. The segment parts of the addresses is stored in a set of internal registers. To speed up the translation from logical to physical addresses the most recently accessed segment descriptors are stored on board on a translation lookahead buffer (see paged memory). Figure 4.14 shows the layout of a Pentium segment descriptor.

The base address is 32 bits long and defines the physical start of the segment in memory; this gives a range of 4 Gigabytes for the base (2^{32}). The limit defines the size of the segment, the limit address is the maximum offset that can be defined for the segment. This can be interpreted in two ways: if the granularity (G) bit is zero this can define a segment size in bytes from 1 byte to 1 Megabyte. If the G bit is set to one then the limit is multiplied by 4K and defines a limit from 4K to 4 Gigabytes. D/B double or big flag used to indicate whether operations on this segment should work in 32 or 16 bit mode.

AVL available for use by system software, this flag can be used by the OS, perhaps to help with the memory management.

P Present bit, this bit to one if the segment is stored in main memory and does not need loading from secondary storage.

DPL descriptor privilege level, this defines what privilege is required to access the descriptor, if the processor is currently running at a lower privilege than the descriptor it tries to access then a fault will be generated. This allows the computer to protect system critical information from being corrupted by a faulty program.

S System, this bit is set to zero if the descriptor is a system descriptor (beyond the scope of this book).

TYPE defines if the segment contains code or data or a special system descriptor.

4.6.4 PAGED SEGMENTED MEMORY

In this model segmentation and paging are combined. The process of converting a segmented address to a physical address has to go through two stages. First the logical address segmented is converted to a logical paged address and then the logical paged address is converted to a physical address

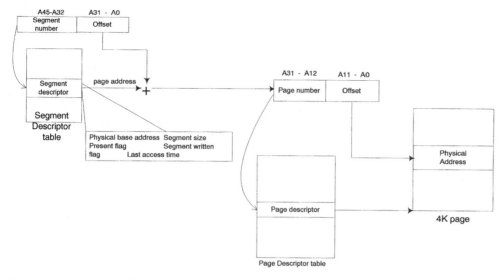

Figure 4.15   Paged segmented memory

(see Figure 4.15). This has the advantage that, even though the program sees the memory as a segmented model, the handling of information to and from the disk is done in fixed size pages (a lot easier to implement).

4.7   MEMORY TECHNOLOGIES

Different implementations of ROM and RAM are available, each with individual characteristics.

4.7.1   TYPES OF ROM

Ordinary ROM stores the information when the chip is manufactured; each memory bit in the chip is connected to logical 1 or 0 depending on the required data pattern.

PROM (Programmable Read Only Memory)

PROM is supplied empty: the data can be programmed into the chip by blowing fuses. Information can be written but once only. PROM, therefore, is a WORM (Write Once Read Many) type of device.

EPROM (Erasable Programmable Read Only Memory)

With an EPROM the data can be programmed into a chip. The chip package is constructed with a window on top. The data can erased by exposing the chip to ultra violet light for about 10 minutes. EPROM chips are very popular for embedded applications and are recognisable by the paper label that covers the window in normal use (*note* without this label UV light from sunlight might cause data loss).

EEPROM (Electrical Erasable Programmable Read Only Memory)

Like EPROM, but the data can be erased using an electrical signal. This allows the data to be modified while the system is running. One application of an EEPROM is to store non-volatile data for an embedded application, e.g., a telephone directory in a mobile phone.

Flash memory

This is the same as EEPROM but has the advantage that data can be written in blocks instead of 1 byte at a time. This makes it faster to write to.

4.7.2 TYPES OF RAM

RAM technologies are classified in two groups, depending on how the data is stored within the chip. With Static RAM or SRAM, each bit of data is stored in a flip-flop. This type of memory can be very fast: access times as low as 5 nanoseconds are possible. Static RAM does have a number of drawbacks, however: it is relatively expensive and, because each bit requires a whole flip-flop circuit, the capacity per chip is more limited than its rival DRAM.

Each bit of data in a Dynamic Ram or DRAM is stored as a charge on a special transistor called a FET (Field Affect Transistor). Since only one transistor is required per bit this has a very high packing density yielding memory with high storage capacities. Since the charge used to store the information leaks away, the chip needs refreshing on a regular basis. This requires extra circuitry to be added to the chip. DRAM is also much slower than SRAM typical; the fastest access times available for DRAM are about 50 nanoseconds.

Memory access

Both static and dynamic memory lay out the individual memory cells as a two dimensional array. Each cell is enabled by two lines (row enable and column enable), Figure 4.16 illustrates this with a 256 bit memory. The reason for wiring memory this way is economy. For example, a 1 Megabyte chip with 2^{20} memory cells, if they were laid out as in Figure 4.2 (1 dimensional array) would require a decoder with more than a million outputs! The same memory chip laid out in 2D would have two decoders each with just 1024 (since $1024 \times 1024 = 1M$) outputs – a lot more feasible.

Error checking and correction

Some systems include one or more extra data bits when storing a data word to allow the processor to detect memory errors (i.e., a bit that was stored as a zero being read as a one or vice-versa). The simplest technique available is called parity checking. In this an extra bit is stored, which ensures the total number of bits set to one is even or odd. For example, if we were storing the binary pattern 01110000 in an even parity checked RAM, the parity bit will be set to 1 to make the total number of bits set to 1 equal to 4 (an even number).

Parity checking adds cost to building the system, since each byte will have to be stored in 9 bits (1 extra for the parity bit) instead of the usual 8. Some systems provide both error detection and correction but since this requires even more redundant information it will add even more cost. *Note* modern RAM chips are extremely reliable and for this reason many systems do not use parity checking at all.

DRAM performance

Because of the speed limitations of DRAM a considerable amount of effort has gone into optimising its performance. Some of the more common techniques used are outlined next.

Interleaving

This involves splitting the DRAM into individual banks. Since the DRAM needs a small amount of time to recharge after each read access, interleaving allows the processor to access one bank, while the other bank is recovering

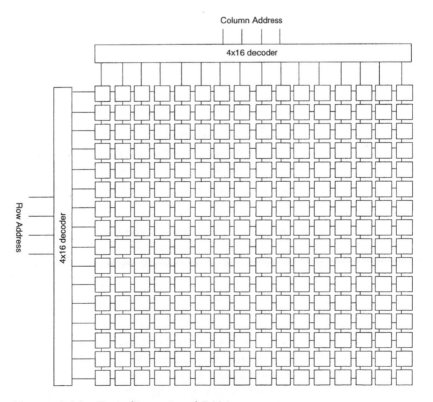

Figure 4.16 Two-dimensional RAM access

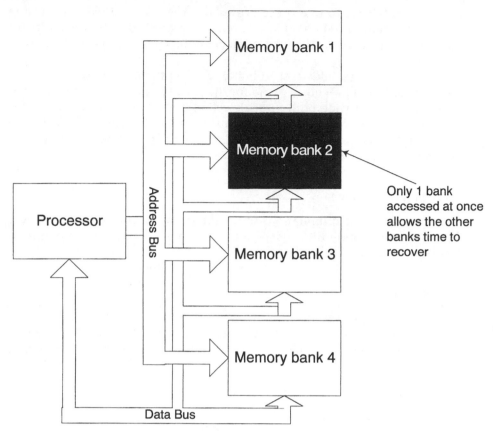

Figure 4.17   Interleaved memory

from the last access (see Figure 4.17). Many memory modules (for example, SDRAM modules) now use interleaving as standard.

Extended data out RAM

EDORAM starts to read the next location from memory, while the current value is still being presented on the data bus.

Burst mode

This is where the memory chip starts the next memory access cycle before the processor requests it. The DRAM can be programmed to deliver a burst of data (from consecutive locations) to the processor without having to have each individual address latched onto the chip. This mode relies on the fact that the processor very often is reading from (or writing to) a set of sequential addresses. Since a lot of the delay involved when accessing RAM is incurred when setting up the row and column addresses, this provides a considerable performance enhancement.

Synchronous versus asynchronous RAM access

When the processor is accessing RAM, two modes of operation are possible.

Asynchronous mode

In this, the processor puts an address onto the address bus and signals the start of the bus cycle. When the memory system has latched the address and successfully read/written the data to or from the memory location, it signals to the processor the end of the bus cycle by sending the READY signal. In this arrangement the memory system can slow the processor down (e.g., it is using slow memory chips) by delaying sending the READY signal.

Synchronous mode

In this mode there is no ready signal but the memory system is expected to respond within a given time interval (less than the bus cycle time). The reading/writing with synchronous RAM is controlled solely by the bus clock cycle, which is generated by the processor.

SDRAM or Synchronous DRAM is expected to synchronise with the system bus its performance is not specified in terms of a delay in nano-seconds but a clock rate in Megahertz. Typical ratings available are 100 MHz and 133 MHz. To achieve this high performance SDRAM uses techniques such as interleaving and bursting to allow the relatively slow DRAM chips to keep up with the system bus.

Rambus

This memory access technology, developed originally in 1992, has been proposed as the next generation of memory to be used for general purpose personal computing, and is already being used by many high performance personal computer systems. To connect the memory chips to the Rambus memory control it uses a cut down data bus of only 16 (or 18) bits which is clocked at 800 MHz (the clock is 400 MHz but the system transfers data twice for each clock cycle). This allows for a maximum theoretical transfer rate of 1.6G bytes per second. Figure 4.18 shows how the Rambus Asic Cell (RAC) is connected to RDRAM modules which are referred to as RIMM (Rambus Inline Memory Modules).

The data bus size of 16 bits, at first glance, would appear to be unusual (most data access channels for PCs are at least 64 bits wide), but keeping the bus narrow allows for the specification of bus timing to be a lot tighter. This consequently allows the bus to be clocked at a much faster rate with standard SDRAM clocked at 100 MHz with a 64-bit data bus provide a maximum theoretical data of 800 Mbytes per second, only half of the performance of Rambus. It is also possible to have a system with multiple Rambus channels (many systems now use two channels) and later generations of RIMM will allow even higher clock rates, increasing the performance still further.

The column and row address information is sent to the RIMM modules from the RAC via the control bus. The bus can send row information to one

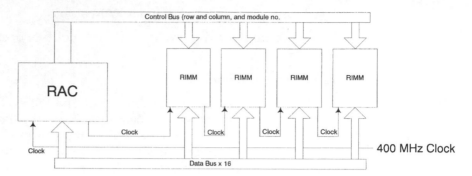

Figure 4.18 RAMbus architecture

RIMM, while sending column information to another; this allows the chips to go on working decoding the addressing information in parallel, allowing even greater improvements in performance. All the RIMM modules contain multiple banks of memory between which access can be interleaved.

All in all, Rambus provides impressive performance improvements over SDRAM but there are some question marks still over its future as the next PC DRAM. The fact that RIMM chips consume a lot a of power (and therefore generate a lot of excess heat), are hard to manufacture (i.e., prohibitively expensive) is some cause for concern.

Double data rate SDRAM

This type of DRAM, sometimes called DDR SDRAM, is a lot less revolutionary than Rambus and is not as efficient but does provide a considerable performance boost over standard SDRAM. Double Data Rate SDRAM transfer data on the rising and falling edge of the system clock; this doubles the data rate over standard SDRAM. Even though it does not have quite the same performance enhancement of Rambus, it does have the advantage of being a relatively safe technology being only an evolutionary step from SDRAM and, for that reason, being better understood and easier to implement.

RAM and system performance

When looking at the performance of the system as a whole, it may be surprising to discover that DRAM performance is not as critical as one might think. This is due to a number of factors, probably the most important of which to note is the use of the processor cache. If the cache is performing well with hits rates greater than 90–95 per cent then the DRAM will only be accessed for 10 per cent of the time. This means that we are only optimising 10 per cent of the processor's memory cycles when we improve the DRAM's performance. Another aspect of the computer's performance is how the virtual memory operates. Remember, as the virtual memory area fills up, the data must be swapped to the hard disk to make room for more pages. This will slow the system down a lot more than sluggish DRAM. Therefore providing more memory will often improve a system's performance a lot more than providing faster DIMMs.

4.8 SUMMARY

In this chapter we have looked at how memory is used in the computer system to provide storage for code and data. We have discussed different types of memory and various ways technology is used to speed up memory storage systems.

4.9 EXERCISES

1 Why would a computer system be equipped with 268,435,456 words of storage rather than 250,000,000 or 260,000,000 which are much easier to remember?

2 For the following memories calculate the total size of the address space in bytes.

Address lines	Cell size in bits
24	8
30	16
16	8
20	32
24	32

3 Describe two ways in which a memory could be organised so as to allow individual words to be read only, read/write, or execute only.

4 Explain how the principle of an interleaved memory can be used to increase access speed to a memory.

5 Investigate how modern computer systems utilise memory techniques in their design. How has this improved the performance of each system?

6 Give two reasons why increasing the speed of the main dynamic memory will not always result in an improvement of the computer's performance.

7 Find out how the cost, speed and size of memory has varied over the past seven years.

8 Describe how a cache is used to improve performance without greatly increasing cost.

9 You want to improve the performance of a system's memory. Describe how the following may affect performance.
size of cache;
speed of cache;
size of main memory;
speed of main memory.

10   A computer with a cache memory uses the direct mapping technique for cache organisation. The following are pertinent parameters:
Main memory   512 M words with a cycle time of 5 nanoseconds
Cache memory   256 K words with a cycle time of 2 nanoseconds
Specify the number of bits in the tag field and describe the process involved with a cache hit and a cache miss.

11   What does the level of a cache mean? Where would you usually find a level 1 cache?

12   Describe how virtual memory using pages can be used to protect memory from unauthorised access.

13   Explain how an operating system detects and reacts to a page fault in a demand-paged virtual memory system.
Consider a demand-paged virtual memory system in which the memory access time is 10 nanoseconds, the page fault service time is 1 millisecond and, on average, 5 memory accesses out of 10,000 causes a page fault. Calculate the effective memory access time for this system. If we require less than 10 per cent degradation in memory access time, due to demand paging, what is the maximum page fault rate that can be tolerated.

14   Describe the main functions performed by a memory management unit.

15   Compare and contrast the two memory technologies RDRAM and DDRAM.

16   What type of memory could be used to store a program for an embedded system that may require software updates after manufacture.

Instruction sets and computer software

As mentioned in Chapter 1, computer systems use lists of instructions called software to enable them to perform tasks. In Chapter 2 we looked at how data is represented within the computer system. This chapter will look at how instructions are stored in the computer's memory, the types of instructions that are available and how the data that the instructions act upon (operands) is handled. We shall also describe some of the most common types of software required to make the computer system usable.

5.1 INSTRUCTION FORMATS

Each instruction consists of two parts, an operator that tells the computer which type of instruction is being executed and one or more operands that specify the data to be operated upon. For example, if we consider the expression 5 + 6, in this case + is the operator and 5 and 6 are the operands. Here is an example from the Intel Pentium™ processor of an addition instruction:

ADD AX, BX

In this case ADD represents the operator and the operands being added together are the contents of the AX and BX registers. It is not clear, however, where the result will be stored; in fact, for Intel Pentium™ processors the result is generally stored in the left-hand (destination) operand – in this example the AX register.

If we look at the next example the operands are stored in memory location 0010 and the AX register.

ADD AX, [0010]

The square brackets indicate that the value is an address and that the contents of memory location are to be used.

Figure 5.1 shows the contents of the registers and memory before and after execution of the two previous examples. Instructions can use 3, 2 or 1 operands and certain special instructions have no operands at all. Table 5.1 shows some more examples of Pentium™ instructions.

Table 5.1   Pentium instructions

Instruction	Meaning	Example	Comment
MOV	Move or transfer data between pairs of registers or memory and registers	MOV AX, BX MOV AX, [0005]	Transfer BX to AX Transfer contents of memory location 5 to the AX register
INC	Increment or add one to the destination operand	INC AX INC [0010]	Increase AX by one Increase the contents of 0010 by one
DEC	Decrement or subtract one from the destination operand	DEC CX DEC [0200]	Decrease CX by one Decrease the contents of 0200 by one

SUB	Subtract one operand from another	SUB AX, BX
		
		SUB [0005], AX
			Subtract BX from AX, store the result in AX
			Subtract AX from the contents of [0005], store the result in [0005]

Before	AX =	2020		BX =	700
Instruction			**ADD AX, BX**		
After	AX =	2720		BX =	700

				Address	**Data**
Before	AX =	2720		220	2050
Instruction			**ADD AX, [220]**		
After	AX =	4770		220	2050

Figure 5.1   Pentium instruction example

Note some instructions act only between registers and not on memory. If the program can manipulate the data in registers this results in higher performance since extra data is not fetched from or stored into memory (generating bus cycles). Of course, at some point, the data must be fetched from or stored back into memory since the register storage capacity is very limited (usually less than 1 kilobyte).

5.1.1   REGISTERS

The register sets for both the processors we will look at can be classified into two groups, general-purpose and specialised. The general-purpose register sets for each processor are shown in Table 5.2.

Table 5.2 CPU general-purpose register sets

Pentium registers							
Name	Size	Name	Size	Name	Size	Name	Size
EAX	32	EBX	32	ECX	32	EDX	32
EDI	32	ESI	32	EBP	32	ESP	32
PowerPC registers							
Name	Size	Name	Size	Name	Size	Name	Size
R0	32	R1	32	R2	32	R3	32
R4	32	R5	32	R6	32	R7	32
. . .							
R28	32	R29	32	R30	32	R31	32

Note the PowerPC has 32 general-purpose registers against the Pentium's eight. In the examples shown for the Pentium, we will sometimes refer to registers AX, BX, CX and DX, instead of EAX, EBX, ECX and EDX; these names refer to the lower 16 bits of the corresponding 32-bit register. So AX is the lower 16 bits of the EAX register. There is also a set of registers AL, BL, CL and DL; these refer respectively to the lower 8 bits of the EAX, EBX, ECX and EDX registers.

5.2 INSTRUCTION SETS

For each processor there is a set of recognised legal instructions called the processor's 'instruction set'. The type and variety of instructions available tells you a lot about the capabilities of a particular CPU. We will initially look at the most common types of instructions supported by CPUs, broken up into six different classes as follows:

  data transfer instructions;

  arithmetic and logic instructions;

  branching instructions;

  floating-point instructions;

  I/O instructions;

  special system instructions;

The PowerPC is a RISC (Reduced Instruction Set Computer) processor, in contrast to the Pentium which is a CISC (Complex Instruction Set Computer) design. This means that the PowerPC supports less instructions with more simplified modes of operation. We will see that certain types of instruction that are supported on the Pentium are not supported on the PowerPC. This would apparently put the PowerPC at a performance disadvantage; we will, however, see the rationale behind this design approach in section 5.6, when we talk about RISC in more detail and how it can be used to boost performance.

Table 5.3   Data transfer instructions

Processor	Instruction	Function	Data size (bits)
PowerPC™	STB	Move data from	8
	STH	register to	16
	STW	memory	32
	LDB	Move data from	8
	LDH	memory to	16
	LDW	register	32
Pentium™	MOV	Move between memory and registers or from register to register	8, 16 or 32

5.2.1   DATA TRANSFER INSTRUCTIONS

Move data between registers and memory locations or between memory locations.

Table 5.3 shows some data transfer instructions; *note* the PowerPC™, because of its RISC architecture, does not provide direct instructions for transferring data between registers. This can be simulated, in fact, by an add instruction with one of the parameters as zero (see next section). Here are some examples of the instructions:

```
Pentium
MOV AX, BX      ;transfer contents of BX to AX
MOV [0005], AX  ;transfer contents of AX to memory location 0005
MOV AX, 149     ;move the number 149 into register AX

PowerPC
LDW r1, [2500]  ;transfer contents of memory location 2500 into r1
STB r4, [19000] ;transfer lower 8 bits (1 byte) of r4 into memory location
                ;19000
```

5.2.2   ARITHMETIC, LOGIC AND COMPARISON INSTRUCTIONS

Basic integer arithmetic operations such as add, subtract, multiply and divide. Floating-point arithmetic functions because of their complexity, are given a classification of their own. Integer logic operations also include all the basic Boolean operators defined in Chapter 3, i.e., AND, OR, NOT and EOR. The comparison instructions allow comparison between the contents of two registers or a register and memory. Table 5.4 shows examples of arithmetic operations.

Figure 5.2 shows the effect of two operations: multiply for the Pentium™ and logical OR for the PowerPC™.

For the Pentium MUL instruction the result of multiplying the two numbers is stored in the two registers AX and DX as follows:

$2020 \times 700 = 1414000$; this, in hexadecimal, is 00159370_{16}

Table 5.4 Arithmetic logic instructions

Instruction	Meaning	Example	Comment
MUL (Pentium)	Multiply AX by operand Stores result in DX and AX	MUL BX	Multiply AX by BX Product stored in DX and AX
OR (Pentium)	Logical OR between two operands 1st operand stores result	OR AX, BX	Logical OR or bits in AX with bits in BX Result stored in AX
And (PowerPC)	Logical and between two operands 1st operand stores result	and r1, r2, r3	Logical and between bits in r2 with bits in r3 Result stored in r1
Mul (PowerPC)	Multiply between two operands 1st operand stores result	mul r4, r2, r3	Multiply r2 by r3 Store result in r4

Before	AX =	2020	BX =	700	DX =	400
Instruction			MUL BX			
After	AX =	9370_{16}	BX =	700	DX =	0015_{16}

Before	r1 =	00010110_2	r2 =	00001010_2	r3 =	10000000_2
Instruction			or r1, r2, r3			
After	r1 =	10001010_2	r2 =	00001010_2	r3 =	10000000_2

Figure 5.2 Arithmetic instruction examples

AX is used to store the lower 16 bits, which are the lower 4 hex digits, i.e., 9370, DX stores the upper 16 bits which are the upper 4 hex digits, i.e., 0015.

The calculation for the PowerPC instruction is a simple logical OR as follows:

r3	10000000_2
r2	00001010_2
Result	10001010_2

Since the PowerPC™ uses three parameters for its arithmetic instructions and no special instructions are available to move a numeric value directly into a register, direct moves into registers can be implemented using special cases of the arithmetic.

To move the number 20 into the AX register with the Pentium™:

```
MOV AX,20
```

To do the same on the PowerPC with register r1:

```
addi r1,0,20
```

Adds 0 to 20 and stores the result into r1.

Again, with the PowerPC, there is no special instruction to transfer data from one register to another register so this can be done instead using the logical OR instruction. So, to transfer the contents of register r6 to register r7, you use the following:

```
or r7, r6, r6
```

This works since X OR X = X.

Compare instructions

These allow the program to compare a register or memory location with another register, number or memory location. The use of the compare instruction is covered in the next section, since it is practically always in conjunction with the conditional branch instruction.

5.2.3   BRANCHING INSTRUCTIONS

These allow the program to transfer control to another memory location, which then allows the programmer greater freedom when writing software, and provides such structures as conditional statements and loops. It also allows the programmer to add structure to the software through the use of subroutines.

The simplest form of branch instruction is the unconditional branch. The following is how the main loop of a computer game might be written (Pentium™ example).

```
PROGRAM_START :
        CALL READ_USER_INPUT_FROM_KEYBOARD
        CALL CALCULATE_PLAYER_POSITION
        CALL REDRAW_GRAPHICS
        BRA PROGRAM_START
```

When the BRA (branch always) instruction is executed the program jumps back to PROGRAM_START. *Note* this code will loop forever, the use of the CALL instruction is covered when we talk about subroutines.

A more powerful type of branching instruction is the conditional branch. This will only jump if a certain condition is met. Examples of conditions could be: a register containing zero, a register containing non zero, a recent comparison of two registers indicating they were equal.

In the following Pentium example ten numbers out of a table are added together.

```
        LEA    BX,TABLE      ;load the BX register with address of table
        MOV    CX,10         ;CX contains loop count = 10
        MOV    AX,0          ;AX contains sum = 0
ADD_LOOP :
        ADD    AX,[BX]       ;Add memory location pointed to by BX to AX
        ADD    BX,2          ;Move BX to next value in table
        DEC    CX            ;decrease CX by one
        CMP    CX,0          ;compare CX with 0
        BNE    ADD_LOOP      ;if not equal go back and repeat
```

The BX register is initially set to the start address of a table of 2 byte values to be added together. The CX register is set to the number of numbers in the table and the AX register is used to store the result. Each time round the loop the program adds the value stored in the memory location pointed to by the BX register to the AX register; this is done by the ADD AX,[BX] instruction. The next line increases BX by two; this is because each value in the table is 2 bytes and therefore takes up two memory locations. Finally the CX register is decremented and then compared with 0. If CX does not equal 0 then the loop carries on. When the CX register is equal to 0 all ten items have been added and the program ends.

Branch prediction

Many processors contain logic which predicts if a particular conditional branch will be taken (i.e., the condition will be satisfied). This is to allow the processor to pre-fetch (and possibly) pre-execute instructions after the branch to improve overall performance. This technique will be looked at in more detail in Chapter 6.

Subroutines

Subroutines are segments of code which perform a given function and generally need to be executed multiple times. By breaking up the program into subroutines the development of software becomes more manageable and the code more compact. Examples of subroutine functions might be:

read a character from the keyboard;
write a character to the screen;
calculate the average of a table of numbers;
compare the contents of two strings stored in memory.

A special form of the branch instruction is used to jump to the first instruction in the subroutine. At the end of each subroutine another special instruction (called return) is executed which returns the program back to the point just after the subroutine was originally called. Look at the example in Figure 5.3.

When the CALL instruction is executed the program jumps to the KEYBOARD_INPUT subroutine; when the RET (return instruction) is executed the program will return to the CMP (compare instruction) since this is the one following the CALL.

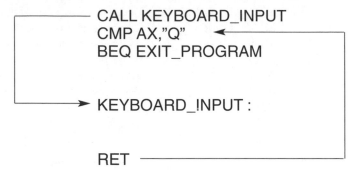

Figure 5.3   Branch to subroutine example

5.2.4   FLOATING POINT INSTRUCTIONS

These perform basic arithmetic and other more complex mathematical operations on floating point numbers. The format of the numbers for both processors follows the IEEE-754 standard. Examples of floating point operations are:

Multiply

Divide

Add

Subtract

Square root

Logarithm

The Pentium processor supports a wider range of floating point functions than the PowerPC, including a large number which can be used to optimise the processing of graphical data. These help the processor to perform functions such as video decompression. For the PowerPC these functions have to be done in software.

5.2.5   INPUT/OUTPUT INSTRUCTIONS

These are special instructions used to send data to and from I/O devices. In fact, the PowerPC does not provide any special instructions for I/O, but uses a technique called memory mapping (see Chapter 10) to access devices. The Pentium supports two instructions, IN to input data from an input device and OUT to send data to an output device.

5.2.6   SPECIAL SYSTEM INSTRUCTIONS

These are instructions which affect the operation of the microprocessor itself. For example, shutting it down, testing its internal function or disabling it from receiving interrupts (see Chapter 9).

5.3   MEMORY ADDRESSING

When fetching data from or storing data to memory, processors usually provide a number of different techniques to generate the address. This is useful since it allows us to use a method suitable for the program we are writing. For example, when we are fetching a single value out of a memory location we may need a different technique than when we are operating on a whole table of values.

The effective address of an operand is the final memory address that is generated by the instruction once the transformations and modifications needed to produce the address have been carried out.

5.3.1   DIRECT (ABSOLUTE) ADDRESSING

The effective address is given explicitly as part of the instruction, for example:

```
MOV BX,[6789]        ;move the contents of 6789 to the BX register
```

Assuming the number 120 was stored at location 6789 then, after this instruction, BX would contain 120. This is suitable when the data is a single variable and the memory location is known beforehand.

5.3.2   IMMEDIATE ADDRESSING

This is where the operand is an immediate value and does not refer to an address at all. The effective address is, in fact, the address of the instruction operand (since this is where it is fetched from).

```
MOV DX,45        ;move the number 45 into the DX register
```

5.3.3   INDIRECT ADDRESSING

The effective address is stored either in a memory location or a register. In this case, first the effective address must be read out of memory (or register) then the operand can be accessed. Here is an example of register indirect addressing:

```
MOV BX,1235        ;set up address in BX register
ADD AX,[BX]        ;add the contents of the address pointed to by BX
                   ;onto AX
```

This is useful because it allows the address of the instruction to be changed (for example in a program loop) or passed into a subroutine as a parameter. Here is an example of a subroutine which determines the length of a null terminated string, the address of the string being stored in the BX register. *Note* null terminated strings store a zero in memory to indicate the end of the string of characters.

```
        MOV AX,0                ;start
STRING_LOOP :
        MOV DL,[BX]             ;get the next byte in the string
```

```
        INC BX              ;add 1 to the BX register (move to next
                            character in
                            ;string)
        INC AX              ;add 1 to the length count
        CMP DL,0            ;have we got to the end of the string
        BNE STRING_LOOP     ;no carry on
        DEC AX              ;adjust AX
        RET                 ;now AX contains length of string
```

The AX register is used to return the result. In the loop the DL register is loaded up with characters in the string pointed to by the BX register. Each time round the loop the BX register is incremented to move it to the next character and AX is incremented to add to the length. When the value in the DL register equals 0, the null has been found and the loop finishes. Since the value in the AX register is always incremented (even when DL = 0), it will count the null character in the length of the string. For this reason, AX is adjusted at the end by subtracting one to get the correct result.

The PowerPC also supports an indirect register addressing mode called register indirect with index. In this case the sum of two registers is used to calculate the effective address. For example:

```
    lwzx   r4, r8, r9
```

If r8 contains 4000 and r9 contains 9000, r4 will be loaded with the contents of memory location 13000.

5.3.4   BASED INDEX ADDRESSING

To generate the effective address a constant base address (called, with the Pentium processor, the displacement) is added to a register called the index. This makes it easy to perform a function such as moving though a table of values in memory. The base address is the start of the table and the register value contains the index of the table entry being accessed. The following program finds the average of the numbers stored in the table called data_items.

```
        MOV BX,0                    ;BX = 0 start of the array
        MOV AX,0                    ;AX contains the sum
ADD_LOOP :
        ADD AX,[data_items + BX]    ;add next item to sum
        INC BX                      ;move to next item
        CMP BX,10                   ;have we reached the end of the array
        BEQ ADD_LOOP                ;if not keep going
        DIV BX                      ;since BX = 10 divide SUM by 10 to
                                    get average
```

The code inside the loop adds up the numbers stored in the data_items' table, with the result being stored in the AX register. When the loop is completed the DIV BX instruction divides the AX register by 10 (the contents of the BX register).

For the PowerPC, based index addressing is called register indirect with immediate index mode. For the Pentium, the programmer can also set a scaling factor and use up to two index registers (Intel refers to these registers as index and base registers). The scaling factor allows the index register to refer to a list of items which are multiple bytes in length (e.g., 4 byte words). The sum of the index registers is multiplied by the scale factor before adding to the constant displacement value. Here is an example of based, indexed addressing for the Pentium with a scale factor of 4:

MOV AX,4*[SI + BX]+start_table

In this case because we have two index registers, we can organise the data as an array of rows and columns, the SI register referring to the rows and the BX register referring to the columns.

5.3.5 REGISTER ADDRESSING

This is where the source operand is just another register. An example of this is:

MOV AX,BX

This type of addressing mode is extremely fast since no memory access is required to retrieve the operand.

Table 5.5 compares the number of different addressing modes of the PowerPC and the Pentium processor. *Note* the Pentium has a lot more addressing modes for each type of instruction, which is typical when comparing CISC with RISC designs.

5.3.6 ABSOLUTE AND RELATIVE ADDRESSING

Absolute address values encoded into instructions define the address from the start of memory, i.e., 2000 means memory location with address 2000. In contrast, relative address values define an offset value from the address of

Table 5.5 Pentium and PowerPC addressing modes

Instruction type	Addressing modes
PowerPC	
Load and Store	4 modes: direct, based index, register indirect with index, register indirect
Branch	2 modes: immediate, register indirect
Arithmetic	2 modes: register, immediate
Pentium	
Move	8 modes; direct, register indirect, immediate, register, indexed, scaled indexed, based index, indexed base (two registers + displacement)
Branch	immediate
Arithmetic	8 modes same as move

Table 5.6   Absolute addressing encoding

Address	Instruction	Opcode	Operand
1400	MOV AX,4560	99	4560
1403	ADD AX,1000	100	1000
1406	BRANCH 1412	65	1412
1409	MOV BX,1234	101	1234
1412	ADD BX,1978	102	1978

Table 5.7   Relative addressing encoding

Address	Instruction	Opcode	Operand
1400	MOV AX,4560	99	4560
1403	ADD AX,1000	100	1000
1406	BRANCH 1412	65	0006
1409	MOV BX,1234	101	1234
1412	ADD BX,1978	102	1978

the current instruction being executed. To calculate the effective address the offset is added to the instruction address. For example, if an instruction is stored at memory address 22000 and the relative address value is 198, the effective address will be 22198. This mode, called relative addressing, is particularly useful for branch instructions. The example in Table 5.6 will illustrate why (*note* the encoding of the program is done using a pseudo machine code to aid understanding).

This program has been loaded into memory at memory address 1400. Now, what would happen to the code if it were relocated to memory address 1500? The operand value 1412 in the third line would have to be changed to 1512 to make the branch go to the same part of the program.

In Table 5.7, we look at the same program encoded using relative addressing.

The encoded value for the operand in line 3 is 0006. This means that we calculate the address of the branch by adding 6 onto the address of the current instruction 1406. So we get 1406 + 6 = 1412 as the destination for the branch. The advantage with this type of encoding is that it allows the whole program to be moved in memory without having to modify the code. This property called relocatability is desirable since computer systems commonly need to put programs in different places in memory at different times.

5.3.7   IMPLICIT ADDRESSING

This is where the operand is not specified in the instruction but is implied by the type of instruction being executed. For example, for the MUL instruction one of the multiplicands is always stored in the AX register and therefore does not have to be stated in the instruction. So MUL BX means multiply AX by BX the AX being an implicit operand.

5.4   INSTRUCTION ENCODING

Each instruction has to be encoded in memory using the format defined by the processor. Figures 5.4 and 5.5 show the formats for both the Pentium™ and PowerPC™ processors. One thing we can see immediately is that the PowerPC format is of a fixed length (32 bits); this is consistent with its cut down RISC architecture and simplifies the instruction execution. In contrast, the Pentium has a variable length, fairly complex instruction format.

5.4.1   PENTIUM INSTRUCTION FORMAT

The first part of the Pentium instruction is called its prefix; this adds more control to the operation of the instruction. For example, the REP prefix allows an instruction to be executed repeatedly. Other prefix values determine which segment register the instruction should use (we looked at segmentation in Chapter 4).

The next part of the instruction is a 1 or 2 byte opcode (the opcode defines the operator part of the instruction, i.e., its function).

After the opcode the field called mod R/M defines the addressing mode and source and destination operands. The SIB field stores a scaling factor and defines any index or base register for the address calculation. The last fields of the instruction are two mutually exclusive values, displacement (for address generation) or an immediate value. Since no instruction on the Pentium allows an immediate value to be placed directly into memory, only one of these fields is specified in any given instruction.

Note that the displacement and immediate fields are 1 to 4 bytes long, allowing the full range of addresses to be generated and immediate values from 0 to $2^{32}-1$ to be specified.

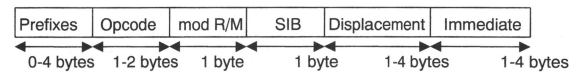

Figure 5.4   Pentium instruction format

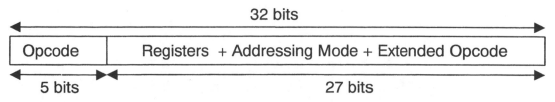

Figure 5.5   PowerPC instruction format

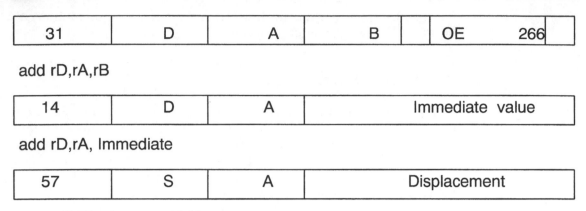

add rD,rA,rB

add rD,rA, Immediate

stwu rS,Displacement(rA)

Figure 5.6 PowerPC instruction examples

Since up to 4 prefixes can be defined (or none at all), the length of the Pentium instruction can range from 1 to 12 bytes. This wide range of instruction lengths will make it more difficult to decode the instruction since its length will have to be determined as it is decoded.

5.4.2 PowerPC INSTRUCTION FORMAT

The PowerPC instruction is packed into 32 bits. The start of each instruction consists of a 5 bit primary opcode and the format of the rest of the instruction is dependent on this opcode value. If the opcode is 31, this defines an extended opcode with the rest of the opcode OE being stored at the end of the instruction word. Figure 5.6 shows three examples of PowerPC instructions: addition of two registers, add register to immediate value and a store word instruction.

For the first two instructions, the field following the opcode defines the destination register rD of the operation; for the last instruction it defines the source register rS, since the destination is a memory location. The next field is used to define the first operand register rA. The last part of the instruction defines the other operand (register rB, immediate value or displacement).

For the register to register add instruction, the action is as follows:

rD ← rA + rB

Note the fields for the register definitions are 5 bits long, allowing references to the PowerPC's 32 general purpose registers.

For the register plus immediate add instruction, the following is executed:

rD ← rA + Immediate value

If the A is zero then rA is replaced by zero giving:

rD ← Immediate value

Note that because of the limited size of the PowerPC instruction field only a 16 bit immediate value can be added. Since the loading of immediate values is carried out using an ADD instruction (see 5.2.2), two instructions are required to load up a 32-bit immediate value into a register. To load up the 32-bit hex value 12345678 into register r5 would require the following two PowerPC instructions:

```
addis r5,0,1234        ; add with shift left 16 positions
addi r5,r5,5678        ; add in remaining 16 bits to r5
```

The final instruction stwu rS,Displacement(rA), stores the value held in register rS into a memory location. The effective address of the memory location is calculated by adding rA to the displacement. So operation of the instruction is:

(rA + displacement) ← Rs

Since the displacement is only 16 bits long rA must be set up with an appropriate address.

5.5   STACKS

A stack is a data structure stored in memory which is accessed in a particular sequence called last in first out. Items can be added to the stack and removed from it. Figure 5.7 shows a stack with items being added and then removed. Adding items to a stack is called pushing onto the stack and removing items called pulling (or popping) from the stack.

In Figure 5.7 the following sequence of operations is represented:

push 55, push 101, push 99, push 76, pop, pop, push 25

Notice how the stack grows downwards in memory and items are removed in the reverse order that they were added. The next item to be removed (and conversely the last item added) is stored at a location called the top of stack. This at first may seem confusing since this is stored in the lowest memory location. All processors provide a stack facility and computer programs use stacks for a number of functions including:

Temporary storage of registers.

Storing the return address when calling a subroutine.

Local variable storage for subroutines.

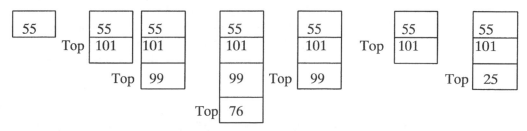

Figure 5.7 Operation of stack

Some machines use an internal stack to store information alongside the internal registers. These machines are called stack assisted; the floating-point unit for Pentium processors is stack assisted. A system that uses a stack instead of registers is called a stack machine. Stacks are useful when doing arithmetic; this can be illustrated with the following example.

To calculate $(A \times B) + (C \times D)$ a stack machine will work as follows:

```
PUSH A
PUSH B
MULTIPLY      (pops 2 items off stack, multiply items, push result back on
              stack)
PUSH C
PUSH D
MULTIPLY      (pops 2 items off stack, multiply items, push result back on
              stack)
ADD           (pops 2 items off stack, add items, push result back on stack)
```

The final result is stored on the top of the stack; *note* the sequence of operations is changed somewhat from the original expression. The expressions inside the brackets are carried out first with the operands being pushed and then operators acting on the data stored at the top of the stack. We can change the sequence of the original expression to:

A B $\times$ C D $\times$ +

We then use the following two rules on each of the items in the sequence in turn.

If the item is an operand push it on the stack.

If the item is an operator, pop the operands off the stack, do the operation, push the result back on the stack.

When the expression is finished the result is found on the top of the stack. The format of the expression is called reverse polish notation and has the advantage that it required no brackets and is easy for a computer program to process.

5.5.1 SUBROUTINE LINKAGE

When calling a subroutine the return address (where the program will return when the subroutine finishes) is saved on the stack. If the subroutine calls another subroutine then the new return address is stored on the top of the stack. When the second subroutine finishes it will get the return address from the top of the stack and return to executing the first subroutine. When the first subroutine finishes it will get its return address from the top of the stack and return to the main program. Figure 5.8 illustrates this process.

Stack pointer

This register stores the address of the top of the stack, i.e., the address of the last item stored or the next item to be retrieved. When an item is pushed

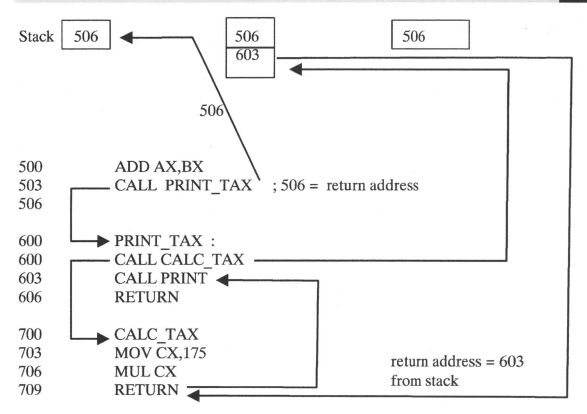

Figure 5.8 Subroutine linkage

onto the stack the stack pointer is decremented and then the item is stored at the memory address referred to by the stack pointer. When an item is pulled from the stack the location pointed to by the stack pointer is read and the stack pointer incremented. Figure 5.9 illustrates this process; *note* this is the same sequence of push and pops as defined in Figure 5.7.

As well as providing a mechanism for handling the return address, the stack is also used by subroutines for temporary storage. For example, when a subroutine starts it might want to save the values of the processor's registers; this can be done by pushing them onto the stack at the start of a subroutine and pulling them from the stack (in reverse order) at the end. Also the stack can be used as an area for temporary variables that the subroutine might need to use. The area in the stack used by the subroutine for this storage is referred to as a *stack frame*. Figure 5.10 shows an example of a stack frame.

To help the programmer keep a track of the frame, a register is usually assigned to point to the start of the frame on the stack. The start of the frame also has a pointer to the previous stack frame. This allows the subroutine to get access to the other subroutine's local variables and is used by programming languages such as Pascal, C++ and Java.

Address

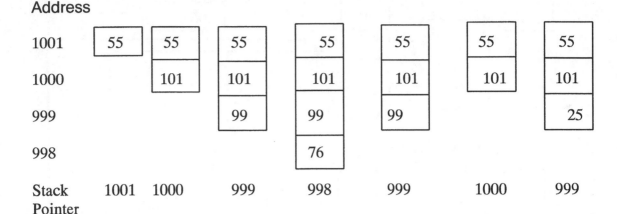

| Stack Pointer | 1001 | 1000 | 999 | 998 | 999 | 1000 | 999 |

Figure 5.9   Stack pointer example

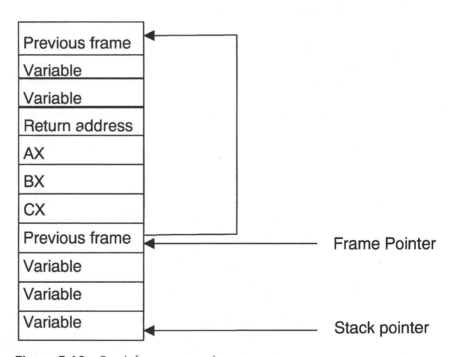

Figure 5.10   Stack frame example

5.6   RISC REDUCED INSTRUCTION SET COMPUTERS

There has been a lot of hype about RISC processing since its invention. The concept of RISC is as follows:

Design a processor with a very limited instruction set, each instruction performing only a simple function but executing very rapidly. Each instruction ideally will run in one machine cycle (or possibly less if multiple instructions are executed at the same time). This is in contrast to CISC or Complex Instruction Set Computers in which each instruction does more work but takes longer to run.

With early computer systems, memory storage was very expensive and of limited capacity. This led to the design of processors with large complex instruction sets so that the program could be coded into less space.

The typical characteristics of a RISC processor are:

relatively few instructions, each with limited addressing modes;

fixed length instructions;

many instructions hard wired (see Chapter 6) with short execution times;

many general purpose registers;

memory access limited to two operations, load and store, other instructions operate only on registers.

To perform the same task a program written for a RISC processor will require more instructions than the equivalent program written for a CISC processor. For each CISC instruction two, three or more RISC instructions will have to be executed. To achieve high performance, the RISC program has to be very carefully written to perform the task with the fewest instructions possible.

The use of many general-purpose registers allows the processor to keep data stored internally and only write back to memory when the result is obtained. This allows the processor to do complex calculations very quickly. Also, having so many registers, it is easier for the processor to work on more than one instruction at a time since each instruction may be working on a different set.

A RISC architecture does not deliver improved performance simply because it is faster, though more instructions reduce the total execution time from that used by slower, though fewer instructions. The important factor is that it requires careful analysis of what instructions are really necessary and the design of the hardware to be undertaken in conjunction with the design of the software (both language and its compiler).

5.7 SOFTWARE DEVELOPMENT

A typical computer program (or piece of software) consists of many thousands of low-level instructions. These instructions (as we saw in 5.4) are stored in memory in the form of binary. This numerical representation of the program's instructions is called machine code (or object code) and is the only instruction form which the processor can execute.

To write a program in machine code you would need to look up each instruction you wanted to execute in the processor's user manual and then enter it numerically into the computer. If your program was 10,000 bytes long you would have to type 10,000 numbers into the computer. The problem of finding and getting rid of errors in your program (or debugging) would be extremely difficult. Imagine trying to debug the following piece of program code:

```
A334A0
304567
409010
```

These codes are actually just random numbers, but you wouldn't necessarily know that until you tried to translate them. In fact machine code is not used to develop software at all since it is very error prone and slow to code.

5.7.1 ASSEMBLY LANGUAGE PROGRAMMING

In assembly language programming, each instruction is represented by a short form or mnemonic. Each assembly language instruction has a one to one correspondence with one machine code instruction. The instruction examples in this chapter are written in assembly language. Even though assembly language is preferable to writing programs in machine code, it, again, is slow to code in and error prone. In general, assembly language should only be used in the following circumstances:

Where performance is highly critical and using a high level language (see next section) will not achieve that performance.

Certain features of the machine are only available when programming at a low level.

A high level language for the processor is not available (for example for new hardware).

Since the processor only understands machine code, before it can be run the assembly language program must be translated. This is done with a piece of software called an assembler. The assembler will take the file containing the assembly language and produce an object file containing the machine code instructions.

5.7.2 HIGH LEVEL LANGUAGE PROGRAMMING

With a high level language the program is written in a form closer to natural languages. Figure 5.11 is an example of a short piece of code written in C. See if you can work out what it does (the * symbol represents multiply). Programs can be written in high level languages much more quickly and debugged a lot more easily than programs written in low level languages. A compiler is used to translate the program from the high level language to machine code.

5.7.3 PORTABILITY

Since the program's high level language instructions do not have a one to one correspondence with the machine language instructions the program can be run on (or ported to) another machine (as long as an appropriate compiler is available for that machine).

For example, the program written in C (Figure 5.11) could be run equally well on a PowerPC or Pentium machine, as long as we had a C compiler available for each. This feature of portability is a major advantage of high-level language programming over assembler. For this reason and the others stated previously, almost all software is written in high-level languages.

Interpreted programming languages

These are high level languages, which, instead of being translated into machine code, are either not compiled at all or are compiled into a form called intermediary code. The program (or intermediary code) is not executed directly by the processor but instead run by a program called an interpreter. The interpreter takes each line of the program in turn and performs the statement on its behalf. Interpreted programs run a lot slower than conventional compiled code but do have a number of advantages:

The program is portable without recompilation.

The program can be controlled very tightly since it is being run using another piece of configurable software (the interpreter).

The program is quick to debug since it does not have to be recompiled/linked when the code is changed.

Java is an example of an interpreted language. The Java interpreter is called the Java Virtual Machine or JVM. The compiled intermediary code in Java is called byte code and can be ported without modification between Java compliant platforms. This makes the code particularly suitable for downloading over a network (e.g., the Internet) where it might have to run on a wide range of hardware and operating system platforms.

5.7.4 LINKERS AND LOADERS

Usually a program will consist of so many instructions that it is sensible to break it up into a number of smaller pieces (typically called modules), each stored in a separate file. Most software development environments provide a standard set of subroutines or libraries that the software developer can use.

```
if (salary>allowance) {
    taxable=salary-allowance;
    tax=taxable * tax_rate;
}
else
{
    tax=0;
}
```

Figure 5.11 C language example

Each program module, when compiled, produces a separate object file. The linker's job is to join all these files (objects and libraries) together to produce the finished program called the executable.

Apart from just joining the object files the linker also has to do two other important tasks:

Resolve external references.

Relocate code.

It is quite common for a program module to call a subroutine or access data defined in another module; this is called an external reference. Since each module is compiled individually, the address of the subroutine or data in the other module will be unknown at compile time. To get round this the compiler inserts a dummy address for the reference which is then filled in with the correct value by the linker later on.

Code relocation is the process of getting the program to work at the given address where it will be loaded in memory. We looked at the problem of relocation in section 5.3.6. Here is another example.

```
1000        MOV BX,VARIABLE2
1003        MOV CX,VARIABLE3
1006        MOV DX,VARIABLE4
  .
  .
  .
2000        VARIABLE1
2002        VARIABLE2
2004        VARIABLE3
```

If the data is moved to another location each of the absolute addresses coded in the move instructions will have to be adjusted to reflect the variables' change in address. At compile time the start address is not known (since it will depend on the number and size of modules in the link) and each module's code is compiled as if it were located at address 0. At link time each module is relocated to the address that it will occupy in the final executable.

5.7.5   LOADERS

The loader is responsible for loading the file into the system's memory from file storage. As the address of available free memory in the computer system will change with time (due to the number of programs already loaded up), the loader will have to be able to get the program to work at any given address. This means that apart from loading the program the loader will also have to modify any code which requires relocation (see example above).

5.8   SYSTEM SOFTWARE

System software provides a basic set of services which makes the machine usable. Without any system software the machine would be essentially useless since you wouldn't be able to even interact with it using the keyboard or monitor. Typical functions of system software include:

controlling hardware such as keyboards, disk, monitor or mouse;

scheduling user programs to run;

providing a file system in which to store data;

providing a graphical user interface (GUI;)

network services;

system security;

allocating memory to user programs.

The complete set of system software for a machine is called the operating system or OS. Examples of operating systems are UNIX, VMS and Windows NT.

Operating systems can be classified as follows:

multitasking or single tasking;

multiuser or single user.

A multitasking operating system can run more than one program at once. In fact the programs run using a process called time-slicing where the computer runs a little bit of one program, then stops it, then runs a little bit of the next program, etc. It switches between each program so fast that it appears as if the programs are running concurrently. All general purpose operating systems in use today provide multitasking. An example of a single tasking operating system is DOS but this is not in widescale use any more.

A lot of modern computer systems have multiple processors where each processor can run a separate program at the same time without time slicing. If an operating system is capable of using multiple processors to run your applications it is said to support SMP or symmetric multi-processing. Each processor is treated the same (symmetrically); this is in contrast with systems which might be using a specialised extra processor to, for example, control the hard disk. Windows NT, Windows 2000 and Linux support SMP.

Multi-user operating systems have to be able to distinguish between different users on the computer and provide secure access for user's data. For example, if a user writes a confidential letter and stores it on the machine they would not want it read by other users. With a multi-user system it is possible to provide file security so that users cannot access each other's files. Before using a multi-user system users must first login, identifying themselves with a username (or userid) and a password. Once logged in the system controls file access dependent on the userid. Most multi-user operating systems allow multiple users to access the system concurrently and run programs at the same time. Windows NT, UNIX and Linux are all examples of multi-user operating systems. *Note* Windows ME is not a multi-user operating system, being based in the single user technology of Windows 95.

Device drivers

Modern computer systems are capable of being fitted with a bewildering array of different hardware, e.g., video cards, TV cameras, scanners, etc. Each of these pieces of hardware needs to be controlled in a different manner. For the operating system itself directly to support each and every different piece of hardware that might be connected, the OS developer would have to include control software for hundreds or even thousands of devices. This is practically an impossible task and would require the OS to be updated to support new hardware nearly every day.

The solution to this problem is for the manufacturer of the hardware to develop a program called a device driver and supply the driver with the device.

The device driver provides a standard interface to the operating system; this is used by the OS to send commands to the hardware (see Figure 5.12). For example, for a network card device driver there will be an operating system command to read the next packet of data into memory. Since the OS interface is standard (for a given OS) the OS does not need to worry about the details of interfacing with the device and only has to know how to talk to the driver. Device driver standards exist for Windows, UNIX and Linux.

Different possible types of device drivers are:

character drivers	keyboard
block drivers	network card
video drivers	graphics interface card

Each of the types of driver has different types of command. For example, a graphics driver would support line drawing commands. This allows an application such as video game to support new powerful hardware without modification. All the application needs is code written to inter-operate with the driver – the hardware can be updated without changing the application at all.

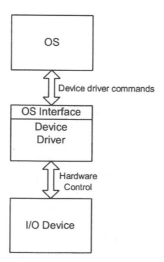

Figure 5.12   Device driver interface

BIOS (basic input output system)

When a computer system is powered up, its memory is empty and it needs a program to start it up. The BIOS is a program stored in ROM (or EPROM or EEPROM, see Chapter 4) that runs as soon as the machine is powered on.

When the machine starts up the BIOS will typically perform the following tasks:

Put a message on the monitor.

Test the operation of hardware including the memory and hard disk controller. This is called the power on self test or POST.

Get the current system configuration out of battery backed up RAM.

Load up the operating system from the hard disk drive.

Release control to the operating system.

The BIOS also provides simple I/O access to some of the hardware on the machine. In fact, on PC systems the BIOS provides low level control to the following devices:

keyboard;

monitor;

disk drive;

printer port;

serial ports.

5.9   SUMMARY

We have seen in this chapter how computer processors support a wide range of instructions and how these instructions are encoded in memory. We have also seen how different types of addressing modes can be used in programs and compared the different approaches taken with both the Pentium and PowerPC processors' instruction sets. We looked at how RISC systems optimise the performance of software with fixed length, simplified instruction sets. Low level programming is inherently difficult, slow and error prone; we saw that by using a high-level programming language, software can be ported between different systems. We also looked at how interpreted programming languages such as Java have provided an even higher level of portability requiring no recompilation.

The need for and the functions and operations of system software was also examined. In particular, the important role that device drivers play in interacting with different types of hardware and providing a standard interface to the OS.

To understand in depth the main principles explained in this chapter the reader is urged to write some simple programs in assembly language and examine the machine code produced. By doing this the reader can fully understand how opcodes and addressing modes are encoded at machine level. The reader is also encouraged to find out more about the capabilities and pros and cons of the various operating systems currently available.

5.10 EXERCISES

1 a   Describe implicit addressing.

   b   What is an effective address? How is it achieved when addressing:
   directly;
   by indexing;
   indirectly.

2   Describe two simple addressing modes in common use. Specify their advantages and disadvantages and give a specific detailed example of each mode from a processor with which you are familiar. Use diagrams where appropriate.

3 a   What factors have to be taken into account when the number of operands in an instruction is being specified and how does this affect the computer's architecture.

   b   Describe four ways in which an effective address can be generated.

4   What type of addressing is used to specify the destination operand for the Pentium multiply instruction?
   What is reverse polish notation and why is it useful to express mathematical expression using it?

15   Show, with examples, how logical operations can be used:
   to set the top bit of 16-bit register leaving the rest unchanged;
   to test for the occurrence of a 4-bit pattern in the least significant nibble of a byte;
   to complement the three most significant bits of a 16-bit register.

6   Investigate the instruction sets of the following processors:
   RS6000   680020   Pentium   PowerPC   ARM
   Determine which are RISC and which are CISC and compare and contrast the approach taken for the instruction set of each.

7   Why is a stack so important for the correct operation of a computer program?

8   How do device drivers make it easier for the hardware to be upgraded on your computer system?

9   What are the advantages and disadvantages in using a language such as Java, as compared to a conventionally compiled language such as C++?

10   Describe the functions of an operating system.

The central processing unit

The central processing unit or CPU is responsible for carrying out lists of instructions (or software) that are stored in memory. The CPU has to read (fetch) each instruction from memory, interpret what the instruction must do (decode) and then after (optionally) reading more data, perform the instruction (execute). For some instructions, data is written to memory as part of its execution (see Chapter 5). In early computer systems the CPU were constructed out of a number of different circuit boards wired together. In modern computer systems the CPU is fabricated on to one chip called a microprocessor. For most purposes the terms microprocessor and CPU are interchangeable.

6.1 COMPONENT PARTS

The CPU can be thought of as being made up of a number of component parts, as illustrated in Figure 6.1. There are a number of special-purpose registers (in addition to the general purpose ones that are available to the programmer): the arithmetic and logic unit (ALU) which performs computations, a bus control and a memory management unit and level 1 cache (see Chapter 4) used to communicate with the memory or I/O. The control unit is effectively the nerve centre of the machine, sending control signals to all the other units. Many CPUs also contain a floating-point unit to execute non-integer arithmetic. There are variations on this model, with many CPUs containing multiple ALUs to allow them to perform more than one calculation at a time.

6.1.1 INTERNAL REGISTERS

A program is made up of a series of instructions; these are stored in the main memory of the computer. To execute this program, the CPU fetches the instructions, one at a time, and arranges for the appropriate actions to be taken. The instructions are fetched from consecutive locations unless a branch instruction is executed. The registers in Table 6.1 support this activity.

Table 6.1   CPU internal control registers

Program counter (PC) (sometimes called the instruction pointer)	This stores the address of the next instruction to be fetched from memory. As each instruction is executed, this register is incremented by the size of the instruction in bytes. If the instruction executed was a branch instruction it may load the PC with the branch address.
MAR	Memory address register; this holds the address that the CPU wants to read from or write to memory.
MBR	Memory buffer register; this holds the data that is to be written to or has been read from memory.
IR	Instruction register; this stores a copy of the current instruction being executed, so that it can be decoded and executed.

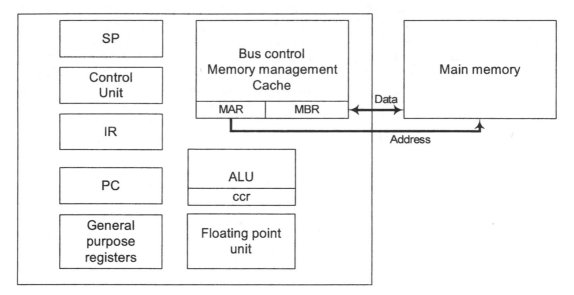

Figure 6.1   CPU block diagram

There are a number of other specialised registers that are commonly used by the CPU when executing its program:

SP	stack pointer points to the top item on the stack (see Chapter 5) used by the CPU when storing the return address of subroutines and by programs to pass parameters to subroutines.
CCR	condition code register, this register; is made up of multiple single bit registers called flags that store information about the results of operations such as arithmetic instructions. For example; most CCRs contain a carry bit which is set if there is an overflow after an addition instruction.

Memory management registers

Other registers used internally by the CPU, and sometimes by the operating system software, include the memory management registers. These store values such as the base address of segments or pages, the address of page of segment tables, cached values of segment descriptors, etc. (see Chapter 4 for a detailed discussion of memory management). These, of course, will only be present on processors supporting memory management which would not be the case, for example, with a simple micro-controller.

Floating point registers

Used to store the final and intermediate values for floating point arithmetic instructions. In many floating point processors these registers are organised as a stack, allowing the programmer to push and pop values in and out of the register set.

6.1.2 ARITHMETIC LOGIC UNIT

The arithmetic and logic unit (ALU) is the part of the CPU where all the arithmetical and logical operations take place. It is constructed from complex digital components, some dedicated to particular functions (such as adders), and some general purpose components such as shift registers. Typical of the operations supported by the ALU are:

arithmetic, such as add, subtract, multiply and divide;

logical and comparison operations such as complement, and, or, exclusive or

bit manipulation operations shift, rotate and test.

The ALU, in general, provides only integer arithmetic (for other types of numbers see the next section on the floating point unit). Addition instructions are carried out using the full adder described in Chapter 3. To subtract numbers the ALU takes the two's complement of the number to be subtracted and adds it to the first number using the adder unit.

Condition flags

The addition of two numbers can result in overflow (see Chapter 2). For example if adding the numbers 100 to 200 in 8 bit registers, the result (300) will be too large to store since the largest number that can be stored is 255. In this case the ALU will indicate the overflow by setting a bit in the condition control register called the carry flag. The following condition flags are supported by most processors (including the Pentium® and PowerPC®).

Zero flag

Indicates the result is zero, particularly useful when using the comparison instruction.

Carry flag

Indicates the result overflowed (or borrow is required for subtraction); this can be used to do multiword additions as follows:

For example, if your ALU can only do 8 bit addition and you need to add 356 to 456, these numbers in hexadecimal are 164 and 1C8. Stored as 8 bit numbers they require 2 bytes each and would be stored as the following byte sequence: 64, 01, C8 and 01. Note the least significant bytes are being stored first.

1 ADD 64 to C8 → 2C and the carry flag set
2 ADD with carry 01 to 01 → 03 (since the carry flag is set this adds an extra 1)

The result is 32C which in decimal is 812 the required result. By stringing together more ADD with carry instructions, numbers of arbitrary length can be added together using this technique.

Negative flag

Set to one if the result is negative in two's complement arithmetic.

Signed overflow flag

Set if the result of an operation resulted in a signed overflow, for example if adding the two 8 bit numbers 100 and 95 the result 195 is greater than 127 the maximum value that can be stored and the signed overflow flag will be set.

Multiplication

To multiply two numbers: this can be done using shifts, bit testing and addition. The following algorithm will multiply two numbers, M1 and M2.

1   0   →   RESULT
2   IF LEAST SIGNIFICANT BIT(M1) = 1 RESULT + M2   →   RESULT
3   M1 / 2   →   M1
4   M2 X 2   →   M2
5   IF M1 IS NON ZERO GO TO 2

The divide by two is the equivalent of a shift right one place and the multiply a shift left. This, plus the addition, can all be carried out in hardware. Due to the looping nature of the algorithm this is more computationally intensive than add or subtract, and therefore takes more time. All these functions (add, shift and bit test) making up the multiply are relatively easy to implement in hardware, and most CPUs do just that. However, some of the low budget 8 bit processors do not do this (due to small transistors budget) and the algorithm has to be implemented in software using shift and add instructions.

It is also possible to carry out multiplication using a dedicated parallel multiplier; this does the whole calculation at once (not using the shift technique) and is therefore a lot faster. Parallel multipliers tend to be too expensive (in terms of transistor count) to be justified by most processors and are, therefore, usually only used in specialised high performance systems such as supercomputers.

Division

Divide uses a similar set of functions as multiply but it uses subtract instead of add and compare instead of bit test. Again most CPUs carry out the instruction within the ALU, with some 8-bit processors requiring the algorithm to be implemented in software.

Logical operations

Logical operations (AND, OR, NOT, etc.) are very simple to implement in hardware since they have exact equivalents in gate form and run very fast. Comparison is equivalent to subtraction but with no result being stored although the condition flags are affected. For example, if you compare registers r1 and r2, the ALU will subtract r2 from r1. If the numbers are equal the zero flag will be set; if r1 is less than r2 then the carry flag will be set. Conditional branch instruction uses the values in the condition flags to determine if a branch will occur; for example, the BEQ Pentium® instruction will only branch if the zero flag is set [i.e., the two compared (subtracted) numbers were equal].

Shift and rotation operations

ALUs support two directions of shift, left or right, and two types of shift operation, arithmetic and logical shift. With logical shift, zero always replaces the bit vacated (least significant bit with left shift, most significant with right shift). With arithmetic shift right the most significant bit is always preserved, i.e., does not change; this ensures that two's complement numbers divide by two correctly. Arithmetic shift right is the same as logical shift right.

Rotate is the same as shift but, instead of losing bits, they are recycled with the top bit replacing the bottom bit (with left rotate) and the bottom replacing the top (with right rotate). All these operations are illustrated in Figure 6.2.

6.1.3 FLOATING POINT UNIT

This provides the CPU with the ability to do floating point arithmetic and other functions such as logarithms and exponents as well as geometric functions such as tangents, sine and cosine. In early computer systems the provision of the floating point unit was often an optional extra (since it was expensive). For systems without a unit, the floating point operations had to be simulated in software. Both the Pentium® and PowerPC® processors provide floating point units built in; both implementations use the IEEE 754 standard to store and represent numbers.

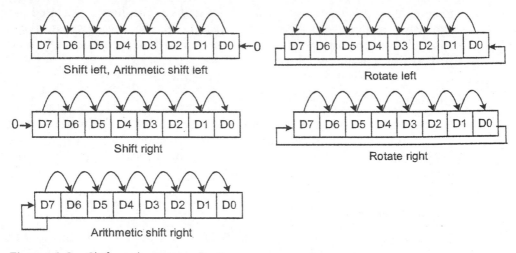

Figure 6.2 Shift and rotate operations

6.1.4 BUS CONTROL AND MEMORY MANAGEMENT UNIT

These are used to control signals on the bus lines that connect the CPU to the memory and I/O. The memory management unit converts logical addresses into physical addresses, fetches segment and page descriptors from memory and controls the protected memory mechanisms described in Chapter 4. The MMU contains all the memory management registers, as well as the MAR and MBR.

6.2 FETCH/EXECUTE CYCLE

The execution of the program is carried out using the following sequence of events, called the fetch/execute cycle.

1 Copy the PC into the MAR and initiate memory read

2 Copy the instruction now in the MBR into the IR

3 Increment the PC by the size of the instruction

4 Decode the IR

5 Execute the instruction

6 Go to step 1

This can be represented by a symbolic notation as follows, where [x] means 'contents of x', and M represents a main memory location.

$$[PC] \rightarrow MAR$$
$$[M] \rightarrow MBR$$
$$[MBR] \rightarrow IR$$
$$[PC] + IR_{length} \rightarrow [PC]$$

Decode IR

Execute the instruction

Decoding the IR involves the control unit examining the opcode of the instruction, working out what it is meant to do, and passing control signals to the other parts of the microprocessor to complete the execution. The execution of the instruction is somewhat simplified in this description; the following section describes it in more detail.

Note for processors such as the PowerPC® the instruction length is fixed at 4 bytes. This means that the PC is always incremented by 4 and the length does not have to be worked out from the instruction. The Pentium® instructions are of variable length making the fetch phase more complex, since the length has to be calculated once the instruction has been read from memory.

6.2.1 EXECUTION OF NON-MEMORY REFERENCE INSTRUCTION

For some instructions there are no extra operands to fetch out of memory, or they are built into the instruction itself (for example, with the immediate add instruction the number to add is encoded into the instruction itself). This simplifies the execution since once the instruction has been fetched from memory it can be executed immediately. A lot of non-memory reference instructions perform manipulation directly between registers; these instruction run particularly quickly.

6.2.2 EXECUTION OF A MEMORY REFERENCE INSTRUCTION

In this case the execution is more complex, since one or more operands need to be fetched from memory before the execution phase can be completed. The execution phase for a direct address instruction (the address field encoded in the instruction field) can be represented symbolically as follows:

$$[IR]_{address\_field} \rightarrow MAR$$
$$[M] \rightarrow MBR$$

The address part of the instruction is transferred to MAR, then the data, read from memory into the MBR.

For a memory write instruction, e.g., 'store the contents of the AX register in addressed memory location', the sequence would be:

$$[IR]_{address\_field} \rightarrow MAR$$
$$[AX] \rightarrow MBR$$
$$[MBR] \rightarrow M$$

In all the examples in the chapter, it is assumed that the action described symbolically as $[IR]_{address\_field} \rightarrow MAR$ involves taking into account the addressing mechanism used by the instruction: for example, immediate, indexed or based index, etc., as described in Chapter 5. It also assumes that the address is translated by the MMU into a valid physical address before it is loaded into MAR.

Some instructions involve both a read from and a write to memory during their execution. Consider, for example, the Pentium® ADD [Var1], AX instruction. In this case, the data must be read from the memory location Var1, the AX register added to the value and the result stored back into the

Var1 location. *Note* the PowerPC® does not support this type of execution mode and only supports simple transfers between registers and memory. Symbolically, a read then write execution sequence can be written like this:

1 $[IR]_{address\_field}$ → MAR
2 [M] → MBR
3 [MBR] + [AX] → MBR
4 [MBR] → M

Some instructions take their address from a register. For example, ADD AX, [EBX] adds the contents of the AX register to the address pointed to by the EBX register (storing the result in the AX register). Symbolic representation is as follows:

1 [EBX] → MAR
2 [M] → MBR
3 [MBR] + [AX] → AX

This is faster than getting the address out of the instruction since the address does not need fetching from memory and is already present in the CPU register.

6.2.3   BRANCHING INSTRUCTIONS

With branching instructions the processor does not always move to the next consecutive instruction and can transfer control to another part of the program.

Consider an unconditional branch instruction. In this case the required effect is to transfer control to the address defined in the instruction operand. Normally, at the end of each instruction's execution the PC points to the address following the current instruction. When a branch executes, the PC has to be replaced by the branch instruction operand. This can be represented symbolically by the following:

$[IR]_{address\_field}$ → PC

Sometimes the branch instruction is a call to a subroutine. This is somewhat more complex since the current value of the PC has to be stored on the stack before the PC is replaced (in fact the same is done when the CPU processes an interrupt, see Chapter 9). Here is the symbolic representation:

1 [SP] → MAR
2 [PC] → MBR
3 [MBR] → M
4 [SP] − 1 → SP
5 $[IR]_{address\_field}$ → PC

The SP register points to the top of the computer's stack. After the PC is stored at the location pointed to by the SP register the SP register is decremented (since the stack grows downward in memory).

Another specialised type of branch is the return instruction. This is executed at the end of a subroutine. This instruction has to retrieve the program counter from the stack so that the program can return to where the subroutine was called in the first place. Here is the symbolic representation:

1 [SP]   →   MAR
2 [SP] + 1   →   SP
3 [M]   →   MBR
4 [MBR]   →   PC

Another useful type of branch provided in the Pentium® instruction set is called the software interrupt. This instruction allows the CPU to jump to a particular address that has been listed in a jump table (called the interrupt descriptor table) (the index into the table is encoded in the instruction). For the Pentium™ the start address of this table is stored in a special register called the interrupt descriptor table register which contains the base address and limit of the descriptor table's segment (see Chapter 4). The software interrupt allows the operating system to provide a standard entry point that the user application can call. The following example shows the sequence for a software interrupt:

[IR]operand field $\times$ 8 + IDTR   →   MAR
[M]   →   MBR
[MBR]   →   Segment descriptor
Segment descriptor base address   →   PC

6.2.4   MEMORY INDIRECT ADDRESSING

If memory indirect addressing is specified in the instruction, this introduces an additional memory read into the sequence of actions.

For example, consider an instruction to fetch some data from memory and perform an arithmetic operation on it when the addressing mode is defined as indirect. The sequence would be:

$[IR]_{address\_field}$ →   MAR
[M]   →   MBR
[MBR]   →   MAR
[M]   →   MBR
Perform appropriate action using ALU

Notice this is a particularly slow way of getting information out of memory since it involves two memory read cycles to get hold of the data. For this reason it has become somewhat out of vogue and is not supported on the Pentium® or PowerPC® for standard data instructions. There is a memory indirect mode supported by the Motorola 60020 processor, however.

6.3   ARCHITECTURAL CONSIDERATIONS

This chapter has so far discussed features of a CPU that are normally found in most computers. From the user's point of view, what makes computers differ from each other is the instruction set provided. From a performance point of view, in addition to the facilities provided by the instruction set, it is important to look at how the basic components are structured and inter-connected. It is in this area that the term 'architecture' can be sensibly applied. The word is directly analogous to the meaning as used when designing buildings. All buildings are constructed from the same basic components: brick, cement, glass, etc. It is the way the components are put together that makes the difference. Similarly, with computer systems the basic components are the same (memory, registers, gates, etc.) but are functionally different because of the way they are put together and inter-connected. These are the factors that determine how a computer will perform. In this section we will consider ways of arranging for the basic components of the CPU to be controlled and connected.

6.3.1 SYNCHRONOUS AND ASYNCHRONOUS PROCESSORS

In section 6.2 we examined the sequence of steps that the CPU must perform in order to fetch and execute an instruction. Certain of these steps must wait until the previous step is complete before commencing. For example, during the fetch phase the instruction cannot be moved from the MBR to the IR until a previous step ([M] → MBR) has been completed, which is dependent on the time for completion of a memory read. This is not necessarily true for all steps, however. The SP, for example, can be incremented (or decremented) at any time after it has been used and its value transferred to the MAR. Since incrementing is an operation purely internal to the CPU and involves the SP and perhaps the ALU, it takes less time to complete than a memory transfer operation. The incrementing of the SP can be done concurrently with this memory transfer.

The total time required to execute an instruction depends on the instruction itself. The fetch phase is the same for all instructions, but the execute cycle may require either one or a number of steps. For example, the multiply instruction will require more steps (and therefore take longer) than a simple addition or a branch instruction. Also instructions that involve memory references will take longer than ones that operate only on internal registers. Of course the time for each of the steps in the fetch/execute cycle for a given instruction is not necessarily the same. The time for a memory transfer step is relatively large compared to the time it takes for a register to be incremented. The timing can be done in one of two ways.

A synchronous processor has an internal processor clock. This is an electronic circuit that generates electronic pulses at regular and accurate intervals of time, and this is usually based on a crystal controlled oscillator for accuracy and stability. Each step must commence operation on a clock pulse and finish at the end of a clock pulse. Since some steps require more time than a single clock pulse to complete they are given multiple clock pulses in which to perform their function. Synchronous architecture leads to simpler processor construction, but has the disadvantage that since not all steps need the same amount of time, some operations cannot commence until the next clock pulse, even though the preceding step is complete.

An asynchronous processor is one where the initiation of the next step takes place immediately the previous step is completed. This will remove any idling of the processor as it waits for the next clock pulse and consequently should result in an increase in speed of the processor. However, this is tempered by the fact that extra logic circuitry is required to detect the end of each event. Not only does this extra logic make an asynchronous processor more expensive but also the end of the previous step has to be detected which takes a little time, offsetting some of the time saved.

Asynchronous operation of the CPU is, however, generally faster but more complex and costly. Another advantage of asynchronous processing is that the CPU consumes less power; this is because the clock itself requires a large amount of power to ensure that it is propagated quickly to all parts of the CPU. It also generates less electromagnetic interference since electrical activity does not occur at a regular interval.

In practice, however, all commercial processors on the market are synchronous due to the fact that they are easier to design and use a better understood technology. At the University of Manchester, however, there has been a project called Amulet, started in 1990, that has designed (and had fabricated) a number of asynchronous processors which are compatible with the ARM RISC processor. The Amulet-2 processor which was fabricated in 1996 was capable of about 40 MIPS (million instructions per second); the current design project is the Amulet-3 processor. For more information on Amulet and asynchronous processing go to www.cs.man.ac.uk/amulet/.

6.3.2 INTERCONNECTION METHODS

The central processing unit is made up of a number of component parts (described in section 6.1). These component parts can be interconnected in several ways; the way the components are connected can have a significant effect on the operating speed of the CPU.

Examine the individual information transfer steps that make up machine instructions as described in section 6.2. Some of the transfer paths for a simple CPU with just one register, known as the accumulator, are shown in Figure 6.3. In this example, there is a requirement for five address transfer paths and seven instruction and operand paths, a total of eleven paths.

These transfer paths can be implemented in one of three ways, either using point-to-point connections, a common bus or a multiple bus structure. If a computer is to achieve a reasonable speed of operation, it must be organised in a parallel fashion. This means that data has to be transferred a whole word at a time and that the interconnections between the components require multiple wires. For a 32-bit processor, 32 wires are required for each path. Such a collection of wires that have a common identity is called a bus.

In the case of a point-to-point bus system a different dedicated bus handles each information transfer path. If we used a point-to-point architecture for the CPU shown in Figure 6.3 we would need a separate bus for each data flow. The advantage of this is that there is no competition (called contention) for the buses between the components and many transfers can take place simultaneously. This leads to a fast CPU but at a high price.

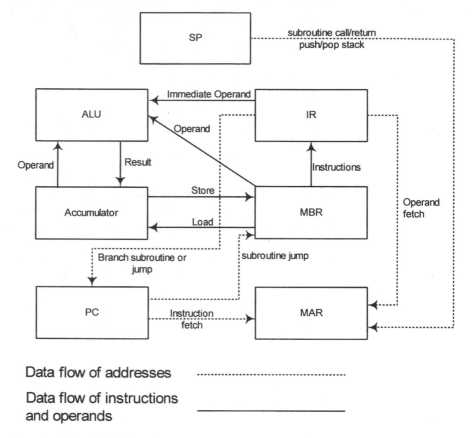

Figure 6.3 CPU data flows

For example if we had 32 32-bit registers (as in the case of the PowerPC™) this would lead to a total bus count of 512 and a total of 16,384 wires just for register to register transfer. Since each register would need 31 dedicated sets of communication electronics to talk to the 31 other registers this would make the construction of the CPU far too complicated and expensive. Consequently a full point-to-point bus system for internal CPU is almost never used.

At the other extreme there could be a common bus. Implemented with a common bus system, the simple CPU illustrated in Figure 6.3 would be as shown in Figure 6.4. All data transfers take place along this common bus. To enable information to be transferred from one register to another there have to be some logic gates which enable only the required registers to be actively connected to the bus at the appropriate time. The advantage of the bus system is that it is inexpensive but the disadvantage is that it is slow since only one transfer can take place at once.

The most common form of internal CPU bus found on machines is the multiple bus system. This is a compromise between the two extremes just described. Here, there is more than one bus to which a number of

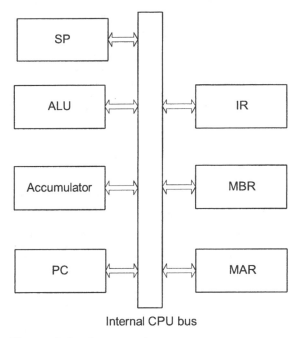

Internal CPU bus

Figure 6.4 Common bus interconnection

components are attached. Some registers are connected by a point-to-point bus: for example, the registers involved in the fetch cycle, since transfers between them are so common. The Pentium® processor has a 64-bit internal data bus, a 32-bit internal address bus and 10 dedicated 32-bit buses used to move data between the data cache, internal registers, ALU and the floating point unit. Figure 6.5 shows how our simplified CPU could be inter-connected using a data and address bus plus two dedicated IR to MBR and PC to MAR buses. The dedicated bus connections allow the fetch execute cycle to be run concurrently with other register transfers.

6.4   CONTROL UNIT

To execute instructions, the CPU must have some means of generating the appropriate control signal to initiate the next step in the correct sequence, as discussed in section 6.2. The various ways that have been developed fall into one of two categories:

Hardwired control

Microprogrammed control

6.4.1   HARDWIRED CONTROL

Consider the sequence of steps in the fetch/execute cycle as defined in section 6.2. Each step will require a time period, defined by the clock if the

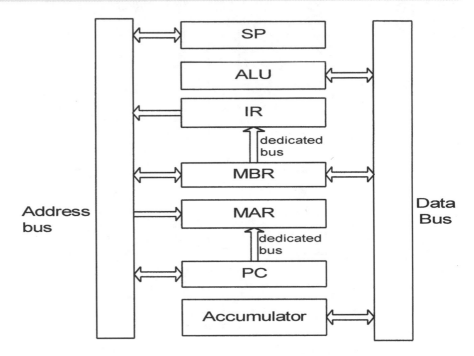

Figure 6.5 Multiple bus interconnection

processor is a synchronous one. The particular action at each step is defined by the state of

1 the output of the decoder – this defines the machine instruction to be executed;

2 the clock, relative to the time period at the start of this machine instruction;

3 any test flags set in the ALU (see section 6.1.2).

The particular operation carried out by the CPU is controlled by a complex logic circuit known as an encoder. The use of this is illustrated in Figure 6.6; it has as input a series of lines from the decoder and the clock. Only one line from the timing decoder will have a signal on it indicating which particular instruction is to be executed. Only one line from the timing decoder will have a signal on it indicating which step period is the current one (the signal reverting back to T0 at the end of the execution of each instruction). *Notice* how the instruction complete signal sent back from the encoder is sent to the reset signal on the timing counter setting it back to 0.

In Figure 6.6 only 4 bits are taken from the IR, which allows you a maximum of 16 instructions. The control lines coming out of the encoder enable the transfer of data from register to register. Each register is connected to the bus via a series of bi-directional circuits (called buffers). The READ register signal enables the buffer in the left to right direction (towards the bus) and the WRITE register signal enables the buffer in the right to left

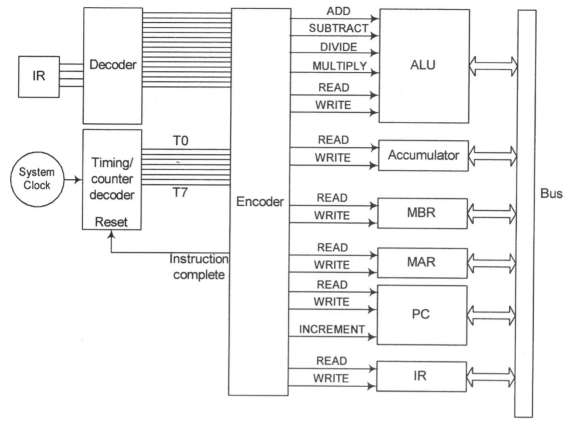

Figure 6.6   CPU control unit

direction (towards the register). For example, by enabling the WRITE line on the ALU and the READ line on the MBR, data will be transferred from the MBR to the accumulator (contained in the ALU).

For arithmetic operations (ADD, SUBTRACT, MULTIPLY and DIVIDE) the ALU operates by acting on the data on the bus and accumulator register.

For example, to add the contents of the accumulator to the contents of the MBR, with the result being left in the accumulator, the following control sequence will suffice.

```
MBR READ      ALU ADD      ;adds MBR to data stored in
                           ;accumulator
```

Another example is an instruction to read the address operand, read the data from memory and then add the result to the accumulator.

```
INCREMENT PC                 ;increment the PC to move to the
                             ;operand
PC READ       MAR WRITE      ;transfer PC to the MAR setting up
                             ;address
```

MBR READ	MAR WRITE	;MBR contains address of operand ;transfer to the MAR
MBR READ	ALU ADD	;add contents of data read in ;MBR to accumulator

Note that the design of the encoder defines the operation of the instruction set; if new instructions are to be added it must be redesigned.

System clock

The system clock controls the operation of the CPU. Each pulse of the clock is called one machine cycle. Instructions may take one or more machine cycles to execute. The maximum speed that this clock can be pulsed defines the processor's speed. The units of the clock rate are measured in MHz (1 MHz = 1,000,000 cycles per second) and now, more commonly, in GHz (1 GHz = 1,000,000,000 cps). The faster the clock rate the faster the processor can execute instructions; however the speed of operation is not determined by clock rate alone. This is because different processors execute similar instructions in different numbers of clock cycles, and also because the processor itself may have to slow down if it is waiting to access memory or I/O.

6.4.2 MICROPROGRAMMED CONTROL

An alternative way of generating the appropriate control signals at the appropriate time is by a software technique known as microprogrammed control. Consider a control word whose individual bits represent the various control signals in Figure 6.6. Since there are seventeen different control signals coming out of the encoder you will need a 17-bit control word. Figure 6.7 shows the format of the control word which has been put in 24 bits so that it is a multiple of 8 (i.e., 3 bytes).

A particular combination of 1s and 0s in the control word corresponds to a particular transfer step. For example, to transfer the contents of the PC to the MAR the following control word (in binary) would be used: $000000000000000000110000_2$.

This sets the bits for PC READ and MAR WRITE.

Compare the previous example, where the number to be added was read from memory, with the following control sequence:

INCREMENT PC	
PC READ	MAR WRITE
MBR READ	MAR WRITE
MBR READ	ALU ADD

Would be encoded as

Code	Comment	
$000000000000000000000100_2$	;INCREMENT PC	
$000000000000000000110000_2$	;PC READ	MAR WRITE
$000000000000000100100000_2$	;MBR READ	MAR WRITE
$000000010000000100000000_2$	;MBR READ	ALU ADD

The individual code words are called micro-instructions and a whole sequence of micro-instructions is needed to perform one machine instruction. A sequence of micro-instructions is called a micro-program. The micro-programs corresponding to the instruction set are held in a special memory called the micro-program memory.

The control unit generates the control signals for any machine instruction by sequentially reading the control words of the corresponding micro-program from micro-memory. To read the control words sequentially, and at the correct time, a micro-program counter (μPC) and a clock is required. In order to take account of the condition of any status flags that exist (see section 6.1.2) there is a need for conditional instructions. For example, the instruction BEQ (branch on equal) would require an instruction that will load the MBR to the PC only if the zero flag is set.

Only a minority of micro-programmed CPUs allow users to write their own micro-programs. Sometimes the micro-programs, which are supplied by the manufacturer, are stored in ROM and cannot be altered as, for example, with the Motorola M68020 microprocessor. The Pentium processor uses micro-programmed control but, as the program is stored in ROM, it is not micro-programmable.

The following points are important:

1 Micro-programs define the instruction set of the computer. If the micro-program memory can be written to, then the instruction set is not fixed but can be changed to suit a particular application (e.g., graphics processing). This can offer flexibility to the designer, particularly if the CPU is to be used in a specialist high performance application.

2 Hardwired control units are inevitably faster than micro-programmed ones because there is dedicated circuitry for control functions and no time is required to read the micro-instructions. For this reason, most

23-17	16	15	14	13	12	11	10	9	8	7	6	5	4	3	2	1	0
Reserved for Expansion	ADD	SUBTRACT	DIVIDE	MULTIPLY	READ ALU	WRITE ALU	READ SP	WRITE SP	READ MBR	WRITE MBR	READ MAR	WRITE MAR	READ PC	WRITE PC	INCREMENT PC	READ IR	WRITE IR

Figure 6.7 Control word

RISC processors that only have to support smaller instruction sets use the hardwired instruction system.

3 Since execution of the machine instruction involves a number of fetches from the micro-program memory, the speed of this memory determines the overall speed of the CPU. For this reason, the micro-program memory is always implemented in a small, very fast, dedicated memory on board the CPU chip.

For CISC processors that need to support a wide range of instructions (some of them very complex) micro-program control is common, since extra instructions are easy to add as they require only more memory (and not complex control logic).

6.5 IMPROVING PERFORMANCE THROUGH DESIGN

Improved technology has led to a dramatic increase in the speed of processing over the years, but the question still remains – given a particular technology (i.e., size and speed of electronic component) – how can the speed of the processor be increased? This section looks at some enhancements to processor design that help to increase speed without changing the hardware technology.

6.5.1 CPU CACHE

Most CPUs have caches (see Chapter 4) to store instructions and data. For some CPUs the data and instruction cache are separate, for others they are integrated. The split cache technique allows the two caches to be accessed independently, speeding up the operation of the CPU. The cache built onto the microprocessor is referred to as the level 1 cache.

6.5.2 LOOKAHEAD PROCESSORS

It can be seen from the earlier part of this chapter that the process of fetching and executing machine instructions consists of a sequence of micro-instructions. During the time of a memory access, the processor is idle (unless there are other things for it to do, such as incrementing the program counter). Conversely, during periods when the processor is busy, particularly when computation is proceeding in the ALU (e.g., a multiply instruction), the memory access mechanism is idle. During these periods the processor could be 'looking ahead' and fetching (and perhaps decoding) the next instruction(s) so that they are already available on completion of the current instruction. Clearly, the number of instructions that can be pre-fetched depends on the time available, and this, in turn, depends on the instruction being executed; between three and12 instructions is quite common.

Effectively the time for the execution of one instruction and the time for fetching the next instruction are overlapped, resulting in an increase in the speed at which the program is executed. The disadvantage of this approach is that it assumes that the next instruction for processing is the next one in sequence in memory. For an unconditional branch this is not true, and for a conditional branch this may not be true. In both these cases the processor may be pre-fetching the wrong instruction.

When this is discovered during the execute phase of the branch instruction, the processor must 'throw away' the instructions that have been pre-fetched and continue to fetch the correct ones. This, in fact, is not always the case, as we see in the next section when we look at branch prediction.

6.5.3 PIPELINING

With a pipelined processor, the idea of overlapping the fetch and execute phases is extended so that each of the following phases has its own processor:

> instruction fetch;
>
> instruction decode;
>
> address calculation;
>
> data fetch;
>
> instruction execution.

This is illustrated in Figure 6.8.

When the machine starts, the first instruction is fetched by the pre-fetch unit. After that, the instruction decoder will decode this instruction, while the pre-fetch unit is fetching the second instruction. At the next step the address calculation is carried out for the first instruction, while the second instruction is decoded and the third instruction fetched, all in parallel. This has the potential for increasing the performance of the machine considerably over conventional sequential machines because of the concurrent operations. However, it requires much more complex hardware to ensure the correct timing of all the operations on the pipeline.

There is the same problem with branch instructions as on the lookahead machine (in fact the lookahead machine is a very simple pipelined

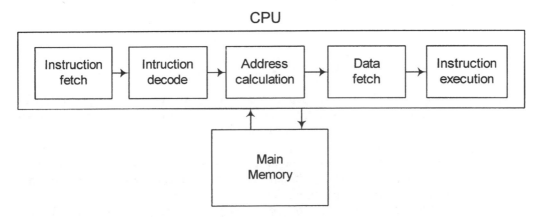

Figure 6.8 Pipeline

machine). If a control transfer occurs as a result of a branch instruction, the pipeline has to be emptied out and a large gap will appear in the instruction stream. Since, on some estimations, about one-seventh of the instructions in software are branches this is a big problem with pipeline architecture.

6.5.4   BRANCH PREDICTION

Most modern processors try and get around this problem by using a technique called branch prediction. When the processor sees a branch in the instruction stream it tries to predict if the branch will be taken (easy for an unconditional branch). If it predicts the branch will be taken it starts to fetch instructions from the branch target; otherwise it carries on fetching instructions sequentially. If it is correct in its prediction then the pipeline is still valid and continues to operate; if the prediction is incorrect the pipeline is flushed out and the instructions have to be fetched from memory.

An enhancement of this technique is used on the Pentium® processors for the pre-fetch phase (see section 6.5.2); two pre-fetch buffers are used, one which always pre-fetches the code sequentially and the second which pre-fetches according to the branch prediction. In this way, both possibilities are covered and it is very rare for there not to be a valid instruction to feed into the pipeline.

The PowerPC® 603 processor handles branch prediction as follows:

If the conditional branch can be predicted because the flags it depends on cannot be affected by any intermediary instructions in the pipeline, then it is predicted and the code pre-fetched. If the branch cannot be predicted for sure then the processor guesses that backward branches will branch, on the basis that they are part of a loop, and loops generally execute at least once. Forward branches will not branch.

It is also possible to hint to the processor what the branch will do in the machine code and reverse the above rules with a special bit set in the branch instruction.

The PowerPC® 604 and Pentium® processors use a more sophisticated technique called dynamic branch prediction. This involves keeping a record of recent branch instructions (and where they branched to) in a cache. The prediction is based on the branch's previous behaviour and has been found to perform extremely well in practice.

6.6   PARALLEL PROCESSING

It can be seen from the previous sections that the way to increase the speed of a computer over and above that which results from improved technology is to introduce parallelism into its operation.

A useful classification of parallel computer systems, known as the Flynn classification, makes use of the ideas of parallelism in the instruction stream and parallelism in the data stream. There are four classes of parallel computer system as illustrated in Figure 6.9.

SISD is a single instruction, single data stream machine. At any given time during the execution of the program, there is, at most, one

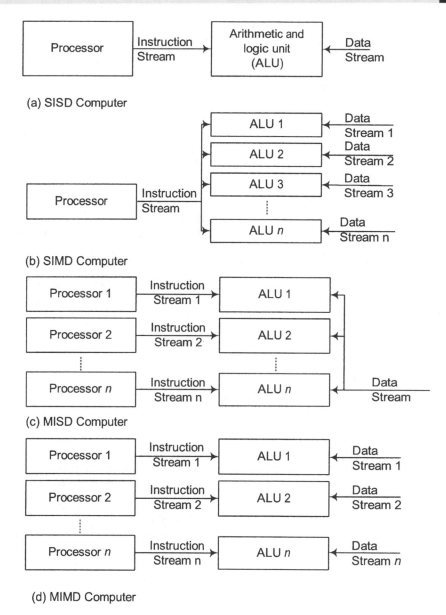

(a) SISD Computer

(b) SIMD Computer

(c) MISD Computer

(d) MIMD Computer

Figure 6.9 Flynn's taxonomy

instruction being executed and that instruction affects, at most, one piece of data.

SIMD is a single instruction, multiple data stream machine. At any given time during the execution of a program, there is, at most, one instruction being executed, but it affects an array of data (a data vector) rather than a single operand. One common application of SIMD is when processing graphics or audio (for example, compression or decompression of a video stream). In this case, the screen is split into regions and the same algorithm is used to compress each region in parallel. Motorola supports SIMD with the PowerPC® chip with its AltiVec technology. Pentium® processors have SIMD instructions as part of their multimedia instruction set extension called MMX.

MISD is a multiple instruction, single data stream computer. Each operand is operated on by several instructions simultaneously. At first glance this does not seem to be a useful concept – one example of an application for this would be in pattern recognition, more than one pattern recognition algorithm could be run over the same set of data. In practice MISD computers are not built; most multiple instruction stream machines also support multiple data streams as described next.

MIMD is a multiple instruction, multiple data stream. There are N instruction streams and N data streams, one data stream per instruction stream. Because there are N processors there needs to be some form of communication between them, so that they can cooperate to achieve the required processing. The MIMD can be implemented so that all the data is stored in a shared memory or each processor could have its own private memory. A common type of MIMD is the distributed system where a number of computers can work together on a single task, communicating using a network.

6.6.1   EXECUTING SEQUENTIAL PROGRAMS IN PARALLEL

Even though the MIMD model for parallelism seems to offer seemingly unlimited power (just add more execution units) to the computer, there are limits on how this can be exploited by any given application. This sometimes has to do with the nature of the problem; for example, imagine calculating the total VAT on a set of ten invoices. Even though it is possible to do some of the addition in parallel, the multiplication by the VAT rate can only be done sequentially at the end.

Another reason that computer programs don't exploit parallel processing is that the language that the program is written in expects the instructions to be executed in sequential order. The exception to this is the language Occam but, since it is now very rarely used, most software is not optimised for concurrent processing.

6.6.2   OUT OF ORDER EXECUTION

All this has led processor designers to build parallelism into their machines which runs sequential instructions in parallel (and therefore sometimes out of their original order) but takes care to resolve any inconsistencies that this might cause. Look at the following examples:

```
MOV AX,200
MUL AX,BX
```

In this case the instructions must be executed sequentially since the second instruction depends on the first, but consider the following sequence:

```
MOVE AX,200
MOVE BX,100
MUL DX,CX
```

All these instructions are independent of each other and can be executed simultaneously without problem and, in fact, both the Pentium® and recent PowerPC® implementations are capable of running instructions concurrently. The Pentium processor itself has two ALU pipelines (the U and V pipeline) and is therefore capable of executing two integer arithmetic operations concurrently.

The Pentium 4 has a highly complex parallel architecture, which includes 4 ALUs, a floating point unit and separate internal caches for both code and data. The processor fetches instructions, which are then decoded into micro-program instructions (or uops) and then stored in a cache. The uops are then fed into the Out-of-Order Execution engine. This tries to execute as many instructions as possible in parallel; the results and status of these instruction executions are then fed to the retirement logic, which ensures that the result of the execution agrees with the original program sequence. The Pentium 4 is capable of retiring (completing execution of) up to 3 instructions for each clock cycle.

The PowerPC 604e is capable of retiring up to 4 instructions per clock cycle and is provided with 3 integer ALUs. It, again, uses some of the same techniques as the Pentium chip, including out-of-order execution.

6.6.3 REGISTER RENAMING

Sometimes it is difficult for instructions to be executed out of order due to register conflicts; look at the following example:

```
ADD AX,BX    ;instruction 1
ADD BX,200   ;instruction 2
```

Instruction 2 cannot complete before instruction 1 due to the fact that instruction 1 needs the contents of the BX register and instruction 2 corrupts it. The completion of instruction 2 prohibits instruction 1; this is called anti-dependency.

To get round this problem many processors (including the Pentium®) use a technique called register renaming where two (or more) internal registers are used to store the value of a particular named register. In the above example suppose we have two copies of BX called BX1 and BX2. The code now becomes:

```
ADD AX,BX1
ADD BX2,200
```

Assuming both copies of the register were valid (i.e., = BX) before running the code the instructions can now be run out of order. When the instructions are retired the last register to be written to (BX2) is transferred back to the BX register.

6.7   CPU PERFORMANCE BENCHMARKING

Providing accurate measurements of processor performance is difficult. Measures such as millions of instructions per second (MIPS) are not always indicative since some instructions do a lot more work than others. For this reason, reasonable effort has been put in to producing standardised benchmark tests. One of the leading players in this field is SPEC (Standard Performance Evaluation Corporation), a non-profit organisation. SPEC licenses a number of benchmark tests in the form of software suites that can be used to test the performance of any given system. SPEC also publishes the benchmark's results of tests that have been performed on various processor, motherboard and memory configurations.

6.8   SUMMARY

The architecture of the CPU is decided by:

The control functions that it is capable of initiating and, consequently, the instruction set that can be provided.

The method of interconnection of the component parts.

The ability of the processor to pipeline or run instructions out of order and/or concurrently.

The size and design of the processor's instruction and data caches.

The type of execution unit (hardwired or microprogram controlled).

Inevitably the design of a particular CPU is a compromise between cost and performance. The faster components and transfer methods tend to be more expensive, and so the designer has to have a clear idea of the requirements for the machine in order to make it process information quickly at a reasonable cost.

6.9   EXERCISES

1   What is a micro-instruction?
  Explain how a micro-programmed processor can be used to emulate a range of different processors using the same basic set of hardware.

2   Using the micro-instruction format given in Figure 6.7, list the set of micro-codes that will be used to add the contents of the accumulator to a memory address location storing the result back in the memory location (for example ADD [0020], A). You can assume the address is coded directly after the opcode.

3   How is register renaming used to improve the concurrent processing power of a CPU?

4   Why is the MIP not always a very useful benchmark when comparing processors? Name a better technique.

5   Discuss and give examples of the Flynn classification scheme for the parallel computer systems, SISD, SIMD, MISD and MIMD. Explain how a pipeline machine fits into such an architecture.

6   What is branch prediction and how is it used to improve the performance of instruction pipelines?

7   Describe what is meant by 'out of order execution' and 'instruction retirement'.

8   Why, by increasing the speed of the system clock by 10 per cent, will the system's performance not necessarily increase by 10 per cent?

9   One of the latest trends in computing is for users to overclock their CPU. This involves running the CPU at a speed higher than the manufacturer's specification. The obvious advantage is the computer system may run faster. Can you think of any problems that may be encountered when using this technique?

10 Translate the following assembly language into the register transfer language introduced in section 6.2:
    MOV BX,2060
    MOV CX,5000
    ADD AX,[500 + AX + BX]

7 Peripherals

In Chapter 1 we looked at the model of the computer system that receives data, processes it and then outputs some type of result. The parts of the computer which are involved in the transfer of data to and from the outside world are known as peripherals devices and can be categorised as follows:

1 Input: used to transfer information into the computer

2 Output: used to transfer from the computer to the outside world

3 Input/Output: used for both the input and output of data

There is a special class of input/output peripherals called storage devices, used to store and retrieve data. Because of the complexity and special role of these devices they are dealt with separately in Chapter 8.

7.1 INPUT PERIPHERALS

The purpose of an input device is to transfer data from the outside world into the computer system. Since the computer system stores information internally in a numeric form (in binary) and the external data is commonly in analogue form, it must be converted. Examples of external data might be text input (from a keyboard), graphics (scanned from a document), or voltage levels (read from a transducer).

7.1.1 KEYBOARDS AND KEYPADS

Keyboards are used to input text. These devices practically always follow the QWERTY standard originally devised for the typewriter. Figure 7.1 shows two QWERTY keyboards, a conventional PC design and an ergonomic keyboard that is designed to be easier to use since its contours follow the shape of the reach of the hand.

Data is typically transferred to the computer system using ASCII code (see Chapter 2). Alternative layouts to QWERTY have been proposed (e.g., Dvorak) which are meant to allow for faster typing but none of these have currently been adopted widely.

Figure 7.1 Computer keyboards *(left* standard PC, *right* ergonomic design)

Keypads are specialised keyboards for devices such as mobile phones (which, of course are a specialised type of computer system). These are designed commonly with a keyboard which suits the purpose of the application. For example, keypads can be designed which can withstand unfavourable conditions such as being exposed to water or heat, for use in a factory environment.

7.1.2 MICE, POINTING DEVICES AND TOUCH SCREENS

Used to interface with a graphics user interface or any other function where two dimensional position has to be input. Mice can come in various forms, the most common of which use a small ball held in a plastic housing. As the mouse is moved across a surface the ball rolls against two rollers which detect the horizontal and vertical components of the ball's movement (see Figure 7.2). The rollers are connected to a shaft that in turn rotates a disk with slots cut into it. An LED is set on one side of the disk and a light sensor on the other. As the disk rotates, light from the LED is interrupted, causing the signal coming from the sensor to pulse. The encoder chip interprets the pulses as movements of the mouse and sends the result back to the computer as a stream of data. In fact, each disk has two sets of LEDs and sensors, so that direction as well as distance can be determined.

The mouse also has a number of buttons that allow the user to activate various components within the GUI (usually Windows). Mice typically have two or three buttons.

Optical mouse

Another type of mouse uses an optical system consisting of an LED and a tiny camera which takes a picture of the surface many times a second. The camera sends the result back to a processor that interprets the change in image and calculates the movement of the mouse. The mouse can be used on any surface that reflects light and is discontinuous. This has the advantage that there are no moving parts to wear out or become clogged with fluff.

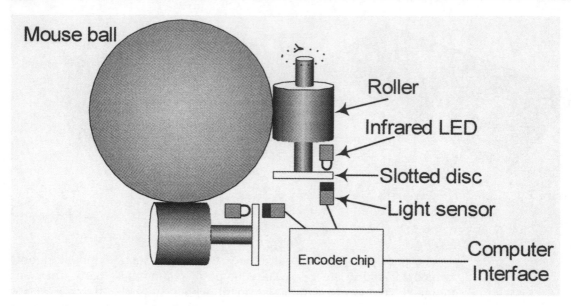

Figure 7.2 Mouse internals

Touchpads and drawing tablets

Another type of commonly used pointing device is the touch pad. This is a pressure sensitive pad, which detects movement of the finger or other pointer across its surface. This is a good alternative for mobile computing devices, which may be used in a place where a conventional mouse might have difficulty finding a decent flat surface. A drawing tablet is just a particularly accurate and probably larger size touchpad. It is used to allow the accurate drawing on the computer as if the user was drawing on paper.

Touch-sensitive screens

These are sometimes transparent touch pads that are overlaid over a conventional display or additional sensor devices fixed to the edge of the display. Three types of touch-sensitive technologies are commonly in use today:

1 **resistive** – two layers of material, one conducting the other resistive, are placed over the screen. If the user presses the screen the layers are pressed together closing the circuit. The resistance measured between the layers indicates the position of the pressure point.

2 **capacitive** – the screen carries a small charge; when the user touches the charge is carried to earth. Four sensors in the corners of the screen measure the drop in potential and the position on the screen.

3 **acoustic wave** – an ultra-sonic sound is transmitted across both the x and y axis of the screen. If the user presses the screen the wave is disturbed, the disturbance of the wave is detected by sound sensors and is used to calculate the position on the screen.

The resistive screen is the cheapest, but has the greatest reduction in light from the screen (75 per cent of the original brightness). The capacitive screen has better light throughput at 90 per cent, but requires the pointer to be conductive (usually the user's finger), so might not work with gloves. The acoustic wave screen does not reduce light output at all, but is the most expensive.

7.1.3 CARD READERS, BAR CODE READERS, ELECTRONIC POINT OF SALE

Generally used for retail transactions but also have a number of specialised other uses; for example, security access systems.

Card readers

These devices will read (and sometimes write) data stored on a credit or cash card. Two types of card are generally supported: simple magnetic strip cards (which just store data) and smart cards which contain a microprocessor. The smart cards are capable of being programmed with security functions that can assist in protecting against fraud and theft. The card reader itself is generally embedded within another device such as an ATM machine or EPOS terminal.

A number of standards have already been developed for data and smart cards, including the ones used for the mobile phone industry. The subscriber identity module (or SIM) card stores the phone number, account details and personal phone book for the subscriber. The SIM data can be locked in an encrypted form so that only the subscriber with the correct PIN can use that account. For more information on SIM card and mobile phone standards you can try the ETSI (European Telecommunications Standards Institute) homepage (www.esti.com).

Bar code readers

Used to read data printed in the form of a series of black strips called bar codes. Since the information can be printed on practically anything that can take ink, this is a particularly useful way of identifying objects to computer systems. Obvious applications are the identifying (and electronic price labelling) of retail goods; others are the coding of television programme times in a magazine, or the marking of the ISBN number on the back of this book.

To read the data the bar code reader reflects a light beam on the printed surface; as the object is moved across the beam the reflection changes with the pattern of the bars. The coding system has been carefully designed in such a way as to compensate for changes in speed of movement, angle between the beam and the barcode and distance of the object. The coding can also contain extra data to protect against errors. By using error detection, the system can make the user scan the item again if the system failed to read the barcode correctly. The example in Figure 7.3 shows a UPC or Universal Price Code barcode. The final digit 3 is the check digit.

Figure 7.3 Barcode

Electronic point of sale

This device usually consists of a display, cash register, card reader, bar code reader and communications link to a central computer that allows a transaction to be validated. A central microprocessor and software that can be tailored to suit a particular application control these components. Many EPOS systems (for example, in the fast food industry) use touch screens to enter the customer's choice.

7.1.4 SCANNERS

Scanners are used to input documents that can consist of graphics or text (or a mixture of both) into the computer system. The document is laid down onto a glass surface and an arm containing a bright source of light and a system of optics is moved underneath the glass. The reflection from the printed page is picked up by a series of mirrors (see Figure 7.4). The image is then split into three parts (using beam splitters); each part is then passed through a lens which focuses the image. Finally it is passed through filters for each of the colour components (red, green and blue) before being picked up by the charge couple device (CCD) array.

The CCD is a collection of light sensitive diodes that converts light into electricity. As the arm moves across the document the picture is read as a series of horizontal lines, each consisting of a number of dots. The total number of lines and number of dots per line defines the resolution of the scanner, with higher resolution devices producing a more faithful representation of the original.

7.1.5 CHARACTER RECOGNITION

This allows text from the printed page to be transferred directly into the computer. Two forms are currently commonly in use: optical character recognition, where text is identified from the printed page and magnetic ink character recognition where the ink itself is magnetic and is commonly used to read the data printed on cheques.

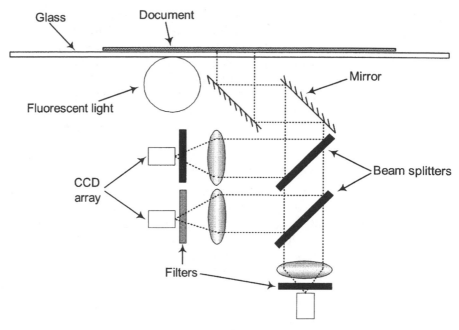

Figure 7.4 Scanner function

Optical character recognition is commonly provided as software bundled with scanner products (higher level professional level products are also available). The OCR software can usually cope well with high quality printed characters, but success with handwriting recognition systems can be poor (due to the varying quality of the input).

Magnetic ink character recognition is used in the banking industry to read the details on cheques. It has the advantage that it is difficult to forge (unless you have the special ink available), can be hidden from the casual observer (the ink can be covered in another layer and still be read magnetically) and difficult to alter.

7.1.6 MULTIMEDIA INPUT (VIDEO AND AUDIO)

With the growing use of multimedia in computer systems the need for peripherals which allow the input of data in the form of video images and sound has become vital.

The reader will probably know of the device which allows sound input, the microphone. It converts sound pressure waves to an electrical signal. This signal has to be sampled and converted from an analogue to a digital form. This process, called A to D conversion for a lot of systems, is carried out using a sound card (which is also used for audio output). Once the signal has been read into the computer it can then be optionally compressed before storage.

Video input into the computer system is generally done using a digital or analogue video camera. With a digital camera the camera itself converts the video signal into a digital form and the data can then be transferred to the computer on a high speed digital link; for example, IEEE 1394 (Firewire) connection. If the camera is analogue, the connection to the computer is via a video capture card. The capture card converts the analogue video signal into a digital signal and optionally compresses it at the same time. Video input and video capture has an exciting range of applications including such things as iris identification (where the user is identified by the unique patterns in the iris), image recognition and robotic control.

7.1.7 BODY INPUT DEVICES

With the advent of virtual reality, a number of input devices that detect the movement and position of the body have been developed. These include data gloves, eye tracking and head movement sensors.

The data glove detects movement of the hand to allow the user to operate within a virtual world as if they are really there. An example application might be the remote control of a robotic hand in a hazardous environment (or at a long distance – for example on the moon) or the control of objects within a virtual environment simulated completely within the computer. The most sophisticated gloves are capable of exerting back pressure on the hand to simulate the feeling gained when holding an object; these are called force feedback gloves.

Eye tracking devices are used to detect where the eye is looking at any given time. They consist of a video camera and computer which tracks a feature of the eye and determines where the eye is looking. Systems are available in a remote and head mounted form (where the camera is connected to a headset worn by the user). These are commonly used by people who have limited movement, researchers looking at how people take in visual information (for example, what interests people on a web site) and military and aviation applications which allow for hands free control.

Head tracking detects movement of the head. This, again, is ideal for users with limited limb movement or hands free operation within industries such as aviation. An example of a hands free product is a head mouse; for more information go to www.microscience.on.ca.

7.2 OUTPUT PERIPHERALS

Output devices allow the computer system to output data to the user in the form of hard copy (for example, on paper) or on a graphical display (with a VDU). The output device may work in text only mode (for example with a line printer) but this is not common nowadays with most systems providing some form of graphics. Another type of output device is the sound system; most systems provide some form of audio output in the form of a sound card.

Printers come in various forms. With impact printers a head is struck against an ink impregnated ribbon which transfers the image to the paper (much like a typewriter). Impact printers can be characterised into two groups, character printers which print text letter by letter and line printers which print a whole line of text in one go. Line printers are evidently much faster. Non-impact printers transfer the ink to the paper without the use of ribbon; two non-impact technologies in common use are laser and ink jet. Impact printers tend to be noisy and this can cause some problems in the office environment.

VDU devices allow the user to see graphical and text images; the technologies are the same as those used in the television set, namely the cathode ray tube and the liquid crystal display.

7.2.1 LINE PRINTERS

Line printers are impact printers that print a whole line of characters in one go. In fact, some so called line printers do not manage a whole line of text immediately but only multiple characters at a time.

Three versions of line printer are the band, chain and barrel printer. The band printer has the whole of the character set attached to metal uprights that are in turn attached to a band containing sprockets (see Figure 7.5). The band is moved horizontally across the paper and a set of hammers hit the characters onto paper as the band moves. The band moves at a very fast rate and band printers are capable of very high production rates as high as 2,200 lines per minute.

With a barrel printer a number of cylinders each containing the full character set are put together to form a barrel. For each line of text the cylinders are rotated and the hammers then actuated to imprint onto the paper. The barrel print is very fast but because of its great expense of manufacture has been superseded by high speed laser printing. The chain

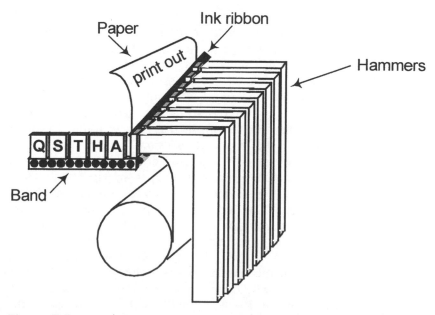

Figure 7.5 Band printer

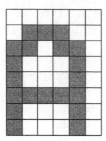

Figure 7.6   Dot matrix letter A

printer is similar to the band printer but the characters are linked together to form a metal chain; again chain printers have fallen out of use.

Line printers are ideal for high volume, text only applications; for example, printing bills. The stationery for line printers is generally continuous so they are not suitable for presentation quality material. Line printers in general will not produce complex graphics.

7.2.2   DOT MATRIX PRINTERS

These use a row of pins that impact on the paper to produce the image as a series of dots. Figure 7.6 shows how the letter A would be produced using a dot matrix printer with a 6 × 8 matrix. Dot matrix printers are slow and a bit noisy; they have mostly been superseded by superior technology such as the ink jet. Dot matrix printers can print both graphics and text.

7.2.3   INK JET PRINTERS

Developed originally in the 1960s by Dr Sweet of Stanford University, ink jet printers use a special head which fires ink onto the paper. In general, ink jet has superseded most other technologies in general-purpose low cost printing. Ink jet provides low cost, high quality and both colour and monochrome output. The only other types of commonly used computer printing technologies are laser (for high speed) and band printing for specialist applications such as form printing. The one major drawback of the ink jet is that it is relatively slow.

The original ink jet printer used an electrical field to accelerate a stream of ink droplets towards the paper (see Figure 7.7). This ink stream is deflected into a gutter and recycled when ink is not required on the paper using a high voltage field set up between a pair of deflection plates.

This continuous stream technique is still used but mostly in the industrial printing field.

Drop on demand printers only release ink when it is required; this allows the head mechanism to be simpler since no deflection or acceleration plates are required. Figure 7.8 shows how the bubble jet drop on demand print head works. Ink is stored in a chamber with an outlet pointed towards the paper. An electric current is passed though a resistor (heater) at the back of

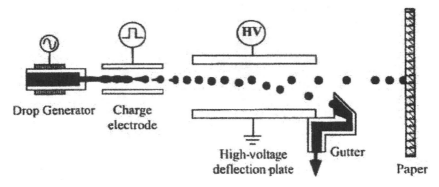

Figure 7.7 Continuous ink stream printer

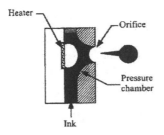

Figure 7.8 Bubble jet head

the chamber and, as the ink warms up, a bubble forms which pushes an ink droplet out of the chamber. When the electric current is removed, the bubble shrinks and more ink is dragged into the chamber.

The ink for bubble jet printers has to have particular properties, such as a low boiling point. Bubble jet printers are the most common ink jet printers used today. This is the technology used by companies such as HP and Canon.

Another type of drop on demand ink jet head uses piezoelectric crystal to force the ink out of the chamber (see Figure 7.9). Piezoelectric crystals change their shape if they are placed in an electric field. The head shown in the figure is called a bend mode design. When electric current is switched on, the crystal expands and, as it is fixed to the diaphragm it has to bend to accommodate this increase in length. This forces the ink droplets through the outlet. This type of head is used in printers produced by companies such as Epson and Sharp.

Ink jet technologies have advanced a long way since their original invention. Printers are currently on the market that can deliver so-called photorealistic quality which some companies claim can compete with photo print.

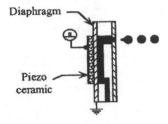

Figure 7.9 Bend mode piezoelectric print head

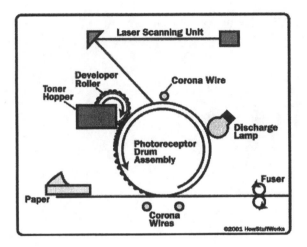

Figure 7.10 Laser printer mechanism

7.2.4 LASER PRINTERS

The laser print technology uses a similar technique to the photocopier, in which toner is bonded to the paper using a heated drum (see Figure 7.10). As the drum rotates a wire with an electric current passing through it (called the corona wire) sets up an electrical charge on the drum's surface. The laser scans the drum in the horizontal axis and, as the laser is switched on and off, this etches out a pattern on the drum. When the laser is switched on this discharges an area of the drum.

The toner is delivered to the main drum from the toner hopper using a toner roller. Since the toner is also positively charged it only sticks to the parts of the drum's surface that have been discharged by the laser. The paper is given a negative charge before it is rolled against the drum; this makes sure that the toner sticks to the paper more than the drum to ensure that it is transferred across. Another set of wires, called the detac corona wires, discharge the paper soon after it has picked up the toner, to ensure that it doesn't stick to the drum. Before the paper leaves the printer it is passed between a set of heated rollers which fuses the toner onto the paper.

Laser printers used to be a very expensive, high quality option and there was some competition from certain cheaper impact printers for the higher quality office print market. More recently, their plummeting cost has meant that they have become the standard workhorse print option for most offices. Laser printers are cheaper to run and faster than ink jet printers, but laser colour options are still very expensive and, for this reason, the ink jet still holds the majority market share for home computer users.

For smaller personal use laser print speeds of about 14 pages per minute are typical. However office printers are available which will deliver about 45 ppm and data centre laser printers over 200 ppm.

Colour printing

Because the colour of paper is determined by the light wavelengths that are absorbed (instead of transmitted), the primary colours used for printing are the complements of the light primary colours (red, green and blue), namely cyan, magenta and yellow. Cyan is the complement of red, magenta the complement of green and yellow the complement of blue (see Figure 7.11). This means that cyan ink absorbs red light, magenta absorbs green light and yellow absorbs blue light. By mixing the inks together you get ink that will absorb more than one of the primary colours. For example, mixing cyan ink with magenta ink you get ink that will absorb both red and green light resulting in blue. By changing the amounts you can change the hue of the colour.

If all three inks are mixed together, in theory, this should give you black (absorbing all three colours); in practice perfect black is very difficult to achieve and the result often looks a little muddy. For this reason, many colour printers also use black ink. This results in black and white printing being clearer, cheaper (since only one ink is required) and quicker, since no mixing is required.

For ink jet printers the head itself is loaded with different colours and the head either puts dots of different colours close together or layers of ink on top of one another. For colour laser printers only one drum is used which has

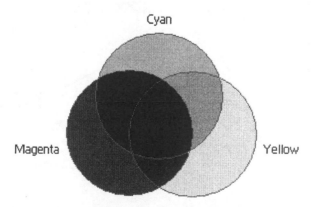

Figure 7.11 Printing primary colours

to print the different colour toners one at a time. This process, of course, is slower than a black and white laser and typically at least four times slower for full colour printing.

7.2.5 VISUAL DISPLAY UNITS (VDUs)

These are used to display text and graphics to the user of the computer system. Two types of technology are currently used: cathode ray tube (CRT) and liquid crystal display (LCD), the former being lower cost mature technology which has been used for television since its invention. The second, LCD technology, consumes a lot less power and is more compact and, for this reason, is used for portable computers; displays are also available for desktop machines but they are considerably more costly than their CRT counterparts. The smallest addressable unit of display on the screen is called a pixel. *Note*, for a colour screen each pixel consists of three dots on the screen, one for each of the primary light colours (red, green and blue).

Cathode ray tube VDUs

CRT displays fire a beam of extremely small particles called electrons at a phosphor covered screen. When an electron hits the phosphor it is energised and emits light. For colour displays there are three types of phosphor that emit the colours red, green and blue. The mixing of different amounts of these primary colours produces the full spectrum of visible light. For example equal amounts of red and green produce the colour yellow. Figure 7.12 shows a simplified schematic of a CRT tube; *note* there are three guns, one for each of the primary light colours.

The electrons leave the cathode and are accelerated towards the anodes using a positive voltage (the electrons are negatively charged and attracted

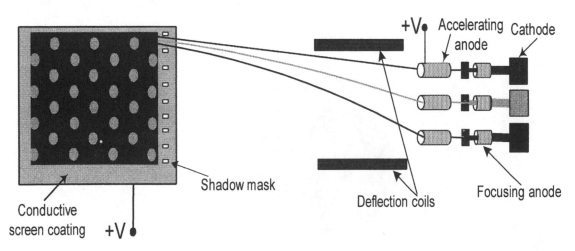

Figure 7.12 Operation of CRT display

to a positive voltage). The focusing anode concentrates the beam and, as they exit, are passed through a pinhole aperture. By adjusting the width of the beam, the focusing anode can adjust the number of electrons that get through the pinhole and therefore reach the screen – more electrons results in more light from the phosphor. The accelerating anode boosts the speed of the electrons. The paths of the electron beams are moved across the screen using steering coils. There are two sets of coils for the vertical and horizontal axis.

Before the beams hit the screen they have to pass through a mask with holes in it – this ensures that the dots on the screen have clear edges to reduce smear and improve picture clarity. The inside of the CRT screen is coated with a conductive coating (called aquadag coating) attached to a positive line; this ensures that electrons that hit the screen are taken away and do not build up.

This picture is scanned as a zigzag from left to right, top to bottom in a process that is called the raster scan. There are two possible types of raster scan, interlaced and non-interlaced. With interlaced scan the screen is scanned twice, first displaying the odd lines and then the even (see Figure 7.13); this is the technique used for television signals. With non-interlaced scan the screen is scanned only once per picture. Non-interlaced display will produce a clearer image with less flicker.

The parameters for CRT displays include the following: dot pitch, resolution, size and refresh rate. Dot pitch is the space between display pixels; some displays support values as low as 0.25 mm, the lower the value the better the quality of the image. The resolution is defined as the maximum number of pixels displayable in the horizontal and vertical axis. The resolution is always written as the horizontal multiplied by the vertical, e.g., 1280×640. The size of the screen is measured diagonally.

The refresh rate is the number of times the screen is redrawn every second – a higher refresh rate will result in less screen flicker. For higher vertical resolutions it takes longer to redraw the screen (since there are more lines to draw); this means that higher resolutions sometimes result in a lower refresh rate. When configuring your display, therefore, there is a trade off between resolution and flicker.

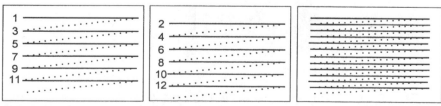

Interlaced odd scan   Interlaced even scan   Non-interlaced scan

Figure 7.13   CRT scanning

Liquid crystal displays (LCD)

LCD technology does not use an electron beam but, instead, relies on the special properties of a substance called liquid crystal that changes its light transmission properties (in particular the direction it polarises light) when subject to an electric field. LCD displays use a lot less power, are more compact than CRT and are, therefore, used widely in portable computer systems. They are also more expensive. Figure 7.14 shows a diagram of a liquid crystal cell. It consists of a lamination of polarised filters and liquid crystal; *note* it has three separate filters to make up the three primary light colours.

The two polarised filters in the LCD cell are set at 90° to each other. In the normal course of events this would create a filter that would block all light. However, the layer of liquid crystal is in a twisted state and it acts to change the polarity of the light moving from the first to the second polarised filter by 90°, thus allowing the light to pass through. When a voltage is placed across the liquid crystal it untwists, the light remains 90° out of phase when it hits the second filter and it is therefore blocked. By varying the voltage the degree of untwisting can be controlled and therefore the amount of light let through.

For computer displays the cells are set out on a two dimensional matrix – a column and row lines are used to control each cell. Two types of display are available, passive and active. To activate a cell within a passive matrix display the drive electronics need simply to send a voltage down the column and connect the row of the cell to earth.

For active matrix LCD panels, the cells are also laid out on a matrix, where each cell is controlled by a thin film transistor, that consists of a transistor and capacitor. By applying a voltage across the row and column of a cell the transistor is switched on and the capacitor receives the charge.

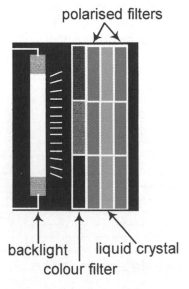

Figure 7.14 LCD cell

By carefully controlling the amount of voltage the capacitor receives it is possible to control the degree of twisting of the crystal so that varying amounts of light can be let through.

The active matrix display allows a higher degree of voltage control (and, therefore, screen resolution) than the passive display. Neither does it suffer from the ghosting problems (where an image will persist after it has been removed) that sometimes are a problem with passive displays. On the whole the active display is a superior (albeit, more expensive) LCD solution.

7.2.6 HEAD MOUNTED DISPLAYS (HMD)

Head mounted displays are a pair of LCD displays (one for each eye) mounted in a headset. Since each eye is receiving a separate image then special effects such as 3D imaging can be achieved. This would, for example, allow the user to view a virtual world project or to examine a landscape realistically that was being filmed by a robot, even if the robot was deep under the ocean or at the scene of a fire, allowing the user to keep a safe distance. HMDs also provide the ultimate in computer display privacy. Figure 7.15 shows an example of a head mounted display produced by Olympus.

7.2.7 SOUND CARD

Used to convert data into audio output. Two techniques are common: FM synthesis and digital audio. With the FM synthesis method the original sound source (let us say, a guitar) is analysed to work out its harmonic components; these components are stored in a table (so called wave table). When the sound is to be reproduced the table is used to reproduce the original sound. As well as the guitar's harmonics, very often the way the amplitude of note changes is stored. This is called the envelope.

For digital audio, the original sound source is sampled, converted to a digital form and then stored in the computer. When the sound is to be

Figure 7.15   Head mounted display

reproduced the sound samples are converted to analogue and fed to the loudspeaker. Digitised audio gives a better quality of reproduction but uses up more storage space on the computer.

7.3 INPUT/OUTPUT PERIPHERALS

Used to provide both input and output to the computer system. In the early days of computing many systems would use devices called terminals. These have now been superseded by separate keyboards and displays. The two most common types of I/O peripherals used today are communications equipment and transducers.

7.3.1 COMMUNICATIONS EQUIPMENT

Used to allow the computer system to communicate with other computer systems. Since these are dealt with in more detail in later chapters, we will only describe them very briefly.

Modem

A modem converts the digital signals that the computer produces to analogue signals that can be sent down telephone lines. The most common use of the modem is to allow users to connect their machine to the Internet. Modems exist that allow connection via the mobile networks as well, allowing the computer to communicate via a wireless connection.

Network Interface Cards

Network Interface Cards connect the computer to a fast, small scale network (typically less than 1 km) allowing it to communicate with other computers in the same building or site. The most common type of cards support a standard called Ethernet.

7.3.2 SPECIFIC TRANSDUCERS

Input/output devices that can be used to convert energy from one form into another. As input devices they can be used to read information in a particular environment such as temperature, pressure, switch inputs or movement. As output devices they can be used to control switches, lights, solenoids, robot arms and many other types of electrical and electronic components.

They are used commonly in factory control systems, in which the computer is responsible for the automation of the production process. For example, when manufacturing paper in a mill, the thickness of the paper has to be kept within certain tolerances. As the paper moves through the rollers a transducer will measure the thickness of the paper and the data will be fed back to the central control computer. The computer system will then pass data to another transducer that will adjust the pressure on the rollers, increasing the pressure if the paper is too thick, decreasing it if it is too thin. Of course, the changes in pressure have to be made very carefully to avoid over compensating which could result in a system becoming unstable with the paper never being the correct thickness. Most systems use some form of damping which measures the average paper thickness over a length of time to reduce this problem.

Other applications for specific transducers might be used to read temperature and humidity levels within a building to allow for the automatic control of heating and air conditioning systems within a building. The computer system will then send data to transducers that will turn the air conditioners on when the temperature is too high and heating on when it becomes too low. These systems, for large buildings, can be very complex, with the software having to model the heat movement for the whole environment. For example, if the heating is on and the temperature is rising then the system will have to switch the heating off before the target temperature is met so as to avoid overheating the building (and using excess fuel).

7.4 PERIPHERAL INTERFACING

All the peripherals mentioned in this chapter have to be connected to a computer system to allow them to operate. A number of different options are available, including general purpose serial and parallel ports, wired and wireless options and dedicated interfaces.

7.4.1 SERIAL VERSUS PARALLEL I/O INTERFACE

Serial interfaces send data a single bit at a time. To transmit one byte, it takes 8 ticks of the transmission clock. A parallel port (or interface), on the other hand, will transmit many bits at a time (typically 8); for this reason, serial interfaces (of a similar specification) will always be slower than their parallel counterparts. On the other hand, with a serial port you only need one pair of transmission wires per channel to communicate, making them a lot cheaper in terms of wire and electronics. With the enormous increase of available transmission speeds serial has overtaken parallel as the interface of choice for most modern peripherals, the exception being external hard disk drives which require very high throughput. General purpose serial ports for most computers follow the RS232 standard and are used to connect external modems and sometimes dumb terminals if the system is multi-user.

7.4.2 USB PORT

Another type of general purpose serial port that is becoming very popular for peripheral manufacturers is called USB or universal serial bus. This allows the computer to connect to the peripheral at a speed of 12 Mbps. More than one device can be connected to single USB port on the machine with aid of a device called a USB hub.

7.4.3 CENTRONICS PARALLEL PORT

Used to connect PCs to printers, but can also be used to connect other peripherals such as zip drives.

7.4.4 WIRELESS OPTIONS

Many computer systems provide infrared ports that allow the system to communicate with another computer or to a peripheral without cable. The problem with infrared is that it requires line of site, i.e., the peripherals' infrared ports have to be directly pointing at each other. Increasingly, mobile phone and keyboard and mouse manufacturers are providing wireless options. Most use a radio receiver that plugs into a port on the main computer. Radio does not require line of site and provides a better communications channel than infrared.

7.4.5 VIDEO PORTS

These provide the connection to an external monitor, usually with a signal in the form of red, green and blue (RGB) components and a synchronisation signal (for the vertical scan).

7.4.6 KEYBOARD CONNECTORS

A number of dedicated keyboard ports are available, the most common of which follows a standard developed for the IBM PS/2 machine.

7.4.7 PCMCIA SLOTS

An interface provided with laptop computers that accepts a credit card size peripheral. The peripheral communicates using a direct connection to the computer memory and therefore can transfer data at very high speed. Most PCMCIA slots support a feature called hot-swap where the devices can be added or removed while the machine is still powered up without risk of damage.

7.5 SUMMARY

In this chapter we have looked at the most commonly used peripherals for computer systems to date. We looked at output devices that produce hard copy, such as printers and plotters, display devices (CRT and LCD) and a wide range of input devices, many dedicated to particular applications. The reader is encouraged to research further in this area since it is rapidly progressing, with developments in print and display technologies and new and improved ways to interface with the computer system.

7.6 EXERCISES

1 Find out how the cost of running a laser printer compares to the running costs of an inkjet printer.

2 What are the primary colours used for printing? Why are these colours chosen, and would it be possible to use others?

3 What advantages does LCD display technology have over CRT displays?

4 Describe, in brief, the operation of a laser printer.

5 Why is a colour laser printer slower than a black and white laser printer?

6 Describe the following:
head mounted display
data glove

7 Describe the two different techniques that are used to produce audio from a sound card.

8 File storage

In Chapter 1 the file storage of a computer system was introduced as a means of holding information in bulk. Also referred to as secondary storage, it is used to hold both programs and data. There are two primary reasons for storing data in secondary instead of primary storage. The first is that primary memory is volatile and loses its data when the power is switched off. For this reason any data that needs to be kept after the machine is powered down must be stored in secondary storage. The second reason is that secondary storage is much cheaper (per unit of storage) than primary storage. Even if you could keep power supplied to the machine continuously it would be prohibitively expensive to keep large amounts of information in this way.

As well as being used for on-line storage, many systems have been developed for backup purposes, allowing data to be saved and then recovered in the case of system failure or loss due to fire, flood, computer virus attack, etc. Archiving is another application for computer storage. This is distinct from backup in that the files are moved from the on-line storage to a remote media, to keep a copy in its current form. An example of this is television production companies that keep massive archives of finished programmes as well as raw video material as a resource for future work.

Media is the actual material used to store the information (for example, the media of this book is ink and paper). Computer storage media options available include: magnetic media (disks and tapes), optical systems and solid-state devices. Each of the storage devices used to read/write this media (e.g., a disk drive) has to be connected (interfaced) to the computer system. In this chapter we will describe various forms of media commonly used and their applications, how storage devices are interfaced and how all the stored information is organised into a file system.

8.1 FILE ORGANISATION

8.1.1 BLOCKS AND CLUSTERS

Since the secondary storage handles large amounts of information and needs to do this at speed, instead of accessing data byte by byte, most devices read and write information multiple bytes at a time. The smallest unit of data that can be written to (or read from) storage in a single go is called a block. The size of these varies from media to media, although a typical value for a hard disk drive is 4 kilobytes. Many types of secondary storage allow the data to be stored and retrieved using block addressing. In this way the first block is numbered 0, the second 1, the third 2, etc. Sometimes blocks are grouped together to form a larger unit of data more suitable for the operating system to handle; these are referred to as clusters.

8.1.2 FILES AND DIRECTORIES

As all the information in the computer system's RAM is lost every time it is switched off, all the software (both system and applications) required must be loaded up from secondary storage on power up. This means that file storage must be capable of storing and organising large amounts of very varied information including user data, applications and system software.

The operating system organises information in secondary storage in the form of files; each file contains a distinct block of data, can be of variable size and is identified by a text name. Files can contain anything from a word-processing document to an executable program file. Since many thousands of files can be stored, the system needs a way of keeping track of all the files that are available. It does this by keeping a special data file, called the directory, up to date. This contains a list of the files' names plus other details (called the file's attributes) such as: file size, date created, the file's owner, etc. and, most importantly of all, where on the media (at which blocks) the file can be found. A directory is said to contain its files; this is analogous to the way a filing cabinet contains paper files and provides details about them on the outside of its drawers.

Since a directory is just a special type of file, it has the same characteristics: file name, length, etc., and therefore it can be listed in (contained within) another directory. The contained directory (called the subdirectory) can also have subdirectories of its own, which in turn can have subdirectories of their own, etc. The whole directory structure forms a tree, with one directory at its root, appropriately called the root directory. This is not contained within another directory but is stored in a special place where the operating system can find it. Figure 8.1 shows an example of how the files can be organised in a directory tree. This whole structure of files and directories is called the file system and allows the files to be organised into an appropriate structure depending on the user's requirements.

8.1.3 FILE SYSTEM STRUCTURE

Since each block on the media might be being used to store a file (allocated) or free for use, this information also has to be kept. The table that stores this information has various names, and different formats, depending on the OS in use: Block Allocation Table (Mac OS), File Allocation Table FAT (Windows®) or I-node table (UNIX® and Linux®) are some examples. *Note*: Windows NT and Windows 2000 also support another format called NTFS (i.e., NT file system) which provides support for multi-user file ownership.

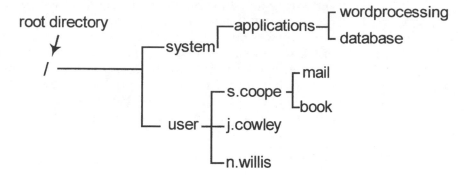

Figure 8.1 Directory tree

Each file entry in the directory points to an entry in the block allocation table, which in turn points to a block(s) on the media where the file is stored.

Figure 8.2 illustrates (in a simplified form) how this is done for the UNIX operating system and Windows FAT32 format (*note*: in the case of UNIX the file's attributes, file size, date created, owner, etc. are stored in the inode not the directory entry). Also of note is that, for the FAT32, the pointers are arranged as a linked list (each entry points to the next entry for that file). The FAT has a one for one correspondence with the clusters so that FAT entry 0 refers to cluster 0, entry 1 cluster 1, etc.

This allocation table, plus other media specific information such as the block size or the number of tracks, sectors on a disk (see 8.2.2) is usually stored at the beginning of the media so that the operating system knows where to find it. The format of all this information defines the structure of the file system and is dependent upon the operating system used.

Formatting

Before the media is used, in most cases it must be formatted. This involves testing all the blocks, clearing them of information, setting up the block allocation (or FAT or inode) table, writing the media specific options and setting up an empty root directory. Since the format and layout of the data written is dependent on the OS used, media formatted using one OS (e.g., UNIX) may not be readable by a computer system running another (e.g., Windows). Some systems (e.g., Linux) get round this problem by providing bridging software that allows the user to read/write files that are stored in 'foreign' file system formats.

8.1.4 FILE SECURITY AND PERMISSIONS

Since information stored within computer systems can often be of a sensitive nature – for example, medical records or financial records – it is very important that only authorised users can access the information. All systems that provide secure file access, store the owner of the file as one of its attributes (this is usually the person who created the file but does not have

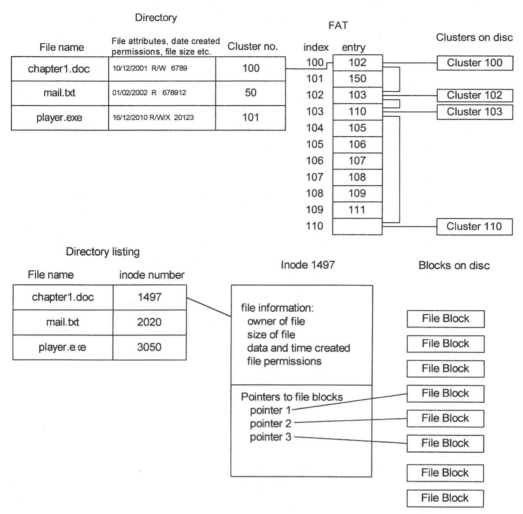

Figure 8.2 UNIX (*bottom*) and FAT32 (*top*) file systems

to be since ownership is transferable). The simplest model of security would only allow the owner of the file access but this would be highly inflexible since it would not allow a number of users to share a set of files (for example, with collaborative teamwork). Most systems allow the file's owner to control a set of file permissions that will apply to other users. A typical minimal set of permissions provided (each of which can be granted or denied) would include:

Read permission	;used to control the opening or copying of a file
	;denied to keep information confidential
Write permission	;used to control modification of the file
	;if denied stops a user writing to the file
Execute permission	;controls a file from being loaded up as program
	;can be used to deny certain users from running
	;certain applications.

For example, if you need to distribute a document to other users but don't want anyone else to change it, you would grant read permission and deny write. If you were sharing a document with another user with you both working on it collaboratively you would grant both read and write.

For the UNIX file system three different sets of permissions are stored and are applied for the following sets of users: the owner of the file (user permissions), users in the same user group as the owner (group permissions) and, lastly, all other users (other permissions). The user permissions allow you to control access to your own files, for example, by removing the user write permission on a file you can stop yourself accidentally changing it.

The user group concept is central to providing flexibility within the UNIX file system security. Each user belongs to at least one user group. Groups can be created based on users' roles within the organisation (e.g., sales, accounts, purchasing, software development, etc.) or created temporarily to support a collaborative team. By granting the group read permission on a document you can share it with all other users in your group. The other permissions control access to the file from all users. In general the only files that will have other permissions granted are system files that need to be accessed by all users. For example, a file containing a word processing application program would probably have the other execute permission granted, so that all users can do word processing.

The Windows® operating system (supported only on the NTFS file system option) uses a more flexible approach, based on a system called access control lists or ACLs. Each file has a specified owner plus a list of access controls, each control defining the permissions for an individual or group of users. This list can be of arbitrary length and, therefore, the control on permissions can be very flexible. In this scheme, for example, it would be easy to add read permission to a file for one other user by just adding the user to the ACL for the file and granting read within the access control. To do this under UNIX is not as easy since the other user may not be in your user group and, even if they are in your user group, may contain users to whom you do not want to give permission.

Finally, this system security is all very well as long as you can guarantee that nobody can steal your hard disk. If they can, they will be able to read the data off the disk directly. To overcome this problem you have to secure the data with a technique called encryption. This involves scrambling the data with a password. The password is required to unscramble the data: a process which is called decryption. Various applications are available that will encrypt/decrypt file data. Within UNIX this can be done with a command called crypt, with Windows 2000® the file can be encrypted by setting advanced attributes in the file's property list.

8.2 STORAGE MEDIA

As mentioned in the introduction, there are many different media options when storing information on computer media. In this section we will describe the characteristics of the media and what they are useful for.

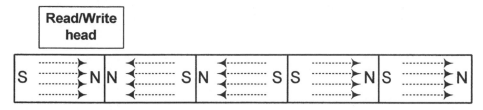

Figure 8.3 Magnetic field recording and the read/write head

8.2.1 MAGNETIC STORAGE

One of the most common ways of storing and retrieving information with computer systems is to use magnetic storage. Most readers will be familiar with devices such as video and audio cassettes, which use magnetic storage to record and playback video and audio signals. The system used within computer systems uses a similar technology to record binary data. In simple terms, a magnetic field can be applied to a magnetic material causing the material to be magnetised in a particular direction. The magnetic field can be arranged in one direction to represent a one and the other direction to represent a zero. In this way binary codes or bits can be stored on the media. Figure 8.3 shows how the number 10011 could be stored using this type of scheme.

Information can be read from such magnetic material by passing the material in front of a detector (or head), which consists of a coil. As the magnetic field changes, an electric current is induced in the coil which is then detected by an electronic circuit. By passing an electric current through the coil, data can be written to the magnetic material instead of being read. Some systems use one coil to read and write, others use separate coils (one to read and one to write). The whole construction is generally just referred to as the read/write head.

Coding techniques (FM and MFM)

Since the head only detects changes on the magnetic field, the scheme illustrated in Figure 8.3 has one drawback: long streams of ones or zeros will result in a constant field (all magnets pointing S → N or N → S) which will result in no current in the drive head. For this reason other techniques of encoding ones and zeros have been developed.

Frequency modulation (FM)

With this technique, two magnetic regions are used for each bit. A one is encoded by reversing the magnetic field twice; a zero is encoded by reversing it once. For example, the bit pattern 0011 would be encoded as shown as Figure 8.4.

Table 8.1   MFM encoding

Bit	Coding
0 (preceded by 0)	RN
0 (preceded by 1)	NN
1	NR

0	0	1	1	
S→N S→N	N→S N→S	S→N N→S	S→N N→S	N = north
R N	R N	R R	R R	S = south

R = field reverse   N = no field reverse

Figure 8.4   Recording 0011 with FM

Modified frequency modulation

In this technique, a zero preceded by a zero is encoded as RN, a zero preceded by a one is encoded as NN and a one is encoded as NR, see Table 8.1. This has an advantage over FM, since it reduces the average number of reversals by half allowing the density of the recording to be doubled. MFM is used to store the information on 1.44" floppy disks (see section 8.2.4).

Run length encoding

This is a more complex scheme again, and actually describes a whole family of techniques which take groups of several bits, encoding them together as patterns of reversals and non reversals. This allows even denser packing of information on the media. Because of its high level of efficiency this technique is used in hard disk drive systems (see next section).

8.2.2   HARD DISK DRIVES

Hard disk drives are the workhorse storage for all modern computer systems. They can store vast amounts of data and read and write at very high speeds. Figure 8.5 shows a top view of an IBM hard disk drive (with the case removed); this can store 36GB of information (36GB = 38,654,705,664 bytes) and retrieve data at a rate of about 30 Megabytes per second.

A hard disk drive comprises of two major parts, of which the first is a set of circular platters made of glass or aluminium mounted on a central spindle powered by an electric motor. The platters are coated with a

Figure 8.5   IBM hard disk drives   *left* 3.5" Ultrastar 367X, *right* Microdrive

magnetic material, usually on both sides. The typical platter diameters are 5.5" and 3.5", with laptop hard drive's platters being 2.5" or less. One of the smallest drives available to date has a platter only 1" across and a storage capacity of up to 1 Gigabyte; the IBM microdrive can be used as storage for handheld devices such as digital camera and handheld computer systems.

The other major part of the hard disk is the read/write head assembly, which is able to move the heads across the surface of the platter while it is made to rotate. In the structure of the hard disk drive (illustrated in Figure 8.6) notice there are two read/write heads for each platter (one for each side) which are attached to a common movement so that all the heads are in the same position relative to the disk surface. Since the whole assembly is very delicate, and the disk read/write process susceptible to even microscopic amounts of dust, the whole assembly is encased in an airtight case. On the outside of the case is mounted the drive electronics which control the movement of the head assembly, drive the motor, and generate the signals required to write/read data to the sectors and interfaces to the computer system to facilitate data transfer.

In order to understand the process of data transfer to and from the disk system it is first necessary to define some terms commonly used. The information on the disk is stored in tracks which are concentric circles placed on the surface of each platter. The tracks are numbered from zero, starting at the outside and increasing as you move to the centre. Modern hard disks contain many thousands of tracks, with some having track densities greater

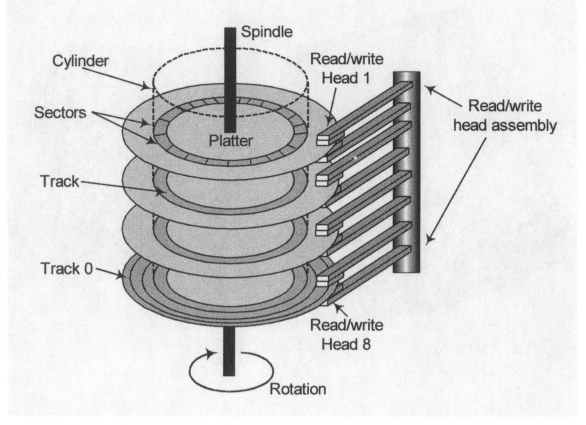

Figure 8.6 Hard disk construction

than 30,000 tracks per inch. A cylinder is defined as all the tracks with the same track number across all the platters in the hard disk assembly. The system shown in Figure 8.6 has 4 platters and therefore 8 tracks per cylinder. The quantity of data stored in a track is too large to be transferred in one operation; a track is therefore subdivided into a number of sectors, a sector being the unit of transfer between the disk and the computer's memory. Typical numbers of sectors per track are from 100 to about 200. Each sector has extra information apart from the data itself, including an id which includes the sector number and a checksum for the data. Each sector is separated from its neighbour with a small gap to allow the head time to get ready to read each new sector. The sector id, plus information about where each track starts, is written to the hard disk by a process called low level formatting; this is distinct from the formatting process described in 8.1.3 which is called high level formatting.

Hard disk addressing

Sectors on the hard disk can be addressed in one of two ways. In CHS (cylinder, head, sector) mode, the sector to be retrieved is defined by its

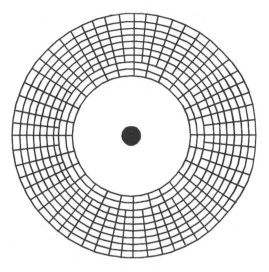

Figure 8.7 Zoned bit recording

cylinder number, head number (defining which head and therefore which platter and surface is being accessed) and sector number (i.e., which sector on the track has been chosen). The computer has to send these three co-ordinates to the disk drive and a request to either read or write a sector. In LBA mode (or logical block addressing), each sector (referred to as a block) is given an index starting from 0 and going up to $N - 1$, where N is the total number of sectors on the disk. To retrieve a particular block from the hard disk all the system needs to do is to send over the block number. LBA is the preferred mode for most hard-disk systems since it is simpler, requires no information about the disk's geometry and scales well for larger disks.

Zoned bit recording

With early disk systems the numbers of sectors per track was constant for the whole disk. This led to inefficient use of space, since the inner tracks are smaller than the outer and can therefore store a lot less sectors. To overcome this problem, hard disk manufacturers started to store variable numbers of track per cylinder with the outer tracks containing more information and the inner less. This technique, called zone bit recording, is illustrated in Figure 8.7.

Interfacing hard disk systems and other storage devices

Two types of hard disk interface dominate the market today: IDE/ATA and SCSI. Both systems involve putting the disk controller electronics on the hard disk, where a standard set of commands is used to talk to this controller using a parallel bus. Both standards define the electrical characteristics, the meaning of the different pins on the interface, different modes (and speeds) of data transfer and the set of commands supported. Even though both these standards were developed originally to control hard disk systems they are also widely used to interface to other storage devices such as tape drives or CD-ROMs.

SCSI: small computer systems interface

First developed in 1979, SCSI is actually a family of standards (SCSI-1, SCSI-2 and SCSI-3) originally designed to interface hard disks, but can be used to connect a wide range of different devices. Many devices can be connected to one SCSI interface. There is a very wide range of SCSI bus width and speed options available; the latest (and fastest) is called SCSI Ultra-320. This provides a maximum transfer rate of 320 Megabytes per second but is still in development. The fastest currently available SCSI on the market is the Ultra-160. This provides a 16 bit data bus clocked at 40 MHz; since the data is transferred on each transition of the clock, the total data rate = $40 \times 2 \times 16 / 8 = 160$ Megabytes per second. Some of the SCSI-3 interface options are listed in Table 8.2; *note* some computer manufacturers incorrectly label Wide Ultra-2 SCSI products as Ultra-2 SCSI.

IDE/ATA

IDE or Integrated Drive Electronics standard was developed to allow manufacturers to put the drive electronics on the hard disk itself. The ATA or AT attachment interface was the name given to the IDE standard when it was approved and adopted by ANSI (American National Standards Institute). Again, IDE/ATA provides a bewildering array of different options but all use a 16-bit wide data bus. Many specifications for ATA are termed Ultra ATA; in fact this defines a number of different speed options depending on the mode of transfer. The slowest is mode 0 (16.7 Megabytes per second) and the fastest mode 6 (133 Megabytes per second).

IDE will only support two devices per connection. To distinguish between these devices one is configured to be the master and the other the slave. Table 8.3 lists some of the options available.

Table 8.2 SCSI-2 options

Name	Data bus width (bits)	Clock rate (MHz)	Maximum data transfer (Mbytes per second)	Maximum devices (per interface)	Pins per interface
Ultra-2 SCSI	8	40	40	8	50
Wide Ultra-2 SCSI	16	40	80	16	68
Ultra-3 SCSI (Ultra-160)	16	40	160	16	68
Ultra-320	16	80	320	16	68

The IDE/ATA interface is a cheaper option than SCSI and is suitable for most small to medium size computer systems. It provides a budget alternative for slower systems. As we have seen the SCSI interface (at a price) can provide a very high level of performance, support many devices on one interface and is particularly suitable for servers, multiple disk systems (e.g., RAID, see 8.2.3) or high end workstations. Both hard disk interfaces make extensive use of DMA (see Chapter 10) to remove data quickly between the memory and the disk system.

Removable hard disks

Removable hard disks allow the user to remove the hard disk and move it from one machine to another. This allows the user to keep data in a secure place, do backups at hard-disk access speeds and transfer data between machines very easily. Hard disk removable cartridges are available with storage capacities as high as 20 Gigabytes.

Summary

Hard-disk drives have advanced a long way since the first PC hard drive was developed just over twenty years ago. That early drive could store only 10 Megabytes of information and cost over $100 per Megabyte. Modern hard disks can provide storage approaching 100 Gigabytes at a cost of less than 1 cent per Megabyte. Whether hard drives will improve by this much in the future has yet to be seen but it is expected that they will be still be the most important on-line storage media for some time to come.

8.2.3   RAID SYSTEMS

RAID, which stands for redundant array of inexpensive disks, is a technique used where a set of hard disks work together under one set of control electronics. The system can be used to improve data performance (by using a technique called data striping) and reliability (by using mirroring).

Here is an example of data striping. Take 8 hard disks and split your data into 8 byte blocks. Put the first byte of each block on the first disk, the second byte on the second disk, etc. When the data is retrieved, if each disk is capable of retrieving data at a given rate say, R Megabytes per second, this will improve performance to 8R since each disk will be working in parallel.

Table 8.3   ATA options

Name	Data bus width (bits)	Clock rate (MHz)	Maximum data transfer (Mbytes per second)	Mode
Ultra ATA-66	16	16	66	4
Ultra ATA-100	16	25	100	5
Ultra-ATA-133	16	33	133	6

The other application of RAID is to improve reliability. This involves a process called mirroring where data is duplicated over more than one drive. If a disk drive fails then the data can still be retrieved from one of the other disks. Most systems also provide a feature called hot swap which allows the failed disk to be replaced while the power is still on. When the faulty disk is replaced, the system automatically copies the data over to the new disk. RAID is commonly used in this way at data centres (for example banks) where very high levels of reliability are essential.

RAID systems come in a series of levels (RAID0, RAID1, etc.) depending on the striping and mirroring techniques used.

8.2.4 FLOPPY DISKS

Floppy disks are a lot cheaper than hard disks due to the lower level of precision used in their manufacture and, for this reason, they are also lower in capacity and data transfer rate. The disk itself, instead of being fixed in the disk drive, is removable. This makes them useful for applications such as backup, so that the data can be removed to a secure place away from the computer system (such as a fire safe). The disk is made of plastic film coated with a magnetic substance and is flexible – therefore the expression floppy disk. To protect it against dust, fingerprints, etc. the disk is enclosed in a protective jacket with an access slot cut into it so the read/write head can access the disk. The access slot is protected with a metal shutter which slides over the slot when the disk is removed from the drive. On the jacket there is also a movable tab which can be used to write protect the disk. The current prevalent standard for small computer systems is the 3.5" floppy disk which has a storage capacity of 1.4 Megabytes.

Data is organised on a floppy disk similarly to that on hard disks (i.e., sectors and tracks) but floppy drives only have one platter in place and therefore only two read/write heads. Floppy disks, because of their lower capacity, have a lot fewer sectors and tracks than hard disks. The standard 3.5" disk is usually formatted with 80 tracks with 18 sectors per track and each sector contains 512 bytes. To calculate the capacity of a floppy you use the following formula:

capacity = heads $\times$ tracks $\times$ sectors $\times$ bytes per sector

For the previous example this gives:

$2 \times 80 \times 18 \times 512 = 1,474,560$ or approximately 1.4 Megabytes

Zip drives

For backup purposes, 1.4 Megabytes is very limited, considering the requirements of modern computer applications. For this reason there is great demand on the marketplace for removable storage with higher capacities. In recent years a lot of advances have been made in floppy disk technology, in part led by a company called Iomega. Its zip drive products are essentially floppy disk drives but with a number of improvements over the standard 3.5" floppy. The disk itself has a higher quality coating, allowing for denser

Figure 8.8 250 Megabyte zip disk

packing of bits. The head is smaller and the positioning mechanism is similar to that used in the hard disk, so that the drive can pack thousands of tracks per inch. The zip drives also use zoned bit recording to improve storage capacity (see hard disk section). All these improvements allow the zip drive to store a lot of data (for a floppy) with current products providing 250 Megabytes of storage. Figure 8.8 shows a picture of a 250 MB zip disk. The zip drive is highly suitable for small system backup but is receiving a lot of competition from other technologies such as CD-R (see section 8.2.6).

Interfacing floppy drives

The standard 3.5" floppy is provided with an interface that was developed over 20 years ago; modern implementations provide transfer speeds as high as 1 Megabit per second. This standard, which is still used today, works well and rarely causes any problems when installing the drive. Zip drives on the other hand offer a range of interface options including SCSI, ATA/IDE, USB and parallel port.

8.2.5 TAPE DRIVES

In the early days of computer systems most storage was provided by tape drives since, at the time, this was already a mature technology developed originally for the music industry. Tape systems are still used today, because of their high capacity and proven reliability, but only for backup and archive purposes (not online storage). Tape drives are available that will store over 100 Gigabytes on one tape cassette. For very large backup and archive applications, auto-loading systems are available that change the cassette over automatically. This allows archives to be handled which contain over 4TB of information (1TB = 1,099,511,627,776 bytes).

One big disadvantage of tape systems is that, because the tape is wound onto a spool, it only provides sequential access, i.e., file by file. This is as distinct from the random access provided with disk systems, where a file location can be jumped to immediately. The following example illustrates the point: imagine you have backed up 10 Gigabytes of information on a tape and have rewound the tape to the beginning before storage. If, the next day, you accidentally erase a file that you need and want to retrieve it from the backup, and the file is near the end of the tape, you will have to wind through the whole tape to find it. This makes tape the slowest computer storage media in terms of file access time.

Tape drive interface

Many types of interface are provided, depending on manufacturer, including ATA/IDE and USB for smaller drives and SCSI for larger enterprise tape backup solutions.

8.2.6 OPTICAL STORAGE (CD-ROM, CD-R, CD-RW AND DVD-ROM)

The major development in disk storage is in optical disks using laser technology. A number of different optical storage technologies have been developed, the simplest of which is the CD-ROM (compact disk read only memory) which uses the same media as audio CDs. The data for CD-ROMs is stamped on the disk in manufacture and therefore they are only useful when you need to make many copies of the same information; for example: software distribution, electronic dictionary or multimedia application. CD-R (compact disk recordable), on the other hand, contains no data when manufactured; data can be written to the disk at a later date using a CD-R drive. This makes it ideal for backups and archives. *Note*, however, the information can only be written once to these disks and, after that, it is fixed for ever (another name for this type of disk is WORM or Write Once Read Many). CD-RW (compact disk rewriteable) allows data to be written and then written over much like a conventional disk (e.g., floppy or hard drive). In the rest of this section we will describe briefly each of these different technologies and examine some other technical issues relevant to optical storage.

CD-ROM

The compact disk was originally invented by Philips (first conceived in 1969) and developed into a standard by Philips and Sony and released in 1982. The disks themselves are made up of a series of layers as illustrated in Figure 8.9. The first layer is relatively thick and is made of a hard plastic called polycarbonate (which is also used for bullet proof screens and motorcycle helmets). This layer is transparent to allow the laser light to pass through. The top of this layer is stamped with a series of pits and then two more layers are added, first a reflective aluminium coating and then a layer of lacquer for protection. The laser light is directed at the disk as the disk is rotated. When the laser hits an area with no pit (called a land) it reflects cleanly and is picked up by the light sensor but when the laser hits a pit it is diffused. This pattern of pits and lands can therefore be detected and interpreted as a pattern of ones and zeros.

The pattern of pits on the CD is arranged as a spiral with the grooves on the spiral being only 1.6 microns apart (1 micron = 1/1,000,000 metre) – the actual length of this spiral is about 3 miles! Each pit is 0.5 micron across and 0.8 to 3.56 microns long. The pits on a CD are some of the smallest, mechanically fabricated objects ever made (DVD pits are even smaller).

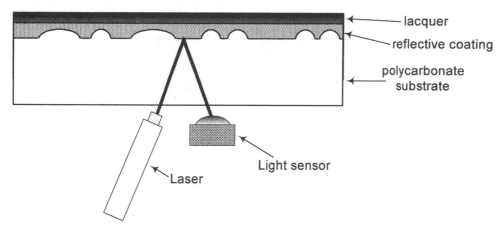

Figure 8.9 Compact disk structure

Error correction codes

Since the size of the pits are so small and the manufacturing process can never be perfect, bit errors are common with CDs. With the audio CD format redundant information called error correction codes is added so that, in the face of small numbers of bit errors, the original data can be recovered. The CD-ROM format extends this by adding even more error correction data to insure against data corruption. More than 10 per cent of a data CD is dedicated to error detection and correction.

Hard disk capacity

Including allowances for error correction codes, a standard CD-ROM can hold about 650 Megabytes of information.

CD-R (compact disk recordable)

The structure of a CD-R disk is shown in Figure 8.10. Like a CD, a layer of polycarbonate is used for the substrate; on top of that is deposited a layer of dye and then a reflective coating of silver or gold alloy, with the whole thing protected with lacquer. Normally the dye is translucent and light will pass through it to the reflective layer underneath and be bounced back. To write data to the disk a laser heats the dye up. This changes its composition so that not as much light is reflected. Heating the dye up is called burning the CD and is a one way process. The dye itself is sensitive to light so it is a good idea to keep CD-R disks out of direct sunlight, particularly if they contain valuable data.

CD-R disks can be read on a conventional CD-ROM drive, making them very convenient as a distribution media. CD-R disks normally store the same amount as a standard CD-ROM, i.e., 650 Megabytes, but CD-R disks are available that can store a little more – up to 700 Megabytes.

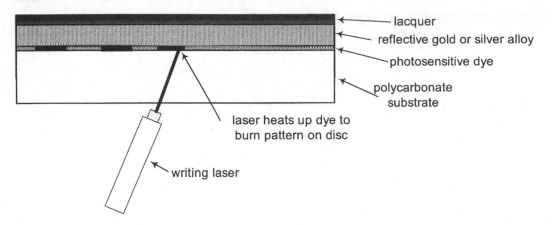

Figure 8.10 CD-R disk

CD-WR (compact disk rewriteable)

With this disk, instead of a layer of photosensitive dye, a special phase changing substance is used to record the pattern on the disk. This substance, when heated up to a particular temperature t1 and cooled down, will crystallise, but when heated up to a higher temperature t2 it will cool down into a non-crystalline form. Since the crystalline form reflects more light than the non-crystalline form, this enables an equivalent to a set of lands and pits to be written to the disk. CD-WR disks again store the same amount as a conventional CD-ROM, but unfortunately cannot be read on many conventional CD-ROM drives because the reflective properties of the substance is not similar enough to a conventional CD. This is a major drawback and, this reason and the fact that the CD-R disks are quite a bit cheaper, makes CD-R a more popular option for many users.

DVD-ROM

In the same way that CD-ROM used an established standard (CD) to deliver data, DVD-ROM uses the DVD or Digital Versatile Disk standard to store information. DVD disks are similar to CDs in that data is stored by using a pattern of lands and pits arranged in a spiral but are capable of storing a lot more information. This is achieved by using two techniques; higher bit density and multi-layering. Firstly the pits on a DVD are much smaller and the tracks much closer together. The distance between tracks is only 0.74 micron and each pit is only 0.32 micron wide and can be as short as 0.4 micron. The consequence of this is that a standard single layered DVD has a data storage capacity of 4.7 Gigabytes. A multi-layered DVD disk is a bit like two conventional CDs sandwiched together, so that the inner layer can be read by the laser, while the outer layer uses a semi-reflective gold layer which can be focused through with a laser onto the second layer underneath. A cross section of a multi-layered DVD is show in Figure 8.11

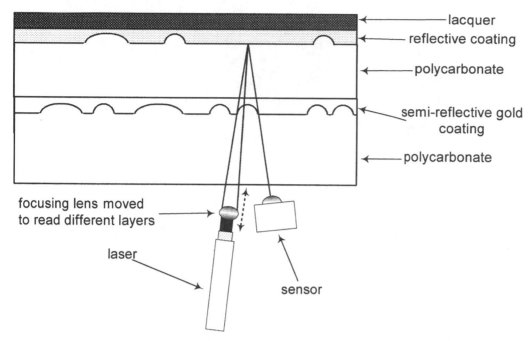

Figure 8.11 Multi-layered DVD

Note the laser beam is focused on the different layers by moving the lens up and down. One might ask why not use more layers to store even more data and, in fact, work has been done in this area but has been hampered by reflective noise. Because the semi-reflective layer reflects some of the laser even if it is focused mainly on the layer beneath, this interferes with the reading of the lower layers. A double-layered DVD disk can store up to 8.5 Gigabytes of information, using both sides a double sided, double layered DVD will hold 17 Gigabytes.

DVD + RW

This is a recordable rewriteable DVD. It uses similar technologies to the CD-RW, but with the increased precision and complexity required for the more complex DVD disk. This format is suitable for small and medium system backup solutions and, since it is also ideal for recording programmes from the television, will finally make obsolete the VHS VCR.

Other optical form factors

Not all optical disks follow the same form factor as the CD, as for smaller portable computer systems and hand-held devices, miniaturised optical disk systems have been developed. Figure 8.12 shows an example of one of these disk systems. The disk is about an inch in diameter, uses a rewriteable phase change media (as in CD-RW) and provides a storage capacity of 500 Megabytes.

Figure 8.12 Dataplay optical disk and drive

Fluorescent multi-layer disk (FMD)

The latest advance to data in optical storage is the Fluorescent multi-layer disk or FMD which uses multiple layers of polycarbonate coated with a pattern of ones and zeros, drawn with a fluorescent dye. When light (of the right wavelength) strikes a fluorescent substance the molecules in the substance go into an excited state; after a short time (a few nanoseconds) the energy which the molecule has absorbed is released and light of a slightly different wavelength is emitted. The FMD can read a pattern of ones and zeros from the disk by focusing the laser on each of the layers in turn. The unfocused laser light passes through the intermediary layers without interference and, since the emitted light is of a slightly different wavelength, any reflected light can be filtered out. The upshot of this is that the multiple layers on the disk do not interfere with each other. This will allow the manufacturer to put a lot more layers in the disk (as many as twenty have been demonstrated).

FMDs will be able to store from 20 to 140 Gigabytes of pre-recorded data on a disk the same dimensions as a CD. In fact, storage of up to 1 Terabyte of information is possible, using a blue laser but this would be expensive. A picture of an FMD disk is shown in Figure 8.13; *note* since the material uses fluorescent instead of reflection the disk is transparent in ordinary light.

8.2.7 SOLID-STATE STORAGE

This is really a form of removable primary storage and not secondary storage. Solid-state removable storage consists of a flash ROM chip mounted on a cartridge. A number of competing formats have been developed from different manufacturers, including Toshiba's SmartMedia™, Sony's Memory stick™ and Iomega's CompactFlash (see Figure 8.14). The devices not only consume very little power (only 5 per cent of the power required by small disk drives) but also contain no moving parts which makes them very robust in applications that might suffer from vibration or shock. Solid-state storage is useful for applications such as mobile computing; devices are available that provide up to 128 Megabytes on one cartridge.

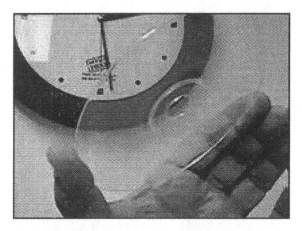

Figure 8.13   Fluorescent multi-layer disk

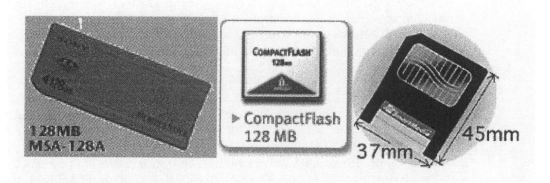

Figure 8.14   From left to right: Memory Stick, CompactFlash and SmartMedia

8.3   ERROR CHECKING AND CORRECTING

During the transfer of data from a disk or tape system, data may become corrupted. It is, therefore, necessary to have some means of detecting errors which have occurred and, possibly, correcting them. These techniques can also be applied to the transmission of data in a communications link. The techniques can be classified into two general groups, error detection and error detection and correction. The first, as its name implies can only detect whether an error has occurred; the second can sometimes repair the data (as long as the damage is not too bad). Consider an example of each type:

Parity checking

With parity checking (an error detection code) an extra bit is added to the data in such a way that the total number of bits set to one is either even (even parity) or odd (odd parity). When the data is received the parity is checked by looking at the total numbers of bits set to one. If the total is even and the scheme being used is odd parity then there has been an error. Conversely if the total is odd and the scheme used is even parity this also will indicate an error. Here is an example of some data bytes with even parity checking.

Data	Parity bit	Total bits set to one
01001111	1	6
01010101	0	4
00000011	0	2

This scheme works well for single bit errors but fails every time there is an even number of bit errors. For example, if the first data item on the list above had a bit error in the first two positions, it would turn into 10001111, plus the parity bit; this would give you a one bit count of 6 (even parity) and the error would go undetected.

For this reason storage systems use error checking which is more robust than simple parity such as cyclic redundancy checks (CRCs), see Chapter 13, which are very robust and can detect long streams of bits in error with very low chance of failure. For example, a 32 bit CRC can detect all error bursts less than 32 bits long and will only fail to detect error bursts longer than 32 bits at a probability of 1 in 4,294,967,296.

8.3.1 HAMMING CODES

Hamming codes are really just an extension of parity checking, which allows for correction as well as detection of bit errors. Hamming codes are generated in the following way: consider an 8-bit value 10111010, add check bits so that the resultant word has a check bit in each position that is a power of 2, i.e., positions 1, 2, 4, 8, etc.). For an 8-bit number we need to add 4 check bits.

So 10111010 becomes:

Bit position	12 11 10 9	8 7 6 5	4 3 2 1
Data with hamming added	1 0 1 1	X8 1 0 1	X4 0 X2 X1

This is called a 12, 8 block code since, for each 8 bits of original data, there are 12 bits of code data.

The check bits are generated as follows:

X8 is set as even parity for positions 9, 10, 11, 12
X4 is set as even parity for positions 5, 6, 7 and 12
X2 is set as even parity for positions 3, 6, 7, 10 and 11
X1 is set as even parity for positions 3, 5, 7, 9 and 11

If a data bit is received in error its position can be calculated as follows: add up positions of the check bits that fail. Let us say, for example, bit position 10 is corrupted; this will result in errors in X8 and X2 (see above); add up 8 and 2 which gives you 10. This allows you to correct the single bit by complementing it. This hamming code will also allow you to detect double bit errors.

The hamming code here is somewhat weak, in that it can only correct single bit errors but many stronger techniques are available. Reed-solomon coding, which was used traditionally on tape drives to improve reliability (and more recently on CDs), can cope with loss of multiple bytes of data.

8.4 SUMMARY

This chapter has described methods by which bulk data storage can be achieved. The organisation of the data, so that it is in a form useful to the programmer, has also been considered in relation to the physical characteristics of the devices. Finally, the concept of error checking has been introduced, and techniques have been described that allow errors to be detected and, in some cases, corrected.

8.5 EXERCISES

1 From current manufacturers' specifications find out the cost per byte of storage of the following storage media:
   hard disk
   floppy disk
   CD-R
   CD-RW
   Zip drive

2 Approximate the storage requirements needed to store the text and graphics of this book, assuming that each picture takes 16 Kilobytes of storage.

3 Describe the operation of a hard disk drive.

4 Why are error correction codes important for backup storage and error detection only is not good enough?

5 How is data written to:
   magnetic media
   CD-R disk
   CD-RW disk

6 Describe a hamming code scheme which would protect a 32-bit data word. How many check bits would be needed and what would be the size of the final protected data?

7 Show how the scheme devised in 6 can be used to correct a single bit error.

8 Why are CRCs used, instead of parity checking, to test for errors on hard-disk drives?

Interrupts

During the execution of a program by a computer, many situations can arise which require prompt attention, either to utilise the whole computer system efficiently or to prevent a serious mishap occurring. In order to ensure that such situations are dealt with as quickly as is necessary, the execution of the current program is interrupted. The computer is then able to execute a program that determines the cause of the interrupt and deals with it accordingly. After this interruption has been dealt with, the original program can be resumed at the point of interruption, unless a computer error or programming error caused the interrupt.

This chapter will describe the interrupt system and how it operates. Not only will it describe ways of handling a single interrupt, but also it will describe techniques for dealing with the situations of either multiple interrupts occurring simultaneously or interrupts occurring before a previous interrupt has been fully dealt with.

9.1 CAUSES OF INTERRUPTS

This section examines several situations that could require the processor to be interrupted. They are not in any order of priority, since the priorities are not the same for every computer system. The question of priorities is dealt with in section 9.4.

9.1.1 HARDWARE FAULT

The hardware circuitry carries out various checks for its own malfunction. Two examples are power failure and memory parity.

The electricity needed to operate a computer is usually supplied by the national or local power company via its existing power distribution system. In the event of a mains power failure, processing must be suspended. It is desirable that when supplies are resumed, processing can continue from where it was suspended. Because of the volatile nature of registers and of some main memory systems, an orderly shutdown procedure is required; otherwise data can be lost, erroneous information can be written into the memory and other malfunctions can occur during the fraction of a second when power is being lost. To guard against such an occurrence, the voltage supplied to the computer is monitored continuously. If it drops to, say, 85 per cent of its nominal value, the assumption is that a power failure is occurring and an interrupt request is generated. If this power fail interrupt is serviced immediately (it will have to be assigned the highest priority as described in section 9.4) there will be sufficient time for the computer to save the contents of all its registers and shut itself down. When power is restored the contents of the registers can be reloaded (either by the operator or, some-times, automatically) and operation resumes from where it was interrupted. If the main memory is non-volatile, the registers can be stored in special memory locations reserved for this. In the case of a volatile main memory, the situation is more difficult. Back-up battery supplies are often used, switched on by the power fail detector. The battery will enable the data to be held for several hours. (Uninterruptible Power Supplies are described in section 16.1.3.)

For detecting memory errors, a parity bit is provided for every word in the memory. If, on a memory access, either a read or write, one of the bits of a stored word is written into or read from incorrectly then the word transferred will not have the correct parity. In this case, an interrupt is generated.

The action on receipt of this interrupt could be to try the memory transfer again a number of times. If this is successful, processing can continue from where it was interrupted. Alternatively, if it is not successful the original program cannot be continued because either incorrect data would be used in a calculation, or an instruction that differed from that intended by the programmer would be executed.

9.1.2 PROGRAM ERRORS

There are a number of errors that can be committed by a program, as a result of an error situation introduced by the programmer.

Errors that occur while using the arithmetic and logic unit often generate an interrupt. An overflow error is one such condition. Usually an overflow occurs because the programmer did not anticipate that a computed result would exceed the range of the machine. On receipt of this interrupt the action would be either to terminate execution of the program or to transfer control to a user-supplied subroutine which might allow processing to continue despite the overflow condition.

Another condition is that of memory protection violation. It is possible for a program to generate an address that is outside the range of that program. Some areas of memory should be protected, such as the operating system routines used by many programs. Obviously a program must be prevented from overwriting such an area of memory. A memory block is protected by the supervisory programs executing a special *protect memory* instruction and can be unprotected by execution of an *unprotect memory* instruction. These instructions are privileged instructions, which means that only the supervisory programs can execute them. If a user program tries to write to an address that is in a protected part of main memory, an interrupt will be generated. On receipt of this interrupt the action is usually to terminate execution of the program and generate an appropriate error message.

Attempts can be made by a program to perform operations on data that is not compatible with the way data is stored. An example would be to interpret the contents of a word as a series of characters when in fact the bit pattern within the word does not correspond to characters in the character code being used. It is also possible to branch to a word, to continue execution from that point on, when the word branched to does not contain a valid instruction operation code. All of these are examples of conditions that could generate an interrupt to indicate that something is wrong.

9.1.3   REAL TIME CONDITIONS

Computers are often used for the monitoring and control of real time processes. These are processes in which the computer is expected to respond to some situation in a realistic time scale (often very quickly).

In medicine, for example, a computer may be used to monitor a patient's heartbeat. If there is a significant reduction in the frequency or power of the heartbeat an interrupt can be generated which enables the computer to take immediate action such as the triggering of alarm bells. This is illustrated in Figure 9.1.

A potentially costly real time situation can occur during the control of a machine tool by computer. If an expensive part is being machined and the cutter breaks, both the part and the machine may be damaged. By detecting that tool breakage has occurred immediately, and putting the equipment onto standby, consequent damage to the part and the machine can be prevented.

9.1.4   INPUT/OUTPUT

Even though most peripheral devices seem to the user to operate at very high speed they actually operate very slowly compared with the rate at which the CPU operates (see Chapter 10). The slower peripheral devices such as printers transfer characters one at a time. In order to be able to make use

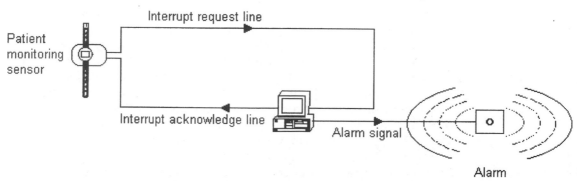

Figure 9.1   Patient heartbeat monitoring

of the CPU during the time the peripheral is transferring the character, it is necessary that the peripheral device is able to interrupt the CPU on completion of the transfer. The CPU can then initiate the transfer of the next character. In the case of faster peripheral devices, such as magnetic disk, a block of characters can be transferred, and an interrupt takes place only on completion of the block transfer (see Chapter 10).

Consequently the interrupt facility is very important as an aid to maximising the use of the CPU during input/output.

9.2 INTERRUPT HANDLING

Suppose the CPU is running a program when it receives a request from, say, a peripheral to interrupt its processing and deal with the peripheral. This will involve transferring control to a second program that will deal with the peripheral. This second program is often called an interrupt service routine. On completion of the interrupt service routine, control will have to transfer back to the original program at the point at which it was interrupted in order for it to continue.

There must, therefore, be a mechanism to allow for error-free switching between the program that is being executed when an interrupt occurs, and another program to deal with the interrupt and go back to the original program again.

Since the main purpose of an interrupt system is to utilise the CPU to the full, it is obviously important that the response to an interrupt be very quick. Since it is totally unreasonable to expect every user program to include an instruction to test the state of some interrupt flag after every instruction in case something requires attention, it follows that the interrupt mechanism must be automatic and provided by the CPU. However, as we shall see, there may be a case for using software to assist the hardware in the provision of the interrupt mechanism.

The problem of transferring control from a program to an interrupt service routine, while remembering the position in the interrupted program so that a return can be made, is essentially the same problem as that faced when writing a subroutine. However, as we have just seen, the transfer of control from the interrupted program to the interrupt service routine must be performed by the hardware automatically on receipt of an interrupt, and not as a result of the CPU executing an instruction. On completion of the interrupt routine, control has to be given back to the interrupted program, and this can be done by software in just the same way as with a subroutine.

In addition to the requirement that the response must be quick, it is also important that it is error free, so that the program is not corrupted. The condition of the CPU must be exactly the same on return from the interrupt service routine as it was before the interrupt occurred.

9.2.1 THE STATE OF THE CPU

In order for the CPU to be in the same state after an interrupt has been serviced as it was before, it is necessary to be able to preserve the state of all the components of the CPU when the interrupt occurs. The CPU consists essentially of a series of registers and lines containing control signals. To preserve the registers will require the execution of some instructions to store the contents of the registers in some area of main memory. However, since the actions required to preserve the control signals would destroy them, the signals cannot be preserved. The solution lies in the fact that in the brief instant between completing the execute phase of one instruction and the fetch phase of another instruction, the CPU control signals are always in the same state, regardless of which instructions have been executed. Consequently, when an interrupt occurs the CPU finishes executing the current instruction before it accepts the interrupt. It is then merely necessary for the interrupt service routine to store the appropriate registers immediately it is given control and to reset the registers back to these values immediately before giving control back to the original program.

9.2.2 A SIMPLE INTERRUPT SYSTEM

In order to see what is required of the hardware when an interrupt occurs, consider in more detail the situation of the CPU executing a program, the only other program involved being the interrupt service routine. We will also assume that there can be only one reason for the interrupt, and that a further interrupt cannot occur while this one is being dealt with. Although this is a false situation, it enables a clear picture to be seen of the actions to be taken on receipt of an interrupt. The other complications are dealt with later. Figure 9.2 shows the program in memory at the point where an interrupt occurs.

Assume that an interrupt occurs while the CPU is executing the instruction stored at the memory location with address n. The PC register will, of course, contain the address of the next instruction to be executed, namely $n + 1$. In order for control to be given to the interrupt service routine, the address of that routine must be transferred into the PC, so that the next instruction fetched is the first one of the interrupt service routine. This, unfortunately, would destroy the address ($n + 1$) already in there, and so the contents of the PC will have to be preserved (by the hardware) in a

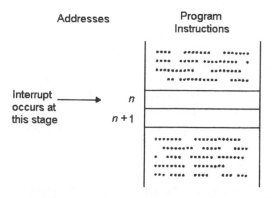

Figure 9.2 A program in memory when an interrupt occurs

particular memory location. Also, it is possible that we may wish to hold the interrupt service routine in any part of memory that is convenient and so the address of the start of it must also be stored in a special memory location. These two memory locations are often at 'one end' of memory, say at locations 0 and 1. This results in the situation where the hardware always uses fixed addresses, but the service routine can be placed anywhere in main memory. To recap, when an interrupt occurs the following events will take place:

1 The CPU will complete execution of the current instruction.

2 The hardware will:
   a transfer the contents of the PC register to memory location 0
   b transfer the contents of memory location 1 to the PC.

3 The CPU will continue by fetching the instruction whose address is in the PC, i.e., the first instruction of the interrupt service routine.

The first instructions in the interrupt service routine will be to store all the general registers in some memory locations. In fact, it is only necessary for it to store away those registers that it is making use of during its processing.

Just before the interrupt service routine is finished, the last instructions will be to restore the general registers from the memory locations used for their preservation. Finally, control can be transferred back to the original program by executing a branch instruction that will branch indirect through memory location 0. This will cause the contents of location $0(n + 1)$ to be put into the PC register, and processing will continue from where it was interrupted.

9.3   IDENTIFICATION OF INTERRUPT SOURCE

To explain the fundamental ideas of dealing with an interrupt, the previous section was restricted to situations where there was only one reason for the interrupt. The mechanism for handling interrupts must now be extended to deal with a number of interrupt causes. Section 9.1 described some of the possible causes of interrupts and, since it is reasonable to assume that the action required on receipt of an interrupt will be dependent on the cause of that interrupt, it follows that there need to be a number of interrupt service routines, one for each cause of an interrupt. Consequently it is necessary to identify the precise cause of the interrupt.

One way this can be done is to have multiple interrupt lines. Each type of interrupt will generate an interrupt signal on its appropriate interrupt line. Each line has its own pair of main memory locations, one of which contains the address of the service routine as described in section 9.2.2. However, there are some circumstances that require more than one type of interrupt on one line. If an interrupt from a particular peripheral device, for example, is considered to be a unique interrupt source then it could have its own interrupt line. But this would mean that the design of the CPU hardware fixes precisely the peripheral devices that can be attached to it. Obviously this reduces the ease with which different peripheral devices can be attached to the same CPU. Consequently, particularly in respect of input/output, it is usual to have a number of devices (interrupt sources) all attached to the same interrupt line. When an interrupt signal occurs on such an interrupt line, the particular device requesting the interrupt has to be identified. This can be achieved either by a software technique or implemented as a hardware function. Because of the potential delay in responding to an interrupt (either because the interrupt is not responded to until completion of execution of the current instruction or because it has to wait its turn as described in section 9.4), an interrupt line actually consists of two lines. One is the interrupt request line, this being the line that will transmit the interrupt request signal to the CPU. The other line is an interrupt acknowledge line. When the CPU is ready to accept it will send an interrupt acknowledge signal so that the interrupt request signal can be turned off by the source of the interrupt.

9.3.1 IDENTIFICATION BY SOFTWARE

When a device signals an interrupt request, the hardware causes control to transfer to a service routine, as described in section 9.2.2. In that section it was assumed that this would be the device service routine. If, however, there can be a number of devices attached to this line, the routine will be an interrupt service routine whose task is to identify the device requesting the interrupt and then to transfer control to that particular device's service routine. In order to determine which device is requesting the interrupt, the routine will examine all the devices on that line, one at a time. This is known as *software polling*. One technique is to make use of a special skip instruction that allows examination of a particular peripheral device interface. On a peripheral device interface there is often a flag bit that is set to one when an interrupt request is generated and back to zero when the interrupt has been dealt with. One of the set of input/output instructions examines this flag and skips the next instruction when it is set to 0.

9.3.2 IDENTIFICATION BY HARDWARE

The above solution to the problem of identifying the source of the interrupt is relatively cheap to implement but slow in operation because of the time taken to execute the instructions, particularly in the case of the device that is polled last. However, in the days when the hardware was expensive, this was an acceptable solution. Since hardware costs are now relatively low, most interrupt systems use a hardware identification system.

This hardware system is called *vectored interrupts*. In general, this name refers to all interrupt handling techniques that allow the interrupting device to identify itself to the CPU by supplying a special code or address to the CPU.

When the CPU is ready to accept an interrupt, it sends an interrupt acknowledge signal. Of the devices attached to that interrupt line, only the device requesting the interrupt will respond. It does so by sending to the CPU an address. This address could be the start address of the service routine for that particular device. However, this would impose the restriction that the interrupt service routine for a given device always starts at the same location. An improvement would be for the address that is sent to the CPU by the device to be that of a word in memory in which the PC can be saved, the following word containing the start address of the service routine. Each device would have associated with it a unique pair of main memory locations.

The following, then, is the sequence of events:

1 A device generates an interrupt request signal.

2 The CPU completes execution of the current instruction and then sends an interrupt acknowledge signal.

3 The device requesting the interrupt will send to the CPU (usually via the I/O data bus) the address of a location in memory and then turn off the interrupt request signal.

4 The CPU hardware stores the current value of the PC in this memory address and loads the contents of the next word in store into the PC and commences processing again. The instruction now being executed is the first instruction of the device service routine.

The name 'vectored interrupts' stems from the idea that the specification to the CPU of a unique memory location for that device causes a specific directed change in processing sequence.

In contrast to the software polling method, the process is very quick, requiring not much longer than the two memory cycles required for the main memory access. Also, the time taken to enter a particular device service routine is independent of the number of devices attached to that interrupt line. The disadvantage is that it requires more specialized hardware, in particular in the peripheral interface.

9.4 PRIORITY SYSTEMS

Section 9.3 extended the mechanism for handling interrupts to allow for a number of interrupt sources, by looking at methods for identifying the source of the interrupt. This section will extend the mechanism even further by examining the situation in which an interrupt occurs before the previous one has been fully serviced, or when multiple interrupts occur simultaneously. Although the chance of more than one interrupt occurring at precisely the same instant is not very high, it must be remembered that an interrupt is not accepted until the machine instruction being executed when the interrupt occurs is complete. During this brief delay there may have been a number of interrupts generated, all of which require servicing simultaneously. Consequently the often-used term of interrupts 'occurring' simultaneously, in fact, refers to interrupts requiring 'servicing' simultaneously. In this latter case the interrupt handling system is faced with the decision of which interrupt to service first. In the other case, that of interrupts occurring before a previous one has been fully serviced, the mechanism must decide whether to finish the servicing of the interrupt it has already started, or whether to leave off and accept and service the new interrupt request. Obviously there needs to be some system of priorities in order to resolve these questions.

9.4.1 NESTED INTERRUPTS

There are many occasions when an interrupt occurs while a previous one is being serviced. If, as discussed later, it is necessary to process this second interrupt immediately, the processing of the first interrupt will have to be suspended. We have already seen (section 9.2.2) that when an interrupt is accepted the address of the instruction that would have been executed next is stored away so that control can be transferred back to it after the interrupt has been serviced. If a second interrupt occurs, that must be dealt with immediately, it is important that the address that is now stored away (the address of the next instruction in the first interrupt service routine) is not stored at the same location as the first address that has been stored away (the address of the next instruction in the original program), otherwise control will not be able to return to the original program. Therefore these addresses must be stored in separate locations. This ability to allow interrupts to interrupt previous interrupt service routines safely is called *nested interrupts*. This is why, in the vectored interrupt system described in section 9.3.2, each device has associated with it a unique pair of main memory locations.

If the computer has a stack facility, the return address can simply be PUSHed onto the stack. This is discussed more fully in section 9.5. Each time an interrupt is accepted the PC will be pushed onto the stack. They will, of course, be POPped off the stack in the reverse order, this being the order in which the interrupt servicing will now be completed. So long as the stack is sufficiently large, interrupt routines can be nested to any depth.

9.4.2 ENABLING AND DISABLING INTERRUPTS

There are a number of occasions when it is necessary temporarily to prevent an interrupt occurring. Consequently there needs to be provision for disabling the interrupt mechanism and also, therefore, provision for enabling interrupts so that they may continue to occur.

There are essentially three levels of interrupt disable:

1 *Disabling of interrupts from a particular peripheral device.* Usually this can be achieved by the inclusion of an interrupt inhibit bit on the device interface.

2 *Disabling of interrupts from sources of lower or equal priority.* When there is a system of priorities given to the various interrupt sources, it must be possible to delay an interrupt that comes from a source of equal or lower priority than that currently being serviced. In some computers, this selective inhibiting of interrupts can be achieved by setting the appropriate bits in an interrupt mask register (see section 9.4.5).

3 *Disabling of all interrupts from any source.* This can be achieved in two ways. The first is a temporary inhibit imposed by the hardware, so that, after acknowledging an interrupt, the CPU will execute at least one instruction before allowing further interrupts. This ensures that the first instruction in the interrupt service routine is executed. If there is a need for more instructions in the service routine to be executed without interruption, the first instruction must be an interrupt disable instruction. This is, in fact, another way of disabling interrupts. An interrupt disable instruction is usually provided, which, when executed, causes the CPU to ignore all interrupts. An example of the use of this can be seen by considering again the software polling system explained in section 9.3.1. The device requesting the interrupt is not acknowledged until it is addressed by the CPU. Since a device requesting an interrupt is not always on top of the polling list, a number of instructions in the interrupt service routine need to be executed before this device is addressed. Unless interrupts are disabled during this period, the device will continue to interrupt the CPU, causing the system to re-enter the interrupt service routine repeatedly.

9.4.3 SOFTWARE ALLOCATION OF PRIORITIES

If the recognition of the interrupt source is achieved by a software polling routine (see section 9.3.1), priority is inherent in the order in which devices are examined or polled. If two devices interrupt simultaneously, the first one that is examined is the one accepted first. Even for interrupts that do not occur simultaneously, it is interesting to note that the one that interrupts first may not be accepted first. If, after having switched to the interrupt service routine because of a device interrupt, an interrupt from another device occurs, and the second device is polled before the original one, then the second interrupt is accepted first.

Because the priority system is determined by the polling order, the priorities can easily be changed by rewriting the interrupt service routine to poll in a different order. Also it is possible for a device with a very high priority to be polled more often than other devices.

9.4.4 HARDWARE ALLOCATION OF PRIORITIES

There are two basic methods of allocating priority by hardware. The first method is concerned with the priority among devices attached to the same interrupt request line. Instead of the interrupt acknowledge line being a common line to which all devices are attached in parallel, the interrupt acknowledge line passes from one device to the next in turn. A signal from the CPU on the interrupt acknowledge line will only be passed to the next device if the current device is not requesting an interrupt, as in Figure 9.3.

This technique, known as *daisy chaining*, has its priority system built into the order in which the devices are attached to the interrupt acknowledge line, those closest to the CPU having the highest priority.

The second method of providing a priority system by hardware lies in the ability to have multiple interrupt lines. Each interrupt source is allocated to one particular interrupt line (there could be a number of interrupt sources attached to the same line). Priority between lines can be achieved simply by a priority arbitration circuit to which all lines are attached. If simultaneous

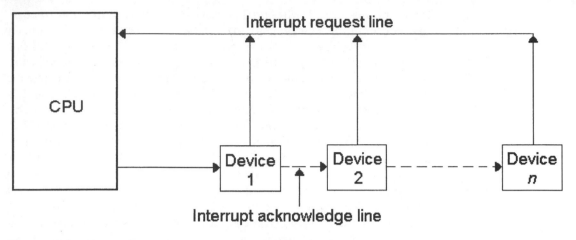

Figure 9.3 Daisy-chained interrupt acknowledge line

interrupt request signals occur this circuit will send the acknowledge signal to the line with the highest priority. The allocation of priority is sometimes fixed and sometimes programmable. If there is only one interrupt source to each interrupt line, total priority between sources is achieved. In practice, it is usual to have a number of interrupt sources (for example, peripheral devices) attached to each line. Priority between lines can be achieved by the arbitration circuit just described, and priority between devices on each line can be achieved by daisy chaining the interrupt acknowledge line between the devices. In this multi-level interrupt system, device recognition is usually achieved by vectoring.

9.4.5 INTERRUPT MASKING

The advantage of a software priority system is that it can be modified at any time merely by polling in a different order. In contrast, however, the faster hardware system is fixed by the wiring of the circuits. In order to combine flexibility with speed, a combined software/hardware system has been developed called *interrupt masking*. Here, all interrupt lines attached to the CPU are associated with a bit position in an interrupt register. If an interrupt on a line is generated, the CPU will recognise it but only if the corresponding bit in the interrupt register is a 1. In order to allow the pattern of bits in the interrupt register to be changed there is an associated register, the interrupt mask register, which is program addressable. This register is permanently ANDed with the interrupt register so that only if there is a 1 bit in the mask register can an interrupt on that line be recognised. If a particular interrupt service routine wishes to inhibit interrupts of a lower priority, then at the beginning of the service routine it must load the interrupt mask register with an appropriate pattern of bits. Only those bit positions corresponding to interrupts that are to be allowed are set to 1; all other bits are set to 0.

9.5 OTHER INTERRUPT FACILITIES

We have seen how it is necessary for the contents of the PC, and any general-purpose registers being used, to be saved at the commencement of dealing with an interrupt, in order to allow control to return to the interrupted program. Stacks can be used for this purpose just as they can in subroutine handling. The CPU can push the PC onto the stack and the service routine can PUSH all the general registers onto the stack at the start of the service routine. On completion of the service routine, these values can be POPped off the stack. If interrupts are nested, the stack mechanism will ensure that the values are retrieved from the stack in the correct order (see section 9.4.1). However, there is still the requirement for a dedicated memory location to keep the address of the interrupt service routine.

We have seen the need to keep the address of the interrupt service routine in a dedicated memory location so that, on acceptance of an interrupt, the CPU can load this address into the PC and then recommence execution by fetching what will be the first instruction of the service routine (section 9.2.2). An alternative to this is to place an instruction in the dedicated memory location. The CPU then merely needs to transfer the contents of this location to the IR and then to continue. This instruction would usually be a branch instruction that would cause control to transfer to the first instruction of the interrupt service routine.

9.6 EXAMPLES OF REAL INTERRUPT SYSTEMS

Having gradually developed the requirements for an interrupt system and seen various alternative ways of implementing such systems, it will be interesting to look briefly at the interrupt handling mechanisms actually used on some existing computers. The examples chosen are from two families of microprocessor. It is left as an interesting exercise for the reader to investigate the interrupt handling mechanism of the computer to which access is available.

9.6.1 THE INTERRUPT MECHANISM OF THE INTEL PENTIUM PROCESSOR

Two classes of interrupt are identified, internal (termed *exceptions*) and external (termed *interrupts*). An *exception* is caused either by the occurrence of a program error such as division by zero or execution of an invalid op-code, or the execution of an INT n instruction to force entry to the operating system in order to use a system routine, perhaps.

Interrupts (i.e., external interrupts) can be signalled asynchronously on one of two lines, INTR and NMI. An interrupt on NMI is not maskable in any way so it can be used to signal some urgent fault condition. Interrupts generated on the INTR line may be inhibited by a bit in the flag register, IF. If the interrupt flag is clear (IF = 0) then it will ignore any incoming signals. Only when the interrupt flag is set (IF = 1) will it respond to interrupt requests.

When an interrupt occurs the processor will save the current status of the machine by pushing relevant information onto the stack (the flag register, code segment register, the offset address of the next instruction to have been executed) and then clear the interrupt flag, so preventing another interrupt occurring.

It also expects to be provided with a one-byte TYPE code, specifying one of 256 interrupt sources. This type code is used to vector into a table of interrupt service routine addresses that is stored in the bottom 1K bytes of memory.

The first five table entries (type codes 0–4) are reserved for specific conditions such as divide by zero, overflow, non-maskable interrupt and single step facility interrupt. In some cases, the interrupt number is defined implicitly by the cause of the interrupt. For example, as indicated above, division by zero uses an interrupt number of 0 whereas the NMI uses an interrupt number of 2. In the case of programmed interrupts the number is specified in the instruction.

When the interrupt occurs on the INTR line, however, the processor expects to be provided with the number via the external bus using an interrupt acknowledge cycle. In order to provide this there is also a support chip that may be used with the Pentium family known as an 8259A Interrupt Controller chip. This support chip can accept up to eight independent interrupt signals numbered 0 to 7. The chip will accord priorities to these inputs and present a single interrupt to the CPU, along with the unique interrupt type code associated with that interrupt source. Interrupt source 0 has the highest priority and 7 the lowest. After the processor has dealt with one of the interrupts any others that have occurred will be presented immediately, again in the order of priorities accorded.

On the PC this support chip is mounted on the system board and provides this interrupt prioritisation mechanism for the following eight interrupt sources:

timer;

keyboard;

colour graphics interface;

secondary serial interface;

serial (RS-232) interface;

fixed disk;

floppy disk;

printer.

This chip also incorporates an interrupt mask register so that interrupt sources can be selectively masked out by writing an appropriate bit pattern into the mask register prior to enabling interrupts.

9.6.2 THE INTERRUPT MECHANISM OF THE MOTOROLA PowerPC SERIES

The PowerPC series microprocessors can operate either in supervisor mode or user mode. The operating system or monitor executes in supervisor mode whereas editors, compilers, user programs, etc., operate in user mode. In user mode certain instructions that would interfere with the operation of the processor are inhibited.

Interrupts are included under the general heading of *exceptions* and, as usual, include hardware errors and program generated interrupts as well as external I/O interrupts. Each interrupt has a vector number n which points to a memory location that stores the address of a service program for that interrupt. At the bottom of main memory is the interrupt table, where the addresses of the interrupt service routines are stored.

When the CPU accepts an interrupt request it suspends normal instruction processing and enters an interrupt response sequence. It first saves the address of the next instruction to be executed in the Save/Restore Register 0 (SRR0). The processor then saves information on the state of the machine from the Machine State Register (MSR) to the Save/Restore Register 1 (SRR1). Next, the MSR is set to a particular value, dependent on the type of interrupt. No matter what type of interrupt is being dealt with, external interrupts are disabled and address translation is turned off. At this point, control is transferred to the appropriate interrupt service routine, which executes in supervisor mode. The addresses of these routines are stored in the interrupt table. When the interrupt has been dealt with, an rfi (return from interrupt) instruction is executed by the interrupt service routine.

9.7   SUMMARY

This chapter has presented the need for, and means of achieving, an interrupt system. In many computer applications it is necessary to be able to interrupt the normal execution of programs in order to service higher priority requests that need urgent attention. Most computers, large and small, have a mechanism for dealing with such situations, although the complexity and sophistication of interrupt handling schemes vary from computer to computer.

However, since the cost of hardware continues to decrease, most systems now provide hardware facilities rather than rely purely on slower software facilities.

9.8   EXERCISES

1   Investigate the interrupt handling mechanism of a computer to which you have access.

2   a   Explain what you understand by:
      (i)   an interrupt, suggesting reasons for the cause of an interrupt;
      (ii) interrupt vector and interrupt service routine.
    b   Explain the sequence of events when the following interrupts occur, assuming that:
      (i)   the second and third interrupts occur before the servicing time of the first interrupt has elapsed;

(ii) an interrupt with priority 1 has the lowest priority.

The sequence of interrupts is:

Interrupt number	Time of occurrence	Priority
1	t1	1
2	t2	2
3	t3	3

3 On a machine using base registers, it is necessary for the interrupt handling routines to save one base register for use by the interrupt routine itself. However, the instruction to store a base register itself requires the use of a base register to address the word where the base register is to be stored. Because an interrupt can occur at any time, the values of all the base registers are unknown at the start of the interrupt handling routine, and this means it has no base register available to use for the store base register instruction. Devise a solution to the problem, and if you are using a base register computer, check to see the manufacturer's solution.

4 Explain why the nesting of interrupts is desirable and what the necessary requirements are of a system that allows nesting. Explain two ways of achieving these requirements.

5 A 16-bit computer has a multi-level interrupt system with 20 levels. Describe how the interrupt priorities of peripheral devices can be resolved by hardware to give each device a unique priority. If the system is vectored, explain how control can be passed to the interrupt service routine of the highest priority interrupt.

6 Assuming a machine with a vectored interrupt system and a stack on which the contents of the CPU registers can be stored, describe the sequence of events from the time when a device requests an interrupt until execution of the interrupt service routine is started. If machine instructions require one to four memory cycles to execute, estimate the maximum number of memory cycles that may occur before the execution of the interrupt service routine is started.

7 A Pentium processor is to be used in a situation where there are interrupts from various sources. Describe the operations that the Pentium goes through when handling any interrupt that may occur.

Data transfer

The architecture of a computer will now be discussed in relation to the ways in which it communicates with the outside world. One of the basic features of a computer is its ability to send and receive data to and from other devices. These range from slow peripheral devices which transfer one character at a time, for example, a modem, to very fast devices which require a whole block of data to be transferred, such as a magnetic disk device or even another computer if the machines are part of a network. Also, the devices may be very close to the computer, in which case connection can be by a simple cable (multi-conductor cable, if information is transferred in parallel), or they may be some considerable distance away, in which case the provision of multi-conductor cables becomes too expensive.

This chapter will look at the above features as they relate to software, for example, input/output as it affects the programmer, and to some of the hardware aspects of peripheral and 'line' transfers. The software aspects of input/output are introduced initially in our discussion of the simpler methods through to the more sophisticated techniques used on higher performance computers (section 10.4). On the hardware side, transferring data over lines is important not only in dealing with input/output along an I/O bus or channel but also in connection with the distribution of processing and data over a network, as we shall see in Chapter 12.

10.1 THE BUS

A *bus* is a data highway that connects two or more communicating devices. *Serial buses* (which send one bit at a time) are typically used for longer distances and (perhaps) lower cost and lower performance. *Parallel buses* send a number of data bits (e.g., 32), plus control and address signals, at the same time. Parallel buses are to be found on the main board (motherboard) of a computer.

10.1.1 INPUT/OUTPUT BUS AND THE INPUT/OUTPUT INTERFACE

Since a number of peripheral devices are usually connected to a computer, there has to be some means by which only one of these devices can be selected to perform some input or output task. This can be achieved through the use of an input/output bus – the I/O bus. In some respects, the I/O bus is similar to the internal CPU bus system described in Chapter 6. Connected to the wires which form the bus are registers in the peripheral device interface. However, unlike registers in the CPU, which are completely under the control of the CPU, those in the peripheral device act in an autonomous way. The CPU initiates their actions, but does not subsequently have any control over their operation.

A bus to which I/O devices are connected consists of three sets of lines used for the transmission of address, data and control signals. When the CPU wishes to send data to a particular I/O device it places a unique identity code, or address, onto the address line. Only the device that recognises that code will respond to the command that is placed on the control line. Figure 10.1 shows a typical structure of a computer system with a single I/O bus. In many so-called 'single bus systems', the I/O interface can be identified uniquely by allocating it a specific memory address (*memory mapping*), and transfers of information to or from a register on an interface can be achieved by any of the appropriate instructions (*port mapping*).

The advantage of memory mapping is that every instruction that can access memory can be used to give commands to I/O devices. The disadvantage: it is more expensive than port mapped I/O. This is because the whole of the address bus must be fully decoded via logic gates for every device.

In port mapping, every I/O device is mapped onto a separate address space. Usually there is a special set of signal lines for port access. The advantage of this system is that less logic is needed for decoding an address, which makes it a cheaper system than memory mapping.

In a system such as that illustrated in Figure 10.1, reading data from a peripheral device and storing it in memory is a three stage process (output being the reverse):

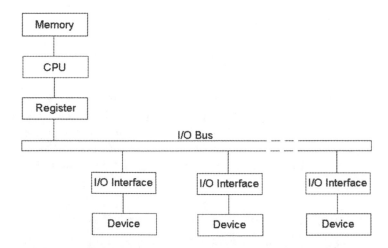

Figure 10.1 A computer system with a single I/O bus

1 Device → I/O interface

2 I/O interface → register

3 Register → memory

A device is attached, by cable, to an I/O interface. The interface is plugged into one of a number of I/O slots, each of which is assigned a fixed address. The interface is the communication link. It includes three basic elements:

1 *A control bit* – is a 1-bit register (flip-flop) which, when turned on, generates a start command to the device to start its I/O.

2 *A flag bit* – is set on by the device when transmission between the device and its interface is complete. It can be tested or cleared under program control.

3 *A buffer register* – is the register in which the data that has been read, or which is to be written, is stored.

When a start command is generated, one character is transferred between the interface buffer register and the device, or vice versa.

10.1.2 THE EXPANSION SLOT ARCHITECTURE OF THE PC

The original IBM PC was designed (in 1981) to be easily expandable by means of slots into which various expansion circuit boards (called *adaptors* or *expansion cards*) could be plugged. Over time, there has been a tendency to put facilities on the main board of the PC rather than in expansion slots (see section 11.1). However, the expansion slots are still an extremely useful way of enhancing the capability of the machine. For example, the PC's graphics adaptor was formerly a separate card which was mounted in an expansion slot. Although nowadays standard graphics adaptor circuitry is included on the main board, if a specialised graphics accelerator is put into an expansion slot the built-in graphics adaptor is ignored and the new, more powerful adaptor takes over. Another expansion card which is commonly added to a PC is the Ethernet adaptor for connection to a network. (See sections 14.2.2, 16.1.2 and 16.1.5.)

The original standard for the PC expansion bus – the *industry standard architecture (ISA)* – took only 8-bit cards and ran at a rate of 4.77 MHz. Through the years, various improvements have been made on this, for example, *peripheral component interconnect (PCI)*, running at 33 MHz and the *advanced graphics port (AGP)*, running at 66 MHz. These alternative buses may all be present in the same machine and each kind of bus will have its own expansion slots. Figure 10.2 shows a typical expansion slot layout. (Compare this with Figure 11.1, which is a photograph of an actual motherboard.)

10.2 EXTERNAL CONNECTIONS

10.2.1 PARALLEL TRANSMISSION

Serial and parallel transmission were introduced in section 7.4. In parallel transmission, each bit position of a word or character code is associated with

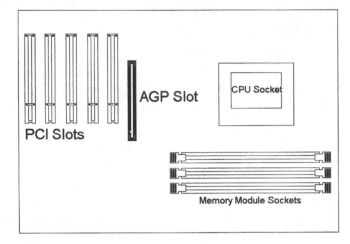

Figure 10.2 Typical expansion slot layout on a PC main board (most details omitted)

its own transmission line. Consequently, all the bits of one word or one character are transmitted simultaneously. Obviously a large number of separate lines are required, and so, although it is a very fast way of transmitting data, its use is usually limited to very short-distance connections. For transmission over long distances, the cost of providing these multiple lines is usually prohibitive. Another problem that limits the distance is *skew*. The propagation delay is not identical for each line (bit) and so the greater the distance the greater the difference in time of arrival of the different bits.

Computer systems sometimes use parallel interfaces for connecting to their peripheral devices. Such interfaces are often provided in the form of a chip, which provides the facilities to control and transfer data between these devices and the processor, e.g., the Motorola peripheral interface adaptor (PIA). There are also some standard interface specifications, such as the IEEE-488, which are also available as chips.

10.2.2 SERIAL TRANSMISSION – ASYNCHRONOUS

If parallel transmission is too costly in terms of the number of lines required, the alternative is to use only one line and to send the bits that make up a character or a word one bit at a time. This is known as serial transmission. Parallel and serial transmission are compared in Figure 10.3

In order that the receiving device can decode a character properly, it must know when to look for a signal and which bit is the first bit of a character. This problem is called synchronisation and there are two techniques used to deal with it. The first technique, asynchronous transmission, is suitable for low speed communications where keyboards or serial printers are directly connected to the line.

Each character transmitted is preceded by a 'start' bit and followed by at least one stop bit (hence it is sometimes called start-stop transmission). Some

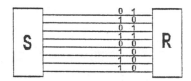

Parallel Transmission

Serial Transmission

Figure 10.3 Parallel and serial transmission

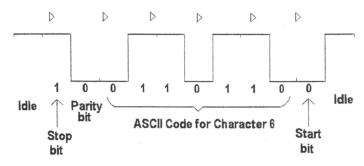

Figure 10.4 Transmission of the ASCII character '6'

devices (particularly electromechanical equipment) will require two stop bits in order to give them time to resynchronise, whereas others require only one. The start and stop bits are always of opposite value. The stop bit is the same state as the line idle state, so that synchronisation can be achieved by the receiver detecting the transition from the stop or idle state to start. Asynchronous transmission of the ASCII character '6' is illustrated in Figure 10.4. (The use of a parity bit in data transmission is explained in section 13.7.1.)

The start bit 'wakes up' the receiver so that the receiver is aware that data bits it needs to record are following. The stop bits allow both the transmitting and receiving devices to get ready for the next character.

The transmission of data from a register in bit serial form down a line, or the receipt of serial bits and the assembling of these into a register, is usually performed by a chip known as a UART (universal asynchronous receiver/transmitter). As an example of the operation of such a device, consider the asynchronous receive process as illustrated in Figure 10.5.

The circuit contains a 16× clock, which samples the incoming line at 16× the anticipated bit rate. It detects the transition from idle to active soon after it occurs. This enables another circuit, which counts eight ticks of the

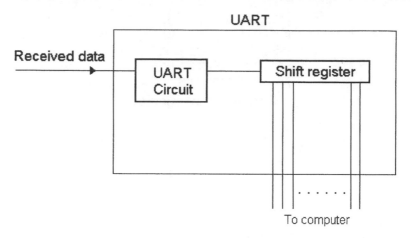

Figure 10.5 The asynchronous receive process using a UART

$16\times$ clock and checks to see if the line is still active. If so, a valid start bit has arrived but, if not, the initial transition was probably due to line noise.

When a valid start signal is detected, a counter is enabled which divides the $16\times$ clock rate by 16 to produce a sampling clock rate, ticking once every bit at approximately the centre of the bit. As bits are received they are clocked into a shift register. When eight bits have been received they are transferred to the processor in parallel.

10.2.3 SERIAL TRANSMISSION – SYNCHRONOUS

The main drawback of asynchronous transmission is that a large proportion (about 30 per cent) of the transmitted bits are not data bits but synchronising bits (start and stop bits). An improved technique, synchronous transmission, is needed for faster devices that send blocks of data rather than individual characters. In this case, the devices are synchronised by the transmitting of a stream of synchronising bits at periodic intervals, between which will be blocks of data.

In order for the synchronising bits to be distinguished from the data bits, they must be sent in a predetermined order and, usually, there will be a number of such timing characters (synchronising bits) so that one of them cannot be generated as a result of random noise on the line.

Various characters are used for synchronisation and message control. There is a definite sequence in which the synchronising characters and message control characters must be transmitted, and this sequence is known as 'hand-shaking' or protocol. It is described in Chapter 15.

As with asynchronous transmission, the mechanism for synchronous transmission and receipt is often provided in the form of a chip. Frequently, this is provided as a system capable of operating in either synchronous or asynchronous format and known as a USART (universal synchronous/asynchronous receiver/transmitter).

10.2.4 SERIAL INTERFACE STANDARD EIA/TIA-232

Because the connection of devices (printers, plotters, modems, etc.) to a computer is such a fundamental requirement, the industry would be in chaos if each manufacturer of such equipment defined their own interface. Hence there are some generally accepted standard interfaces, one of which is known as EIA/TIA-232 (formerly known as RS232-C). Essentially it is the interface between data terminal equipment (a computer or a terminal) and data communication equipment (a modem), employing serial binary data interchange.

The complete standard defines:

Electrical signal characteristics

Interface mechanical characteristics

Functional description of interchange circuits

More details of the use of this in communications are given in section 15.2.2. However, the interface can be used for very simple connections between a device and a computer by using only three of the connecting pins – signal ground, received serial data and transmitted serial data. Thus it has become commonly used to interface devices not connected through a modem.

10.2.5 UNIVERSAL SERIAL BUS

The Universal Serial Bus (USB) was introduced in section 7.4. It can be used to connect many different devices (up to 127) to a PC. One very convenient feature of USB is that it uses only one Interrupt Request (IRQ), irrespective of how many devices are actually attached to the bus. (Interrupts are discussed in Chapter 9 and IRQs in Chapter 16.) IRQs are in very short supply on PCs and nearly all adaptor cards need one. Another useful feature is 'hot-swapping'. This means that a peripheral device can be added or removed without the computer having to be shut down. USB was originally designed for use with low- to medium-speed devices. USB 2.0 supports higher speed peripherals at up to 480 Mbits/sec.

USB can distribute power to many peripherals. The power that is required is automatically sensed and delivered to the device. The two power and two data wires that are provided are shown in cross section in Figure 10.6. Each individual cable can be 5 metres long, but if USB hubs are

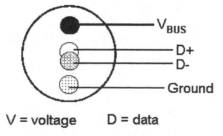

V = voltage   D = data

Figure 10.6 A USB cable

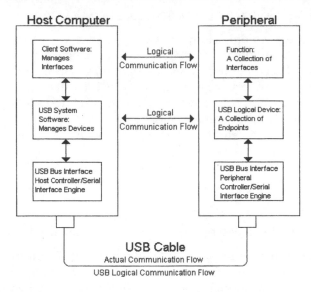

Figure 10.7 Communication flow in a USB system

used, devices can be up to 30 metres away from the host machine. Communication flow in a USB system is shown in Figure 10.7.

Three kinds of data transfer can be performed. A device which sends relatively little data, such as a mouse or keyboard, would use *interrupt mode*. *Bulk transfer mode* is used by bulk devices, such as printers, where error control is necessary. *Isochronous mode* is used for streaming devices such as speakers, where data is to be sent as quickly as possible with no time for error control to be performed. Isochronous (highest priority) and interrupt (second highest priority) devices are allocated regular slots (every millisecond) to carry their data. Bulk transfers use the space that is left over.

10.2.6 IEEE 1394

IEEE 1394 (also known as Firewire® and iLink®) is a serial bus technology that is designed for high-speed audio, video and data transfer applications. Like USB, IEEE 1394 offers hot-swapping and automatic configuration. Unlike USB, it does not require a PC to function. For example, it can be used to send digital data directly from a digital camera to a printer. IEEE 1394 can use a six-wire cable that is made up of two independently shielded twisted-pair conductors and a power supply. The cable is shown in Figure 10.8.

Alternatively, a four-wire cable that consists of just the two twisted pairs without the power supply can be used. IEEE 1394 systems can connect up to 63 devices over a distance of 4.5 metres at high speeds and up to 14 metres at lower speeds. IEEE 1394 is mainly used for multimedia audio/video, whereas USB is mainly used for desktop computer peripheral devices. IEEE 1394b offers a maximum transfer speed of 3.2 Gbps, which is an improvement on the original 1394 standard transfer rate of 400 Mbps.

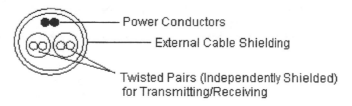

Figure 10.8 An IEEE 1394 cable

10.3 PROGRAMMED INPUT/OUTPUT

Programmed input/output is achieved entirely by the execution of input and output instructions in the user's program. The execution of an input instruction causes data (one character) to be transferred in from an input device to a processor register, whereas execution of an output instruction will cause a character to be transferred from a processor register to a peripheral device. The transfer of a group of characters can be achieved in one of two main ways:

10.3.1 WAIT FOR FLAG PROGRAMMED INPUT/OUTPUT

The simplest I/O system is one in which the processor commands the device to operate and then waits for the completion response. Completion of transfer is indicated when the flag bit on the interface referred to in section 10.1.1 is set. Thus the 'waiting' for a response is in fact a repetitive test of the state of this flag bit by the CPU.

The following two examples (Table 10.1 and Table 10.2) illustrate the sort of code necessary to transfer a single character. They use instructions that refer to the interface at a particular address.

The test and loop instructions cause the processor to test repeatedly the state of the flag bit until it is set to 1, indicating that the transfer is complete. To transfer a group of characters would require a further loop around the above code, since the examples given transfer only one character.

Although this method of achieving input/output is very simple to program, it has the disadvantage of slowness. It might not be obvious, at first, why it is necessary repeatedly to test the flag bit to see if the character has been transferred. Obviously it is important to ensure that one character has been transferred before attempting to transfer the next, but why does the program have to loop, apparently 'waiting' for this to occur? To answer this, consider the following example of the timing of the character transfer process. Suppose the computer is reading data over a low-speed line from a terminal at 1000 characters per second. Further, assume a memory cycle time of one microsecond and that, consequently, the following input code takes, say, 10 microseconds from the time when a character is available (i.e., the IN AL,21 instruction is executed) until the next

Table 10.1   Code to transfer a single character using the wait for flag method

---

INPUT
    WAITING:

IN AL,20	; read in the status register (which includes flag bit)
AND AL,01	; test to see if bit 0 is set indicating interface buffer is full
JZ WAITING	; if bit 0 is zero, jump to WAITING
IN AL,21	; read in character from interface buffer

OUTPUT
    WAITING:

IN AL,20	; read in status register (which includes flag bit)
AND AL,01	; test to see if bit 0 is zero indicating buffer is empty
JNZ WAITING	; if bit 0 is not zero, jump to WAITING
MOV AL,BL	
OUT 21	; output character from register A

Table 10.2   Code to read data from a terminal using the wait for flag method

---

CYCLE:

IN AL,20	
AND AL,01	
JZ CYCLE	
IN AL,21	
MOV Memory,AL	(Store the contents of the accumulator address in the addressed memory location).
JMP CYCLE	(This would actually have to be a conditional branch, depending on whether the end of the data had been reached or not).

---

character needs to be transferred (i.e., the next time it arrives at the IN AL,20 instruction).

The terminal device transferring data at a speed of 1000 characters per second will transfer one character in 1000 microseconds. Consequently, after every 1000 microseconds, the CPU is to take 10 microseconds to deal with the character obtained and then wait another 1000 microseconds for the next character to arrive.

Not only does this explain why an idle loop is necessary (because the peripheral device is so very slow compared to the speed of the processor) but also it illustrates the disadvantage of this method of input/output. In the above example, the CPU is only usefully active for 10 microseconds in every 1000. That is, it is only being used for about 1 per cent of the time and 99 per cent of the time it is idling, waiting for the character to be transferred.

Table 10.3 An interrupt routine for reading characters from an input device

MAIN PROGRAM
Set up address of interrupt service routine

	IN	AL,21	Set control bit to start the transfer of the 1st character.
	—		
	—		
	—		
	—		
Charcount	DEC-50		The number of characters to be transferred.

INTERRUPT SERVICE ROUTINE

	IN	AL,21	Transfer character from interface buffer to A register.
	MOV	Memory,AL	Store this character in memory location
	INC	Charcount	Increment the character count
	JZ	END	All characters are transferred if Charcount = 0
	IN	AL,21	Initiate transfer of next character
	JMP	RETURN	Return to interrupted program
END:	CALL	SUB	Branch to subroutine to process
RETURN:	JMP	0(indirect)	Return to interrupted program.

10.3.2 INTERRUPT PROGRAMMED INPUT/OUTPUT

This method makes use of an interrupt facility (see Chapter 9). It removes the time spent testing the status of the flag bit of the interface by allowing the input/output transfer of data to be initiated by program instruction and allowing the hardware to cause an interrupt when the transfer is complete. In this case, the interrupt service routine would perform the task of transferring the character between the interface buffer register and the processor register (an accumulator, for example) and would then initiate the transfer of the next character. While the character is being transferred the processor is free to be used for other tasks, with the provision that it will be interrupted when the next character has been transferred.

The following example shows an interrupt routine for reading 50 characters from an input peripheral device. The main program has to set up the address of the interrupt service routine, initialise a count of the number of characters to be transferred and initiate the transfer of the first character. While the character is being transferred the processor can continue with another task. On the completion of each character transfer, the interrupt service routine is entered which initiates the transfer of the next character. The program runs as illustrated in Table 10.3.

On completion of the transfer of all 50 characters, it is assumed that some processing of the characters is necessary and so control is transferred to a subroutine, SUB, to do the required processing.

10.4 AUTONOMOUS INPUT/OUTPUT – DMA

Programmed input/output (particularly interrupt driven) is suitable for transferring relatively few characters to or from slow peripheral devices. If, however, there are a large number of characters to be transferred, the CPU will be spending a large portion of its time just dealing with the individual characters, since each character still passes through the CPU and its MAR and MBR on its way to the memory. Also, some of the faster peripherals, such as magnetic disks, may be able to transfer characters at such a rate that there would not be time to process the interrupt service routine for one character before the next character had arrived. Consequently there is a need for some sort of system for allowing a peripheral device to transfer characters directly to memory, without going 'through' the CPU. Such a facility is known as *direct memory access* (DMA). This is achieved by incorporating many of the functions that are performed by software in a programmed I/O method into a hardwired controller. This controller will need:

1 a register for generating the memory address;
2 a register for keeping track of the word count;
3 a register to store the command received from the CPU specifying the function to be performed;
4 a register to be used as a data buffer between the peripheral device and the main memory.

Since DMA is used for connecting high-speed devices it must be remembered that with such devices as magnetic disks there is no need to convert information to and from character format. Consequently the usual unit of transference is a word.

On a single bus computer the memory bus and I/O bus are in fact the same bus. A peripheral device is connected to the bus by the DMA controller rather than by an interface.

On a computer with a separate I/O bus, however, the DMA controller will need to be connected directly to the memory, bypassing the CPU. Figure 10.9 illustrates such a connection. It is still necessary for the CPU to be connected to the DMA in order for control signals to be sent to the DMA controller to initiate the data transfers.

To start an I/O operation using the DMA it is necessary for the program to do the following:

1 load the initial memory address;
2 load the count of the number of words to be transferred;
3 load a control word defining input or output;
4 execute a START command.

On receiving the START command the DMA will proceed with the data transfer independently of the CPU, so enabling the CPU to continue processing another part of the same program or another program altogether. There is, however, the possibility of a conflict when both the CPU and the DMA controller wish to access memory at precisely the same time. Because the transfer of data from very fast peripheral devices attached to the DMA

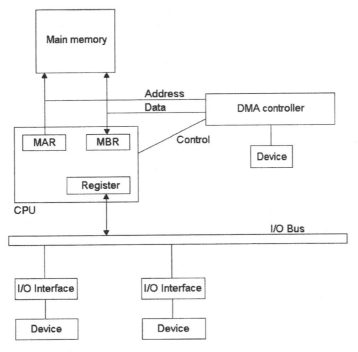

Figure 10.9   DMA controller connected directly to memory

cannot be held up, priority is usually given to the DMA in preference to the CPU. In most cases the CPU will originate the majority of memory access cycles, and hence in the case of contention the DMA can be thought of as 'stealing' a cycle from the CPU. Hence this is often known as *cycle stealing*. It must be remembered, however, that in any program not all the instructions are memory reference instructions, and so, although all instructions involve a memory access to fetch them, only a proportion will access memory during execution. Consequently cycle stealing will take place only occasionally, although it is not possible to predict the effect of the DMA facility on the execution time of an instruction. It therefore follows that the execution time of a program will be unpredictable.

In modern computers *burst mode* is used to speed up data transfers. In burst mode a device is permitted to seize control of the bus. The device does not allow any other devices to interrupt until the transfer is complete.

10.5   SUMMARY

This chapter has dealt with the transfer of data from one device to another from the point of view of the programmer and taking into account the hardware facilities available. It has developed the techniques from the very simple arrangement of busy testing, through more sophisticated programmed I/O, to DMA. These increasingly demand less attention from the CPU, placing more responsibility on other devices operating concurrently. Further aspects of the transmission of data, particularly over long distances, are considered in Chapter 13 in the context of data transmission within computer networks.

10.6 EXERCISES

1 The following question requires you to use a computer to which you have low-level access (machine code or assembler).

   a Write and test a program to transfer a single character from a CPU register to the print device of a terminal.

   b Modify the program so that it repeatedly checks the CPU register for non zero contents and outputs to the print device when non zero.

   c Modify the program so that the character to be output is first input from the keyboard of the terminal.

   d Modify the program to skip round the output code. What is the difference in effect now and why?

2 Compare and contrast the following I/O techniques:

   a programmed I/O

   b DMA

3 A CPU normally allows most interrupt requests to be enabled or disabled under software control. However, no CPU provides facilities to disable DMA requests. Explain why.

4 a Describe the following methods of programming data transfers between a CPU and a peripheral device:

     i executing a program loop to examine a 'ready' status bit.

     ii using an interrupt system to interrupt the CPU when the device is ready.

   b If a peripheral device can transfer data at 10 MBytes per second, explain the relative efficiency in terms of the CPU when the device is used in systems i and ii above, stating any assumptions that you make.

5 Consider a 32-bit processor with both a 32-bit data and address bus. The CPU operates at 10 MHz and a memory access instruction cycle takes two CPU clock cycles. Memory-mapped I/O is used and the CPU supports both vectored interrupts and DMA block transfers. Typical interrupt response time is ten CPU clock cycles. It is necessary to add to the system a disk drive with a data transfer rate of N bits/sec. Estimate the maximum value that N can have if the disk drive is controlled by:

   i programmed I/O;

   ii DMA.

State all your assumptions.

6 Given the following choice of line speeds, 110, 300, 600, 1200 bit/s, which line speed should be used by an asynchronous ASCII terminal that does parity checking and prints at 60 characters/s?

7 How many ASCII characters/s can be transmitted over a 2400 bit/s line in each of the following transmission methods:

   a synchronous;

   b asynchronous?

Building a small computer system

At this point in the book we have already examined all the basic component parts of the computer system. In this chapter we will be seeing how these parts can be fitted together to produce a small computer system. The target system for this chapter will be the IBM PC clone for the following reasons:

The PC is the most prevalent computer system today.

Separate component parts are easy to source.

Components can be obtained relatively cheaply.

11.1 PC COMPONENTS

The PC itself is made up of a number of discrete components, each of which has to be compatible. In this section we will describe each component and explain how they interconnect.

11.1.1 MOTHERBOARD

The motherboard is the centre of the computer system. It holds the processor and provides connection from the processor to the memory (RAM and ROM) and all the I/O (hard disk, floppy disk, CD-ROM and all other peripherals). Practically all PC motherboards provide at least the following as standard:

keyboard port;

mouse port;

floppy disk drive interface;

hard disk drive interface (ATA/IDE provided, SCSI is usually extra);

USB ports (more common these days but some systems may not have this).

Some will provide the following as well:

video port (some may not provide this; if not, you will need a graphics adaptor card);

built-in modem;

built-in network interface;

built-in sound card;

RAID hard disk controller.

It may seem a good idea to have as much functionality built on the motherboards as possible. This is correct but with one proviso: if a built-in component goes wrong it usually cannot be repaired and the whole motherboard has to be replaced.

Expansion slots

Also provided on the motherboard is a set of expansion slots which allow cards to be added to provide extra functionality. An expansion card can be used, for example, to provide an extra interface (e.g., SCSI), or be a peripheral in its own right such as a modem or soundcard. The following types of slots are available on most boards:

ISA   low speed slot (originally provided on first IBM PC, 20 years ago); not used very often (many motherboards do not support this slot anymore);

PCI   high speed slot, current standard for PC cards with most cards fitting this slot;

AGP   very high speed slot designed for use by high end graphics cards.

Motherboards, processor and RAM

Because the motherboard provides sockets for both the processor and RAM, the type of motherboard dictates the speed and type of processor and the total amount of RAM you can use. So, for example, if you want to build a system based around a 800 MHz Intel Pentium III chip with 1.5 Megabytes of 166 MHz SDRAM, you will need a motherboard that will support this processor choice (running at that speed) and will hold that amount of SDRAM. Generally, you will pick the processor and RAM configuration first and then the motherboard. All motherboard manufacturers provide detailed information about their products, many on their websites, so this is not difficult to find.

RAM slots

The motherboard will have a number of DIMM slots to allow memory (RAM) chips to be inserted. You need to check that any motherboard you choose can support enough memory for your current and future needs. Since software is becoming more and more memory hungry all the time (and memory is generally cheaper per byte), it is a good idea to allow for a decent amount of future expansion of RAM requirements. Also, you need to check what type of memory is supported (SDRAM, RDRAM, etc.).

11.1.2 PROCESSOR

The original PC motherboard was designed to use an Intel processor (8066). In the early days of the PC there were a number of competitors producing clones of the Intel product range. This is not so much the case today and the PC processor market is practically a duopoly between AMD and Intel (the Cyrix® III clone is still produced by VIA Technologies, plug compatible clone for socket 370 PIII motherboards).

Both manufacturers make a wide range of processors. In general, you will pay a lot for a latest processor with faster speeds, etc. This is because of low yield – yield is the percentage of processors out of a batch manufactured that work. When a new chip is being made this can be very low (due to the fact that the fabricating process is still being refined).

Remember you must choose the processor and motherboard together, since they have to be compatible.

11.1.3 RAM

RAM is available in various speeds and types. Three types of memory module are currently available for PCs:

SDRAM

Standard PC RAM is available in modules running at 100 or 133 MHz. SDRAM is very cheap but a little slow for higher power systems using processors such as the Pentium 4.

DDRAM

This is similar to the SDRAM module but doubles the effective clock speed (200, 266 or even 333 MHz) and, consequently, doubles the maximum memory bandwidth. Some of the DDRAM modules are named after their maximum data rate: 200MHz RAM is called PC1600 (1600MB/s), 266MHz is PC2100, but 333MHz is called PC333 (2700MB/s).

RDRAM

This is the narrow bus, high frequency RAM described in Chapter 4. The performance of RDRAM memory systems will depend on the number of channels on the motherboard. A single channel RDRAM system running at 800MHz (bandwidth 2×800MHz = 1.6 GB/s) has less bandwidth than a 266MHz DDR (8×266 = 2.128 GBps), a dual channel system (e.g., based on the Intel 850 chip set) will deliver a very high maximum bandwidth (3.2 Gbytes per second). How this impacts on performance can be variable and the reader is recommended to check out the latest benchmarks for any given motherboard.

The speed of RAM for many applications is not probably as important as the amount of it (except perhaps for a file server). This is because, with the operation of the processor's cache, a lot of the time data is retrieved from the cache directly. Considering the current price of RAM, a typical entry system is provided with at least 256 Megabytes. Remember you must choose memory that is compatible with your motherboard.

11.1.4 FLOPPY DISK DRIVE

There is little to say about the 1.4 Megabyte floppy disk drive. It is a standard device with no options to worry about.

11.1.5 HARD DISK DRIVE

There are lot of hard disk drives on the market. You must pick a drive which provides enough storage capacity. This is not difficult since drives are of very high capacity (typically entry level drives start at 20 Gigabytes). Apart from the size and speed you need to decide what type of interface is required. For most systems ATA/IDE will be the most appropriate since most motherboards have this built in and no extra hardware is required. If you are designing a system which will require very high performance then SCSI may be more appropriate but you will probably need to buy an expansion card which will provide a SCSI interface.

11.1.6 CD-ROM DRIVE

Needed to load up most software applications. CD-ROM drives are specified by their speed: for example 16×, 32×, 52×, etc.; this speed is relative to the very first CD-ROM standard speed. Some CD-ROM drives are capable of reading CD-RW media, some are not. CD-ROM drives practically always use the IDE/ATA standard.

11.1.7 DISPLAY

Two options are available, CRT or LCD. An LCD display is more expensive (partly because of low yield problems) but has no flicker and consumes less power. If the motherboard you use does not have a video port built in, you must provide a video card which will need to be inserted into one of the motherboard's expansion slots.

11.1.8 KEYBOARD

There are a lot of keyboards on the market, and all motherboards provide a PS/2 type keyboard connection. Some keyboards can be connected via the USB port, but there are no particular advantages to this.

11.1.9 MOUSE

Again, lots of choice here; the mouse is connected via a dedicated PS/2 port which is provided on the motherboard. Some mice, again, can be connected via the USB port.

11.1.10 POWER SUPPLY AND CASE

The power supply converts mains electricity to a voltage suitable for running the computer system. Mains electricity is provided at between 110 and 240 volts and is alternating (i.e., the flow of current changes direction periodically). The motherboard and other components need lower voltages: for example, 3.5, 5 and 12 volts. For a typical P4 system with 256 Megabytes of RAM and one hard disk, a 300W supply should be sufficient.

Cases come in various forms including flat ones designed to put on your desk, or tower cases. The tower cases are available in a half height model; the problem with these is that they need a special size motherboard, so are best avoided. The case will be provided with internal bays (to mount hard disk drives on) and external bays to mount floppy disks, CD-ROM drives and other removable media. Very often the case is supplied with a fitted power supply.

The motherboards come in various standard sizes as laid down by Intel (size and power requirements for, for example, AT, baby AT, ATX, mini ATX and SFX). These standards also set requirements for certain I/O provision (for example, the ATX board must have an integrated PS/2 mouse connector).

This standard defines what type of case and power supply is required. Most boards currently are ATX form (so require an ATX supply and case). This is the easiest option. If you need to build a smaller PC, formats like SFX are available which is about half the size of the ATX.

A final word on power supplies: try and source a good quality product and preferably a little over specified to ensure no supply problems; lack of power can cause your system to become unstable or crash.

11.2 EXAMPLE SYSTEMS

We are going to specify two example systems: the first is a general purpose machine for budget home PC, and the second is a small file server system. *Note* the parts lists for these systems are examples only and are not meant to be taken as a product endorsement by the authors – many other makes could provide the same functionality.

11.2.1 HOME USER SYSTEM

This system is designed to be of a reasonable cost but with enough expansion potential to allow the machine to be upgraded for some time. The specification is as follows;

Processor	Pentium 4 1.5GHz
RAM	256 Megabytes SDRAM
Hard disk	20 Gigabytes
Monitor	19" CRT
Miscellaneous	CD-ROM, keyboard, mouse, 56K modem

11.2.2 PARTS LIST

Motherboard   Asus P4BS-333 (s478)

This is a socket 478 motherboard and will take the current Pentium-4 processor plus the next generation (up to 2.4 GHz). It supports the current entry level standard DDRAM, which is PC2100 but can be upgraded to PC333 if this is needed. The maximum amount of RAM the board can take is 3 Gigabytes.

Processor   Pentium 4 1.5 GHz

This is the entry level processor for the Pentium 4 range.

RAM   Micron PC 2100

266 MHz DDRAM 1 × 256 Megabytes.

Hard disk space

The drive is a 40GB IBM DESKSTAR 60GXP with an ATA100 interface. This will provide plenty of storage for home use.

Power supply and case

IW-S508i Midi Tower ATX Case with 300W power supply. The power supply supplied with this case has been certified suitable for use with the Pentium 4. This is important as the Pentium 4 has stringent power requirements.

Graphics display card and monitor

The graphics card is a 32Mb Hercules/Guillimot 3D Prophet 2 Geforce 2 MX-400, this is a media budget card suitable for entertainment. The monitor chosen is a 19" Samsung CRT.

Modem

Needed to connect to the Internet, the modem chosen is a Diamond Supra Max 56K USB V90 EXternal V/Fax/Modem. An external modem was chosen so that it can be reset without having to reset the whole machine.

CD-ROM, keyboard and mouse

The CD-ROM drive is a 52× Samsung EIDE model. This is a completely standard type. The keyboard and mouse can be any standard PS/2 compatible product.

11.2.3 FILE SERVER SYSTEM

This machine will only be a single processor system but will be running RAID level 0 (striping only) to boost disk access speed. It also will be configured with a lot of high speed RAM. The specification is as follows.

Processor	AMD ATHLON XP 1600 1.4GHz
RAM	1 Gigabyte of DDR memory
User file storage	40 Gigabytes RAID (2 × 20) striped for performance
System file storage	10 Gigabytes
Monitor	15" CRT
Network Interface	Fast Ethernet
System backup	60 Gigabytes tape system
Miscellaneous	CD-ROM, keyboard, mouse

11.2.4 PARTS LIST

Motherboard   ABIT KG7-RAID

This motherboard has all the basic I/O required except the network interface card and video port. It was chosen because it has support for the processor we specified and can take DDR RAM. It can also control up to 8 hard disks (4 × ATA/IDE slots) and supports RAID (with 4 of the disks). This makes it good as a server since a lot of storage can be handled. The form factor for this board is ATX. The RAID controller supports both mirroring for reliability and striping for performance. For more information go to the manufacturer's website at www.highpoint-tech.com.

Processor   AMD ATHLON XP 1600 1.4GHz

Top of the range AMD processor.

RAM   Kingston ValueRAM KVR266X72RC25/512

266 MHz DDRAM 2 × 512 Megabytes

Hard disk space

The hard disk physical space is split into two domains so that the system can hold the operating system separate to user file server space. This makes it easier to hot swap faulty disks and handle backups. The hard disk to hold the OS and other applications is a 10GB Western Digital hard disk with an ATA100 interface. The user file storage consists of two 20GB IBM DESKSTAR 60GXP hard drives, again with ATA100 interfaces.

Back-up   ONSTREAM 60GB Internal IDE tape drive

This component is capable of storing up to 18 Gigabytes per hour, and would therefore be able to do a full system backup in just over two hours.

Power supply and case

The case is an Antec SX1040B. This has a 400W power supply, two extra case cooling fans and 6, 3.5" drive bays (4 internal, 2 external) for the hard disk drives. This case is specifically designed for small servers.

Since this system is a server, it will be provided with a UPS (un-interruptible power supply). This will allow the server to handle power cuts gracefully, by providing power for some time even if the mains supply fails. A suitable UPS would be the KingPro 625, which has an output of 625W. It is a good idea to have UPS that will provide more power than the power supply, so that the UPS will keep the system up longer. This UPS will keep a system of this size going for about five to ten minutes, enough time for the operating system to close down gracefully (or the power to return).

Graphics display card and monitor

The graphics card is an ATI MOBILITY 8MB AGP. This is one of the cheaper cards since the system is not being used for graphics applications. Any standard PC monitor can be used.

CD-ROM, keyboard and mouse

The CD-ROM drive is a 52× Samsung EIDE model. This is a completely standard type. The keyboard and mouse can be any standard PS/2 compatible product.

11.3 BUILDING THE SYSTEM

The build of a small PC system will follow similar stages, whatever the specification. For this reason this section will describe the build for the file server system, since this will be slightly more complex, involving more hard disks.

11.3.1 ASSEMBLING AND TESTING MOTHERBOARD, PROCESSOR AND CASE

The first stage is to populate the motherboard with processor and memory. All these components are very sensitive to static electricity or ESD (electrostatic discharge). For this reason it is a good idea to connect yourself to earth using a wrist strap. Figure 11.1 shows a diagram of the motherboard.

Inserting the processor

The processor sits in a zero insertion force socket. This has a small level arm which has to be lifted up before the processor can be inserted. When placing the processor in the socket it will only go in one way (do not force it as this may damage the processor). A small mark and flattened corner on the CPU corresponds with a flattened corner on the socket.

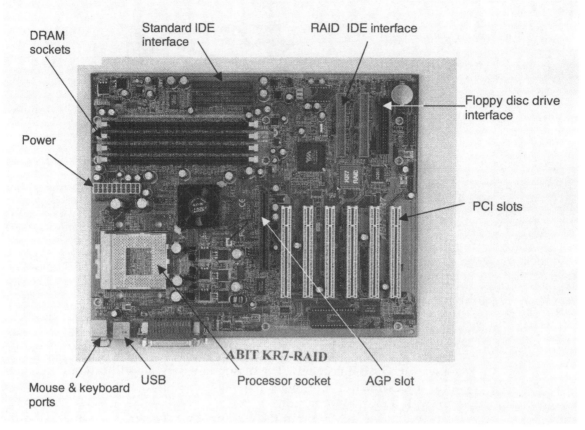

Figure 11.1 PC motherboard

Once the processor is in place you need to attach the heat sink and fan. Without these your CPU will overheat and not last very long. Before attaching the heat sink a small amount (a drop) of thermal compound should be smeared on the back of the processor. Once this is in place the heat sink and fan assembly can be clipped on the processor. There will be a 3 pin plug that will come from the fan. This is attached to the motherboard (see motherboard user manual to find out where).

Inserting the memory

It is important to populate the memory with bank 0 first, then bank 1, etc. – consult the motherboard user manual for more details. When inserting DIMMs great care should be taken. The DIMM can only go in one way and there is a notch on the connector side as a guide. The DIMM should be lined up with the notch and then pushed down into place. Figure 11.2 illustrates the DIMM socket and module.

Once you have the memory and processor in place you can mount the motherboard in the case. The case will be provided with a set of plastic and

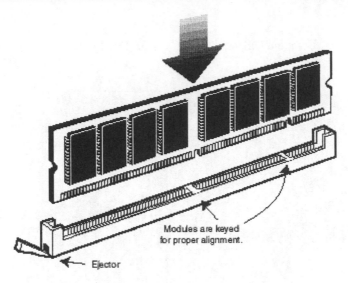

Modules are keyed
for proper alignment.

Ejector

Figure 11.2 Inserting a DIMM

metal mounting fasteners. The plastic fasteners snap into holes drilled on the motherboard. The metal fasteners screw into holes in the case and provide an earth connection.

We now need to install the graphics card. This must be inserted in the AGP slot. The card not only has to fit in the slot correctly but the card has to be exposed at the back of the case to allow the video cable to be connected. Remove any blanking cover that may be covering the access slot on the case. Figure 11.3 shows the front and inside view of the case.

The motherboard has to be connected up to the power supply. For the ATX board this is a 20 way plug. It is keyed to ensure correct insertion; insert this lead carefully (do not force).

There are also a number of female connectors from the front panel that must be connected to the motherboard. These are usually labelled appropriately on the motherboard (if in doubt consult the motherboard manual).

Testing

At this stage (before any more hardware is added) it is possible to test if the RAM, processor and video card are working. Connect the monitor to the graphics card using the video lead, power up the monitor and apply power to the main case. When the power on button is switched on you should get the BIOS start up screen, a correct test and report on the amount of RAM installed and then some error messages (because the I/O is incomplete). If the machine will not start up check all the connectors, that the RAM is secure and the arm on the processor socket is firmly pushed down, then try again. Once the BIOS will start up power down for the next part.

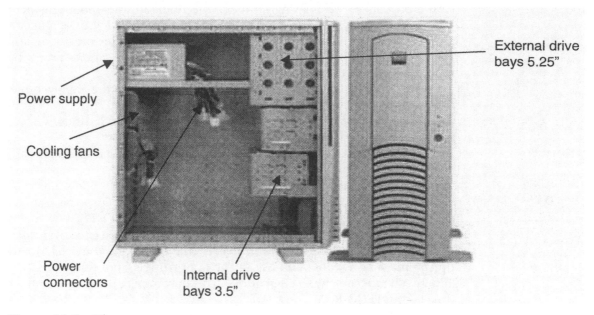

Power supply

Cooling fans

External drive
bays 5.25"

Power
connectors

Internal drive
bays 3.5"

Figure 11.3 File server case

Installing the IDE devices

The IDE interface makes it possible to connect two devices on each connection coming from the motherboard. For each connection one device is termed the master and the other the slave. Before the devices can be connected up as a pair on one connector they must be configured, one as a slave and one as a master.

First configure the Western digital hard disk as a master and the CD-ROM as a slave. This is done by moving jumpers on the back of the drives (consult the user manuals for more information). When this has been done, mount the two drives (not too far apart in the drive bays). Remember to mount the CD-ROM in an external bay positioned behind the access slots on the front of the machine – you will have to remove the blanking plate. Then take the IDE cable, which will have one end with two connectors and one with only one. Connect the single connector to the motherboard primary IDE connector and the other connectors to the two drives.

To install the backup tape drive, first mount it on an external bay (since it will be providing a removable media). This will be configured as a single drive (as it will be connected on its own to the secondary IDE connector – consult the tape drives user manual on how to do this). The IDE cable for the tape drive should be connected between the tape drive IDE connector and the motherboard IDE connector.

The two extra IBM drives should be connected to the RAID IDE interfaces. Since there are two connectors, it would be sensible to connect them to the two interfaces separately so they are not sharing an IDE connection.

Configure both drives as a single drive connection and, after mounting them both in internal drive bays, connect one to the primary IDE RAID connector and the other to the secondary IDE RAID connector. Mount the floppy disk drive on an external bay and connect the floppy disk drive cable between the motherboard and the floppy drive.

Finally, connect power from the power supply to the floppy drive, CD-ROM, all three hard disk drives and the tape drive. The connectors from the power supply are keyed so cannot be inserted incorrectly (if not forced) so take care.

Now the main system has been wired up, connect the mouse, keyboard and monitor.

The hardware has been constructed, so you now need to do some basic configuration of the BIOS. When the machine starts up you will be prompted to press a particular key to set up the BIOS. This will allow you to set up the date and time, tell the BIOS what type of disks you have connected to each of the IDE connectors, etc. Once this has been done you need to start up the machine with a boot disk in the floppy drive – preferably one that allows you to access the CD-ROM drive. This may require the disk to contain drivers for the CD-ROM.

Once the machine has booted up you will need to partition and format each of the hard disks and then install an operating system. The detail of this is beyond the scope of this chapter and will be different for each OS.

For the file server system many operating system choices will do the job (e.g., Linux, Windows 2000, Free BSD and others). Since this is not a book on operating systems we will not be going into a big debate on the relative pros or cons of each of these choices. The reader is encouraged however to read further on this subject.

For the home user system the choice of operating system at the moment will be Windows. The reason for this is the huge base of Windows software available (particularly for the home computer market).

11.4 SUMMARY

In this chapter we have looked at how a system can be built up from a series of component parts. We have looked at some of the actual implementations of technology that we discussed in earlier chapters and seen how these can be fitted together to produce a working computer. The proliferation of standardised I/O, motherboards and CPUs has made it possible for a hobbyist or student to build their own system with only the simplest of tools and a modicum of knowledge. The real challenge is designing a system (i.e., choosing the right mix of components) that will provide high quality, at the right price and processing power that is appropriate for a given application.

11.5 EXERCISES

1 Look at the price and specifications of ready-built systems. See if you can produce the system with at least the same specification and a lower price.

2 Why is it important to provide a high-quality power supply when designing your computer system?

3 When installing memory modules into a motherboard what precautions should be taken?

4 Discuss the relative merits and drawbacks of using RDRAM against DDRAM for you main system memory.

5 Design, on paper, a computer system with the following specification:
Dual Pentium III 800 MHz processors
2 Gigabytes of RAM
400 Gigabytes of hard-disk space with RAID.
For your design produce a full parts list as shown in section 11.2.

12 Computer networks

The earlier chapters of this book have been concerned with developing the concepts of the structure and mode of operation of a single computer. Chapter 10 has been concerned with the techniques whereby some device (typically a peripheral) can be connected to the CPU. In fact, Chapter 10 developed the concept that the devices could become increasingly more sophisticated, taking more of the I/O burden off the CPU. If we allow the remote device to be another computer and then link that to another, and so on, we effectively have a computer network. This leads to a whole new area of application for the users, and new problems for the network designers and builders, which will now be investigated.

12.1 NETWORKS AND DISTRIBUTED SYSTEMS

A very simple definition of a network would be that it is simply a number of connected computers. However, a better definition would incorporate the notion that each device being connected should be capable of some autonomous processing. Thus a computer network is an interconnected collection of autonomous computers.

A distributed system, on the other hand, usually means that some other function, in addition to the hardware, is distributed. For example, in a simple network of computers linked together it would probably be the case that each of the computers has its own operating system and its own copy of all the communications software necessary for it to communicate. With a distributed system, however, there might be only one copy of the operating system although the different components of that one operating system might in fact be located on different computers. In this case it may well be that when a particular operating system function is being used the user is not aware that a different processor is carrying it out.

However, this text is principally concerned with the underlying hardware and software that allows computers to communicate, and, hence, it will concentrate on a study of the basic principles of computer networks.

Having established what is meant by the term 'computer network' it is important to understand the motivation behind linking computers together. Historically, early computer systems were very large (physically) devices to which all the users and their data had to come in order for some processing to be carried out. Clearly this is not now the way most organisations work. In many businesses, regardless of whether they are commercial in nature, such as an insurance company, or industrial like a car manufacturer, they often occupy many sites which may be distributed geographically.

There is usually a need for some local processing and then communication with one or more of the other sites. Rather than having one massive computer at some 'central' site that performs all of the processing for all of the sites, the developments in communications enable the computing functions to map the organisation of the company. That is, computers at each of the sites linked to the others as necessary. It is true, of course, that the remarkable reduction in the price of computers enables this to be more cost-effective.

On the other hand, there may be cases where there does exist a very large and powerful computer whose cost can only be justified by making it available to many users who may be geographically remote. A similar argument may apply to software. It is clearly easier to maintain one single copy of a large database on a 'central' computer and provide access to it from many places (perhaps world wide) rather than to face the problems of maintaining multiple copies of it spread over the world. An alternative solution to this database problem would be, in fact, to distribute the database amongst the network hosts. If the database is huge there will obviously be significant problems in keeping all the data in one location and providing many concurrent accesses to it. If the database is distributed there may be a 'natural' distribution. For example, personnel records of staff employed by a large multi-plant company could be kept at each local site with one site occasionally communicating with another. In other cases an organisation may wish to keep a copy of a database at another site for increased security, for example, a bank with its head office (and database) in an earthquake zone.

All of these examples should illustrate why so many computer networks have been developed. Because such networks may span both manufacturer and international boundaries there has also been significant work involved in reaching agreements on international standards for various aspects of networking.

12.2 WIDE AREA AND LOCAL AREA NETWORKS

Connecting multiple computers that are situated some considerable distance apart, and allowing any of them to communicate with any other is a difficult task. It also requires a very sophisticated data communications network to provide the facility for carrying data from one host computer to another, as illustrated in Figure 12.1 and discussed further in Chapter 14. Such a network, because it is physically spread over a wide geographical area, is often known as a *wide area network* (WAN).

Many of the resource-sharing arguments for computer networks might equally apply to relatively small computer systems that are located close to each other, such as in the classroom or in a group of offices. Although the

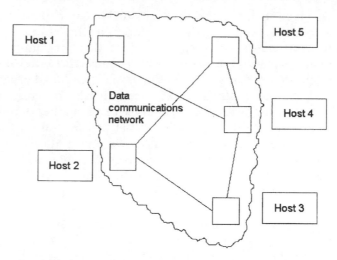

Figure 12.1   A data communications network

computers themselves may be inexpensive and it is cost-effective to have one, say, in each office, some of the peripheral devices, such as high-speed colour laser printers, are not inexpensive, and are also unlikely to be in continuous use. If all these small computers were linked in a network, together with an expensive printer, each computer could use this resource as it wanted it, making its provision much more cost-effective. Clearly the network itself needs to be inexpensive also; otherwise there is no saving. Such a network of computers, situated relatively close to each other is called a *local area network* (LAN).

Chapter 14 explores characteristics of WANs and LANs in much more detail.

12.3   NETWORK TOPOLOGIES

Many different topologies are possible for a computer network, regardless of whether it is a wide area or local area network. As will be seen, some topologies are more resilient to failure of some node or communication link, but they may be more expensive. Generally the compromise to be reached when deciding on a topology is a trade-off between the reliability of the network (its resilience to failures) and the cost of the various links.

In general terms there are two types of communication channel:

Point-to-point channels

Broadcast channels

12.3.1   POINT-TO-POINT TOPOLOGIES

As its name suggests a point-to-point channel is one where individual computers in the network are linked by communication channels to one or

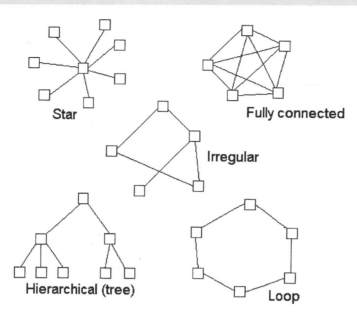

Figure 12.2 Network topologies for point-to-point systems

more (but not necessarily all) computers in the network. If two computers that are directly linked wish to communicate they can do so directly. If two computers that do not share a link wish to communicate they can do so but indirectly via other computers. Figure 12.2 illustrates some possible topologies for point-to-point systems.

With a *star* system the various nodes can communicate simply with each other but only 'through' the central *hub*. Hubs vary in complexity but, in their most basic form, they merely regenerate network signals to allow them to travel a longer distance over the cable. It is easy to add a new node to the network if the hub has a spare port. If a particular node fails this does not affect the other computer communications at all, but if the hub fails the whole network is unusable.

With a *fully connected* network every computer is linked to every other computer in the network. The effect of a failure of either a computer or a communication link is minimised since all the rest can continue communicating. There are no obvious throughput bottlenecks. However, the cost of the network is very high and since every computer has to link directly with every other, the size of the network (the number of computers) is linked to the number of ports on each computer. Because of this very high cost it is generally impractical for most applications. It is used only in situations where it is vital that there is no break in communications, for example in the control system of a nuclear power station.

An *irregular* network is similar to the fully connected network except that the requirement of connecting every computer to every other is removed. That is, the connections are irregular. The cost of the network and the flexibility to add a new computer to it are very reasonable since the new computer can merely be connected to its nearest physical neighbour (it may be advantageous to connect it to some of the others as well if they are regularly to communicate, but it is not strictly necessary). The effect of a failure and likely bottlenecks depends on the exact topology of the network and may vary from serious to unimportant. The Internet (described in section 12.6) is connected in this fashion.

A *hierarchical* topology is a special case of an irregular network. The difficulty inherent with irregular networks is the problem of routing a message from a computer to a remote computer. There may be a number of alternative routes and whatever algorithm is used will have to be adaptable to a changing topology in case a node fails. With a hierarchical network the routing problem is simplified because there is only one route from a node to the next node higher up the tree (or nearer the root) (see Chapter 14 for more on routing).

In a *loop* topology (not to be confused with a ring network described in section 12.3.2) a message is passed to the next computer in the loop in its entirety before being retransmitted. It is also possible for a different message to be on each link in the loop. The cost of the network and the flexibility to add a new node is reasonable since it would merely be necessary to connect it to its two adjacent neighbours. The effect of a failure can be serious, preventing communication continuing; the bandwidth of the loop is an obvious bottleneck.

A *cellular* topology, in which a geographical area is divided into cells, is used for wireless transmission. The cellular topology is not a 'topology' in the same mathematical sense as the other topologies mentioned. However, this is a convenient way of describing a layout that is commonly used for wireless transmission. The topology consists of circular or hexagonal areas with a node (Base Transmitter Station) at their centre. In this topology there are no physical links, only electromagnetic waves. A device such as a cellular phone can be used on the move, transmitting and receiving via the Base Transmitter Station to which it is nearest. The disadvantages are that the signals are sometimes disrupted and that it can be difficult to provide adequate security. Usually, the cellular topology is combined with other topologies. For example, the cellular radio system uses landlines as well as cells.

12.3.2 BROADCAST TOPOLOGIES

A broadcast channel is a single communication channel shared by all the communicating computers. Any message sent by one computer is received by all the other computers; hence the message must contain the address of the intended receiver so that all the other computers can ignore it. Figure 12.3 illustrates possible broadcast topologies.

With a *bus* topology all the computers are connected to a common bus and, at any time, one computer is allowed to transmit onto the bus, all the others being required to receive, not transmit. Since two or more computers may try to transmit simultaneously there needs to be some arbitration mechanism to resolve such conflicts. The cost of adding a new node to the network should be reasonable since it does not matter at which point it is added. The effect of the failure of a computer is unimportant, whereas the

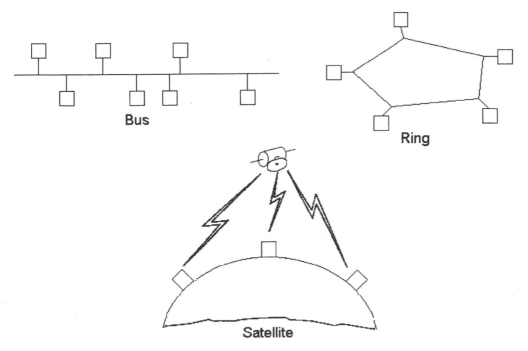

Figure 12.3 Broadcast topologies

failure of the bus is serious. The bandwidth of the bus is a potential bottle-neck. This topology has become a common LAN topology (see Chapter 14).

A *ring* topology involves the bits (or bytes) of a message being trans-mitted round the ring without waiting for the rest of the message to which they belong. Indeed, it may be that consecutive groups of bits or bytes actually belong to different messages and are intended for different nodes, so that the messages are being interleaved and hence the bandwidth of the ring is shared out. Like all broadcast systems, some mechanism is necessary to arbitrate simultaneous access. Again the effect of failure of a computer is unimportant but that of the ring is fatal. The bandwidth of the ring is also a potential bottleneck. This is another common LAN topology (see Chapter 14).

With *satellite* broadcasting each computer may be able to receive data from the satellite (in practice it need not be all the computers in the network but only one in each locality, the other local ones being connected to it more conventionally). All the computers can hear the output from the satellite. Satellites are a useful way of broadcasting over long distances.

12.4 STANDARDS

In the 1970s computer manufacturers were not only developing their own distinctive computer architectures but also they were predicting a huge market in the 1980s and 1990s for communication systems. Fortunately they also began to realise that future systems might well involve computers from more than one manufacturer communicating with each other. To continue developments in a totally uncoordinated way was clearly going to lead to major problems. However, the process of standardisation is inevitably one of compromise and consequently the procedure for developing standards is a complex and lengthy one.

Every country has its own standards body concerned with setting standards for a wide range of products which are sold and used in that country. For example, in the UK it is the British Standards Institution (BSI) (URL: http://www.bsi-global.com/index.html) and, in the USA, it is the American National Standards Institute (ANSI) (URL: http://www.ansi.org). Each of these organisations has representatives on the International Standards Organisation (ISO) (URL: http://www.iso.ch) based in Geneva. ISO has taken the pragmatic view that it is coordinating standards activity world-wide and hence it will adopt existing valuable standards that may have been developed by other organisations, as long as there is support and agreement within ISO. Three other very important standards organisations in the communications field are the ITU-T, IEEE and IETF.

ITU-T is the International Telecommunication Union (Telecommunication Standardisation Sector) (URL: http://www.itu.int/ITU-T) and is made up of telephone and telecommunications organisations. It publishes its computer communications standards labelled with an X followed by a number, e.g., X.25, X.400. IEEE is the Institution of Electrical and Electronic Engineers (URL: http://www.ieee.org/) in the USA. It proposes standards in the area of communications, labelled numerically, and submits them to ISO through ANSI. As an example, there is a series of standards known as the 802 series, concerned with local area networks (802.3 is the Ethernet standard). IETF is the Internet Engineering Task Force (URL: http://www.ietf.org/). It is concerned with the evolution of the Internet and its smooth operation. Network designers, operators, vendors and researchers are members.

12.5   NETWORK MODELS

Although the processing functions of various applications that need to access a network may be very different there are only a limited number of types of network and the problems of communication from one host computer to another are, in the main, independent of the application process. In other words, the problems to be faced when reliably conveying a message (data) from one computer to another are not concerned with what that message is. In addition, as has been discussed in section 12.4, in order to allow for computers from different manufacturers to communicate it is clearly useful if there is some international consensus as to what the problems of communication are and how they can be resolved in a 'standard' way.

A very simple view of the communication problems may be as follows:

There needs to be some agreement as to the form of exchange of the physical signals that allow bits to pass from one computer to another.

Assuming that bits can be transmitted and received, can the receiver be sure that the bits it is receiving are those being sent? In other words, some form of error detection and recovery is necessary.

If a message is reliably received by a computer, is the message for it or should it pass it on to another node and, if so, which one?

If the message is for this node is there a user program here that is able and willing to receive it?

This very simplistic view introduces the concept of 'layers' into the communication process. In fact, we may use the term 'higher' and 'lower' layers in much the same way as they are used with respect to programming languages, that is lower layers are nearer the fundamental machine or network. In the list above each of the different points illustrates a layer that can be imagined to be a set of rules, or a protocol, defining how the two computers will communicate at that level (for more details of protocols see Chapter 15).

This introduces two important concepts:

1 The protocols that are in each layer and the boundaries between layers should be sufficiently well defined so that any changes necessary can be made to that level without affecting any of the other levels. For example, a new error detection mechanism could be introduced without the other software in other levels being aware of any change.

2 The protocol at each level appears to communicate only with the corresponding level protocol in the remote computer (peer level processing).

In practice, data is not transferred from one machine to another at any layer or level other then the 'lowest' one. Each layer only communicates with the layers above and below it, passing information down to the lowest layer or up from the lowest layer.

This concept of structuring the communication process into layers has been adopted by the standards organisation ISO (see section 12.4). ISO has developed and published a formal architecture of protocols for OSI (connecting heterogeneous computers) known as the *ISO OSI reference model*. This model was intended to be used as a framework for the design of standard protocols and services, rather than as a definition of the protocols. It was intended to be the framework within which most future protocols would be developed. Though several useful protocols were produced by ISO, in fact the TCP/IP family of protocols has come to be very much more important. This is mainly because the TCP/IP protocols are the protocols of the Internet. The OSI reference model remains an important tool for thinking about protocols, however.

The ISO OSI reference model incorporates seven layers. Figure 12.4 illustrates the logical structure of this model incorporating the seven layers: the physical, data link, network, transport, session, presentation and application layers. The lowest three layers are network dependent and are essentially concerned with the protocols to be used by the various nodes making up the data communications network being used to convey information from one host node to another. The upper three layers, however,

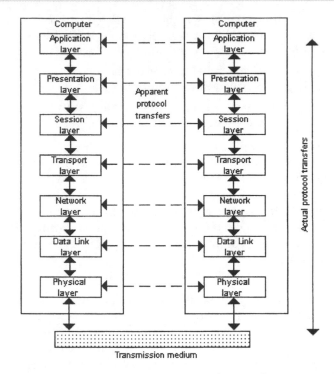

Figure 12.4 The ISO/OSI seven-layer reference model

are concerned with the protocols the two end user applications will use in communicating with each other over the (transparent) data communications network. The middle layer, the transport layer, is the link between the communications network and the end user application layers. It builds on the services provided by the actual data communications network (the lower layers) to provide the applications layers with a network-independent message exchange service.

The purpose of each of the seven layers will now be described.

12.5.1 THE PHYSICAL LAYER

This layer is concerned with the mechanism for transmitting bit patterns over a communication link or channel. It is concerned with the physical aspects of things such as the voltage levels used for representing 0 and 1, and the control signals indicating the status of the physical circuit, in order to be able to synchronise the exchange of data. It also defines the mechanical properties of connecting plugs and pin assignments. Much of the material covered in Chapter 13 is concerned with this physical layer. There are also some internationally agreed standards applicable to this layer, such as EIA/TIA-232, as described in section 15.2.2.

12.5.2 THE DATA LINK LAYER

This layer uses the raw transmission facility provided by the physical layer and makes the communication channel appear free of errors. It incorporates some form of error detection mechanism and handles the problems associated with re-transmitting that information that has been corrupted. Part of Chapter 15 is concerned with data link layer protocols (sections 15.3, 15.4 and 15.5), HDLC being an internationally agreed one (see section 15.5.1).

12.5.3 THE NETWORK LAYER

Whereas the bottom two layers are essentially concerned with communication between two adjacent machines in a network, the network layer is concerned with routing 'packets' across a network. It essentially takes a message from a host machine, splits it up into packets and organises the transmission of packets across the network to the desired destination. In doing so it is responsible for the sequencing and flow control of the packets. The Internet Protocol (IP) is the most important network layer protocol (see section 15.5.4).

12.5.4 THE TRANSPORT LAYER

The transport layer's primary task is to hide all the network-dependent characteristics from the layers above it. This means that it provides transparent data transfer. That is, a user on one host computer may communicate with a user on another host computer without having any concern at all about the underlying network structure being used to convey their messages. The implication of this is that all protocols defined for the transport layer will only need to be implemented on the host computers, not the intermediate switching computers in the network.

The services provided by the transport layer are essentially connection management and the transfer of data. The user of the transport layer (i.e., the layer above) can use the transport layer to establish and maintain a logical connection to the corresponding transport layer user in a remote computer, during which time the transport layer will also transfer data between the two users over this connection. TCP (see section 15.6.1) is the most important transport layer protocol.

12.5.5 THE SESSION LAYER

The period of time for which a pair (or more) of users remain logically connected (even though they may not be continuously transmitting or receiving) is known as a *session*. The session layer is concerned with establishing and managing a communication path between two users. In many ways it can be seen as being analogous to the logon and logoff procedures that are necessary on a conventional time-sharing system. It may, for example, be necessary to authenticate the users to ensure they are bona fide, and to enable the appropriate party to receive the bill for the communication session.

12.5.6   THE PRESENTATION LAYER

The presentation layer is concerned with the format of the data being exchanged by communicating parties. It could be argued that the concern of the presentation layer is really associated with the user's application, but there are a number of common features of many applications that make a presentation layer sensible.

One area of concern is code conversion. It may be, for example, that one of the communicating parties uses the ASCII code for internal character storage, whereas the other one uses EBCDIC. The presentation layer would perform the appropriate conversion.

If, in a particular system, the messages being exchanged contained a lot of commonly occurring words or expressions, for example, *credit* and *debit* in a financial system, these words or expressions could be coded to reduce the amount of information being exchanged. For example, the use of an eight-bit code allows one byte to represent 256 different words or expressions. Other more sophisticated text compression mechanisms are clearly possible.

On a network where data security (confidentiality) is of concern the presentation layer could perform some form of data encryption operation on the data to be transmitted, performing the reverse function on the data being received.

12.5.7   THE APPLICATION LAYER

This is the highest layer in the reference model and is the environment in which users' programs operate and communicate. It would appear that because this layer is concerned with the user, the details of such communication are dependent on the application, and will be different for every application. For some applications this will be true and hence the user will design appropriate protocols at this level. However, there are a number of common application areas where work has been done to define standard protocols for such applications. A fairly common requirement would be that of a file transfer application, e.g., a network of relatively small single-user workstations each with some local limited file storage facility, connected to a large multi-user system that has a very large file store. The File Transfer Protocol (FTP) is the most important protocol of this nature (see Chapter 15). Other examples include electronic mail document transfer. The Simple Mail Transfer Protocol (SMTP) is the major protocol for electronic mail.

12.6   THE INTERNET

The Internet is a network of computer networks that uses the TCP/IP family of protocols (see sections 15.5, 15.6 and 15.7). From its beginnings in 1983, as a mainly academic network, it grew rapidly into the huge agglomeration of interconnected computers that we see today. The IETF (mentioned in section 12.4) issues Request for Comment (RFC) documents, which define Internet protocols. The Internet Corporation for Assigned Names and Numbers (ICANN) has overall control of Internet addresses. There are three international organisations that oversee the administration of Internet addresses on a regional basis. Réseaux IP Européens (French for 'European IP Networks'. URL: http://www.ripe.net) (RIPE) is the regional address registry that has control over European Internet addresses. The American Registry for Internet Numbers (ARIN) (URL: http://www.arin.net) and the Asia Pacific Network Information Centre (APNIC) (URL: http://www.apnic.net) are the other two regional address registries. The *World Wide Web* provides a graphical user interface to the Internet.

An *intranet* uses Internet technology to create a restricted access Web site or set of Web sites. The company to which it belongs can rigidly control its content and access to it. One possible use of an intranet is to publish electronically internal company documents that would otherwise need to be wastefully duplicated on paper.

12.7 SUMMARY

This chapter has set the scene for computer networks by introducing the concept, identifying the idea of wide area and local area networks, looking at a variety of possible topologies, describing an internationally agreed model within which standardised communication systems can be designed and, finally, introducing the Internet.

The remaining chapters will follow this model in the sense of describing the physical transmission of data (the physical layer), the techniques of communication protocols (the data link layer) and a variety of network types (the network layer).

12.8 EXERCISES

1 a Summarise the main functions of the various layers of the ISO model network architecture.
  b Explain how peer protocols in a layered architecture make possible direct virtual communication between processes in the same layer. Trace the transformations a message undergoes as it passes across the network from one application process to another.

2 Review the various topologies that are possible for interlinked computers, paying particular attention to their advantages and disadvantages.

3 Discuss the role of the transport layer of the ISO 7 layer model, identifying the problem it addresses.

Communication technologies

Chapter 11 presented a developing sophistication of input/output methods to cater for the different requirements of small and large computer systems. Chapter 12 has developed these ideas to the concept of networks of communicating computers, and it is now necessary to consider just how data is to be transmitted along a line, whether the line is physically short for the devices in the immediate vicinity of a CPU, or long for devices or computers situated at remote locations.

Data transmission involves the transfer of information between various pieces of computing machinery. This information is usually coded as patterns of bits. In order to transmit such data two voltage levels could be used to represent the two bits, say 0 volts and +5 volts. The use of such binary signals leads to so called square waves, since, when it is displayed on an oscilloscope, the signal has a characteristic square shape, as illustrated in Figure 13.1.

The form in which messages, consisting of sequences of bits, are conveyed falls broadly into one of two classes: parallel and serial systems. These systems are described in section 10.2.

Earlier, the term 'line' was used to refer to the medium of the transmission system. As discussed later, in section 13.6, the medium could take the form of various types of cable, optical fibres, microwave links or even satellite communication. Consequently the general term channel will be used to indicate the link between a transmitter and a receiver.

One of the characteristics of the transmission of signals down a channel that is clearly of great interest is the speed at which the information can be

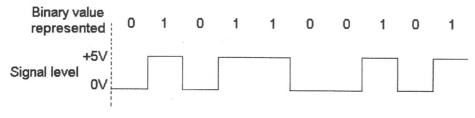

Figure 13.1 A square wave

transmitted. A major deciding factor in this is the characteristics of the channel itself. To establish these, an understanding of the major results of some information channel theory is necessary.

13.1 SIMPLE INFORMATION CHANNEL THEORY

Waves are used to carry information through most media, e.g. sound waves, light waves. One of the simplest waveforms is that of a sine or cosine wave, as illustrated in Figure 13.2.

The major features of such a waveform are its amplitude, frequency and phase. The amplitude is the height of the wave, measured, for example, in volts if the wave is a voltage wave or millibars if it is a sound wave. Its frequency is the number of times the waveform repeats itself in a second [measured in Hertz (Hz) where one Hz is one cycle per second], and the phase is essentially the difference in time between two separate waves of the same frequency.

As indicated in the introduction to this chapter, a voltage applied to a wire to represent logic 1, and 0 volts to represent logic 0 produces a square wave as illustrated in Figure 13.1.

It can be shown, using a branch of mathematics called Fourier analysis, that any waveform is actually made up of a summation of simple sine and/or cosine waves. That is, any recurrent waveform of frequency F can be resolved into the sum of an infinite number of sinusoidal waveforms having frequencies F, $2F$, $3F$ . . . to infinity. In particular, a square wave is actually made up of the sum of a series of sine waves having frequencies:

$F + 3F + 5F + 7F \ldots$

Although at first sight this may seem very strange, an understanding of the truth of this can be obtained graphically from Figure 13.3, which shows the resultant waveform of adding together a wave of frequency F with waves of frequency $3F$ and $5F$. It can be seen that the resulting wave is tending towards a square wave.

The first important result, then, is that in order to transmit a perfect square wave it is necessary to transmit an infinite number of frequencies. Unfortunately all transmission media (and often the sending and receiving equipment) are limited in the frequency range that they can cope with, some more than others. The range of frequencies that a particular channel can

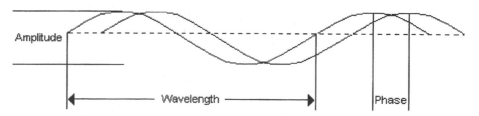

Figure 13.2 A sine wave

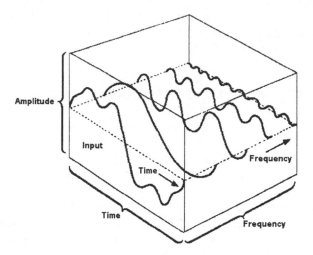

Figure 13.3 The composition of a square wave

cope with is called its frequency range. The difference between the upper and lower limits is called the *bandwidth* of that channel.

Some commonly encountered frequencies are:

human voice	100 Hz to 10 000 Hz
human hearing	20 Hz to 15 000 Hz
the telephone	300 Hz to 3400 Hz (restricted by telephone companies for practical reasons)
mains electricity	50 or 60 Hz.

Since an infinite range of frequencies will never be transmitted, the resulting waveform will be distorted. Thus, for example, a square wave will never be exactly square. The amount of distortion will clearly depend on the bandwidth of the channel and the base frequency of the waveform.

This leads to another very important result. If the bandwidth of a particular channel will only cope with frequencies up to, say, X Hz then a square wave of frequency X Hz cannot be transmitted, since it will require waveforms of frequency X, $3X$, $5X$, etc., which the channel cannot transmit.

Hence, if there is a limit on the frequency capacity of a channel (bandwidth), there is a limit on the frequency of the square wave; that is, the rate of transmission of the data. Alternatively, the greater the bandwidth the faster information can be transmitted.

These arguments merely confirm the following theories developed by the mathematicians Nyquist and Shannon some years before computers were first developed. If we define the information content I as:

$$I = \log_2(M) \text{ bits}$$

where M is the number of different symbols or characters, then, for example, with 128 ASCII characters:

$$I = \log_2(128) \text{ bits}$$
$$= 7$$

That is, 7 bits are required to represent 128 characters.

The capacity C of a channel is the maximum rate at which information can pass through. So, if T is the minimum time to transmit one symbol then:

$C = 1/T$ symbols/sec
$C = 1/T \log_2(M)$ bits/sec

It can be shown that the bandwidth W of a channel is given by:

$W = 1/2T$

Thus $C = 2W \log_2(M)$ bits/sec.

Another way of expressing this is that the channel capacity is proportional to the bandwidth.

This, unfortunately, is only true for a perfect channel. It has to be modified for noise, those random imperfections that reduce the information rate by introducing errors in the information being transmitted.

Shannon's equation modifies the above equation to:

$C = W \log_2(1 + S/N)$ bits per sec

where S/N is the signal to noise ratio, and S is the power of the signal and N is the power of the noise.

Signal levels are commonly referred to in terms of decibels, where:

decibel value $= 10 \log_{10}(S/N)$

As an example of the application of Shannon's equation, consider the maximum information rate (channel capacity) of a channel with a frequency range 300 Hz to 3300 Hz and an approximate signal to noise ratio of 20 dB (this is typical of the analogue portions of the public telephone network):

$dB = 20$
$\quad = 10 \log_{10}(S/N)$
Thus $(S/N) = 100$
$\quad C = 3000 \log_2(1 + 100)$
$\quad = 3000 \log_{10}101 / \log_{10}2$
Therefore $C = 19963$ bits per second

This is, in fact, only an approximation since the dB value of 20 is an average value. In practice transmission on telephone lines takes place at much lower speeds for a variety of reasons.

13.2 BAUD RATE AND COMMUNICATION CHANNELS

A common term used in communication technology is that of *baud rate* and it often appears to be synonymous with bit rate, bits per second.

However, the term baud rate refers to the signalling rate, or the number of times the signal may change per second. If the signals are sent using a 2-bit code (0 and 1) then the signal could change after every bit (010101 . . .), so in this case the baud rate is equal to the bit rate.

If, however, a four level code is used, say 0V, 5V, 10V and 15V, then each signal could represent two bits, 00,01,10,11.

In this case, with every signal level change, two bits of information are being transmitted so that the bit rate is twice the baud rate. (See section 13.3.1 for another example of the bit rate being twice the baud rate.)

Types of channels can be classified as follows:

Simplex   Communication can only take place between the sender and the receiver, whose designations cannot change, i.e. transmission is in one direction only.

Half duplex   Communication can take place in either direction, but not at the same time.

Full duplex   Communication can be taking place in both directions simultaneously.

Simplex transmission is useful if the line is connected only to a device that has either input or output capability but not both, e.g., an input device (such as a transducer) used at a remote site to collect and transmit data to a computer centre could use a simplex line. The choice between half and full duplex is a compromise between cost and speed. A full duplex line requires either two simplex lines in opposite directions or a line with two non-overlapping frequency bands so that there are two independent transmission facilities, one in each direction. Half duplex requires the same sort of transmission line as simplex, but with switches at each end to connect either the transmitter or the receiver, but not both, to the line.

Consequently, full duplex transmission is usually more expensive to provide than half duplex transmission. A large number of computer applications require the computer to receive data, perform some computation and then return the results. This is essentially half duplex operation, and many interactive terminal systems are of this nature.

There are other situations, however, such as data being transmitted over a communications network (see Chapter 12), where messages travelling in opposite directions often bear no relation to each other and can therefore be transmitted simultaneously if the line is full duplex.

13.3 ANALOGUE TRANSMISSION AND MODULATION TECHNIQUES

In the early days of computer communication, when it became necessary to connect together computers that were some considerable distance apart, there was already in existence an extensive network of cables carrying information, namely the telephone system. Thus it was an obvious medium to adopt to carry data as well as speech.

In order to use lines from the public switched telephone network (PSTN) as the transmission medium, it is necessary to convert the electrical signals from the computer, or terminal, into a form acceptable to the equipment used in the PSTN. This is designed for speech communication and audio frequencies in the range 300 to 3400 Hz (see section 13.1). Although most of the telephone network has been digital for some time, the so-called 'local loop', between the customer premises and the local exchange, is commonly analogue.

Figure 13.4 How modems are used

A carrier wave (a sine wave within the above frequency range) is transmitted and one of its characteristics altered in order to represent the 0s and 1s of the desired binary transmission. At the receiving end is a device that converts this signal back into its binary form. The circuit to perform the transmission alteration is known as a *modulator* and that to perform the reverse function is a *demodulator*. Since each end of a transmission line usually both sends and receives data, the combined device is known as a *modem*. This is illustrated in Figure 13.4.

13.3.1 MODULATION

As discussed in 13.1, the three characteristics of a waveform are its amplitude, frequency and phase. Three possible modulation techniques are known as amplitude modulation (AM), frequency modulation (FM) and phase modulation (PM). Figure 13.5 illustrates the principle of each technique.

Amplitude modulation involves varying the amplitude or signal level of the carrier wave between two specified levels. Although a simple principle, it is very prone to the effect of noise on the line and hence is not used on its own.

Frequency modulation concerns changing the frequency of a carrier wave (which has a fixed amplitude) between two fixed frequency values. It is sometimes known as *frequency shift keying* (FSK). Since this technique is less prone to errors it is more commonly used. However, there are a number of problems.

The chosen frequencies must be significantly (measurably) different.

To detect the frequency at least half a wave needs to be transmitted. Thus the lowest frequency must be greater than the baud rate.

Certain frequencies on the telephone network are used by the switching equipment and so are prohibited for general use.

The actual frequencies chosen for modems are in fact agreed internationally by the ITU-T (see Chapter 12, section 12.4). This is a part of the United Nations and coordinates the activities of the telephone companies throughout the world.

Note that the results of channel theory, explained in section 13.1, indicate that there is a limit to the frequency that can be used on a PSTN line, since the bandwidth is limited to 3100 Hz. For example, a 9600 bit/second speed cannot be used on a normal PSTN line using frequency modulation since the bandwidth is insufficient.

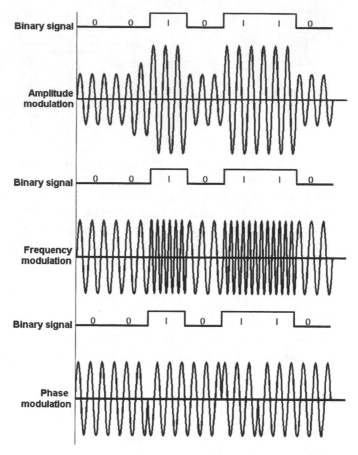

Figure 13.5 Amplitude, frequency and phase modulation

With phase modulation, the amplitude and frequency of the carrier wave are kept constant but the carrier is shifted in phase to represent each bit being transmitted.

In principle, the simplest phase modulation scheme – known as phase shift keying (PSK) – would use two carrier signals to represent binary 0 and binary 1 with a 180 degree phase change between them (see Figure 13.6 (a)). This requires a reference carrier signal at the receiving modem against which the phase of the incoming signal can be compared. In practice this is very susceptible to random phase changes from noise, and the demodulation circuitry is complex. Hence an alternative phase modulation – known as differential phase shift keying – is often used (see Figure 13.6 (b)). Here, a phase shift of 90 degrees could represent a binary 0 and a shift of 270 degrees a binary 1. The advantage is that there is a change in phase for each bit transition determined by the state of the next bit relative to the current bit. The demodulator only needs to detect the size of each phase shift rather than its absolute value.

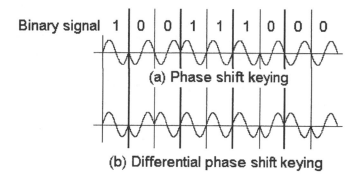

Binary signal 1 | 0 | 0 | 1 | 1 | 1 | 0 | 0 | 0

(a) Phase shift keying

(b) Differential phase shift keying

Figure 13.6   Phase shift keying and differential phase shift keying

A more complex phase change scheme can be employed to increase the transmission speed. For example, four different phase changes could be used so that each change represents two bits. A '00' results in a phase change of 0 degrees, a '01' in a phase change of 90 degrees, a '11' of 180 degrees and a '10' of 270 degrees. This means that, since for each signal change two bits are being transmitted, the bit rate is twice the baud rate (see section 13.2).

In high-speed modems, for example those that offer the ITU-T's V.92 standard, a complex combination of phase and amplitude modulation is used. Techniques such as echo-cancellation need to be applied also to reduce distortion of the signal to a minimum.

13.4 DIGITAL TRANSMISSION AND MODULATION TECHNIQUES

The modulation techniques discussed in section 13.3 were required to make use of the analogue portions of the existing PSTN, which was originally designed for transmission of voice (audio) signals and with a limited bandwidth. If use could be made of, say, a private line, then the original signal (known as the baseband signal) could be applied directly to the line and transmitted. There is, of course, still a relationship between speed at which the transmission can take place and the bandwidth of the transmission media that renders some media more suitable than others for high-speed transmission lines (see section 13.6). However, even with ordinary copper cabling, much higher transmission rates are possible than is the case with the old PSTN. Also, if the line is long, *attenuation* becomes a problem. Since electrical transmission along media involves electrical resistance, energy from the transmitted signal is used to make the current flow against this resistance. The energy available gradually decreases as the signal travels along the line, and this loss of energy is known as attenuation.

If the line is long and the attenuation becomes large, the received signal may be very distorted, and so the signal will have to be regenerated at intermediate positions on the line. With an analogue signal involving an infinite number of signal levels (a continuously varying modulated sine wave), reconstructing the signal exactly is very difficult, whereas with a digital signal having only two discrete levels, it is easy. Hence the use of digital transmission over long distances has significant advantages for transmitting data. As the volume of data transmitted nationally and internationally has grown and as the advantages of digital transmission have become understood, the national and international telephone companies have invested very large amounts of money into converting the existing (and often old) analogue telephone equipment into digital technology. The advantages for transmission of data are clear.

If speech (audio) signals can be converted into digital form to use these digital networks (see section 13.4.1) what are the advantages for the telephone network?

The effects of noise and attenuation are considerably reduced since the signal can be reconstructed exactly.

Since all the signals are digital (binary), all the switching taking place in exchanges can be done by computers and done very quickly.

Software can be developed for these computers that allows considerable intelligence to be built into the telephone network.

Multiplexing techniques can be used to make full use of very high bandwidth transmission media (see section 13.5).

Speech signals can be coded into digital form by a technique known as *pulse code modulation*.

13.4.1 PULSE CODE MODULATION (PCM)

The principle of pulse code modulation is that the analogue speech signal is sampled at regular intervals and its amplitude at that point is represented by a binary number which is then transmitted. In order to represent the waveform adequately, but not require the transmission of too much data, there is a compromise reached on the number of levels into which the waveform amplitude is divided.

Figure 13.7 illustrates this sampling process. In this diagram, for clarity, only eight amplitude levels are shown, each of which therefore requires three binary digits to represent it. In practice, a typical sampling rate is 8000 times per second, with a total of 256 amplitude levels, giving 8 bits per sample. This generates therefore 64,000 bits per second for a single PCM channel (a number of channels may share a very high bandwidth medium as described in section 13.5). Since the continuous analogue signal is being sampled, it can never be reconstructed exactly, hence the resulting signal will involve some error that distorts the speech waveform. However, with the above sampling rates the resulting distortion is found to be acceptable (remember that on the old analogue telephone network the speech is distorted by restricting the bandwidth of the transmission).

13.4.2 LINE CODES FOR DIGITAL TRANSMISSION

We saw in section 8.2.1 how various encoding schemes are used to represent bit patterns on magnetic media such as disk drives. When a bit pattern is

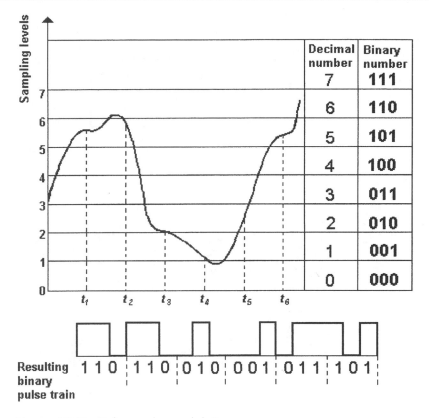

Figure 13.7 Pulse code modulation

transmitted over a network, we also need an encoding system. Many encoding schemes exist but we shall meet just two of these here: Non-Return to Zero (NRZ) and Manchester encoding.

The obvious way to encode the bits would be to use two voltage levels, a high one and a low one, which would represent one and zero respectively. This scheme is known as NRZ. For a synchronous network technology such as Ethernet (see section 14.2.2), NRZ would be inadequate because receiving stations might misinterpret the bit pattern. If NRZ were used there would be no obvious difference to a receiver between the sender sending a zero bit and the sender sending nothing at all. This is because NRZ represents both these conditions as zero volts.

The Manchester encoding scheme that is used in Ethernet takes advantage of the fact that it is easier for the receiving hardware to detect a change in voltage, rather than a value. Rising and falling edges (see section 4.7.2) of the signal are used to encode the ones and zeros. Binary 1 is represented by a high-to-low transition in the signal; binary 0 is represented by a low-to-high transition. The transition always occurs in the middle of a bit period. This makes it easier for the receiver to synchronise with the sender. NRZ and Manchester encoding are illustrated in Figure 13.8.

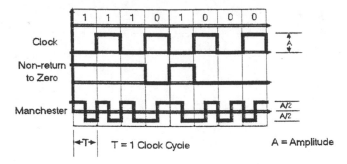

Figure 13.8 Binary encoding schemes

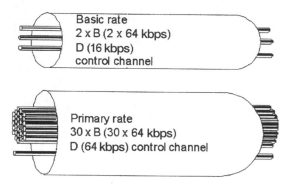

Figure 13.9 ISDN basic rate and primary rate interfaces

13.4.3 INTEGRATED SERVICES DIGITAL NETWORK (ISDN)

ISDN provides an all-digital dial-up service for voice and/or data over standard copper twisted-pair cable. Basic Rate Interface (BRI) ISDN offers two 64 kbps 'B-channels' for sending voice and/or data traffic. There is also a 16 kbps 'D-channel' for signalling. Primary Rate Interface (PRI) ISDN provides up to thirty 64 kbps B-channels plus a 64 kbps D-channel. The two interfaces are illustrated in Figure 13.9.

13.4.4 DIGITAL SUBSCRIBER LINE (DSL)

Digital Subscriber Line technology is a way of making a high-speed link between the customer premises and a telephone exchange over the standard copper local loop. A high-frequency modem is employed to provide a purely digital connection. At the telephone exchange, the DSL circuit is connected to a DSL Access Multiplexer (DSLAM), instead of a standard telephone switch. The DSL circuit is full duplex.

There are several variants of this technology, but the two main types are Asymmetric DSL (ADSL) and Symmetric DSL (SDSL). SDSL uses the entire bandwidth of the line for data transmission. ADSL sends data at frequencies

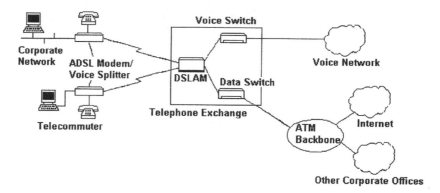

Figure 13.10 Digital subscriber line access multiplexer

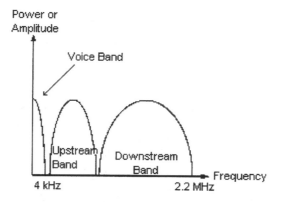

Figure 13.11 How ADSL uses the available bandwidth

of 26 KHz to 1100 KHz, leaving the frequency band of 0 KHz to 3.4 KHz free for analogue voice transmission. The use of a DSLAM for ADSL is illustrated in Figure 13.10; the way in which the available bandwidth is split up is shown in Figure 13.11.

In SDSL the downstream and upstream data rates are the same; in ADSL the downstream data rate (from the exchange to the customer premises) is considerably higher than the rate in the opposite direction. ADSL has been used to give home consumers a fast but fairly cheap connection to the Internet. A rival to ADSL for this market is the *cable modem*, which uses cable TV networks for connectivity to the Internet. SDSL is targeted at business users, offering a cheap alternative to leased lines.

13.4.5 DIGITAL LEASED LINES

Digital leased lines are point-to-point lines rented out to businesses by telecommunications companies. Rather than being paid for by the minute

Table 13.1 T1 and E1 services

Service	Data rate
T1	1.544 Mbps
T3	44.736 Mbps
E1	2.048 Mbps
E3	34.368 Mbps

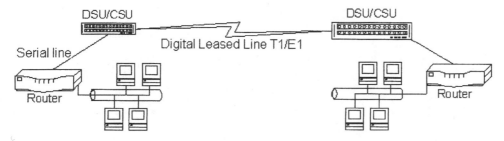

Figure 13.12 Connection to a digital leased line

and second as with normal telephone connections, a leased line is rented by the month. Leased lines can be installed over any distance and are priced according to the data rate and the location of the two ends. The T series of digital leased line services (used in North America and a few other places) and the E series (used in Europe and most of the rest of the world) are extremely important WAN services. They use time division multiplexing (see section 13.5.2) to 'slice up' the available bandwidth and assign time slots for data transmission. Table 13.1 shows the data rates of the T and E series of services. Other data rates are available. The media used are typically twisted-pair copper wire and optical fibre. Leased lines are widely used. The cost is moderate to high.

Digital leased lines such as the T and E series require a Data Service Unit/Channel Service Unit (DSU/CSU) to access the connection. To connect a DSU/CSU to a router (see Chapter 15, section 15.5.4) or computer, a serial line with an interface such as EIA/TIA-232 (RS232-C) is used (see Chapters 11 and 15, sections 10.2.4 and 15.2.2, for a description of EIA/TIA-232). Figure 13.12 illustrates the use of DSU/CSU units to connect to a leased line.

13.5 MULTIPLEXING

Since it costs roughly the same to install and maintain a high bandwidth cable as a low bandwidth (for example, the cost of digging and filling a trench) there are schemes for sharing the high bandwidth channel, a number of users to one line.

There are three ways of dividing the bandwidth: frequency division multiplexing (FDM), time division multiplexing (TDM) and wavelength division multiplexing (WDM).

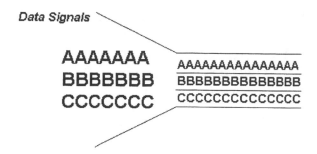

Data Signals

AAAAAAA AAAAAAAAAAAAAAA
BBBBBBB BBBBBBBBBBBBBB
CCCCCCC CCCCCCCCCCCCCC

Figure 13.13 Frequency division multiplexing

13.5.1 FREQUENCY DIVISION MULTIPLEXING

This is an analogue technique that can be used in an analogue telephone system, for example, or to transmit cable television over copper cable. The technique consists of dividing the frequency range (bandwidth) of the high bandwidth transmission line into a number of narrower frequency range channels. Signals from different sources are then modulated onto carrier waves within their allocated frequency range. Thus, the fast transmission line is simultaneously carrying a number of slower transmissions. Frequency division multiplexing is illustrated in Figure 13.13.

Because it is important that the frequencies do not overlap, the main disadvantage of FDM is that it does not utilise the full capacity of the line, e.g., if a slow channel is not in use at any time that frequency range is being wasted. However, it is useful for systems where the channel is in continuous use.

13.5.2 TIME DIVISION MULTIPLEXING

Time division multiplexing (TDM) is achieved by transmitting blocks of characters down the line. Actually, the blocks may consist of 8-bit characters or eight bits representing something else, such as the 8-bit representation of an amplitude level in pulse code modulation (see section 13.4.1). Each sharer of the line (each subchannel) is allocated a character position in the block so that every block is made up of one character from each subchannel. The whole bandwidth of the channel is used to transmit each character in turn (and hence the block) so that it is transmitted very quickly. Each character position can be considered a time slot, so that if there are n subchannels (users) connected to the multiplexer then the time slots are allocated to each subchannel in turn, so that every nth slot contains a character from the same subchannel. Time division multiplexing is illustrated in Figure 13.14.

There is still the potential problem of a subchannel not having a character available, particularly if the multiplexer is used with asynchronous terminal devices and the terminal user is thinking, or typing slowly. In that case the multiplexer inserts a null (pad) character, which reduces the use being made of the very high bandwidth. If the multiplexer is being used on

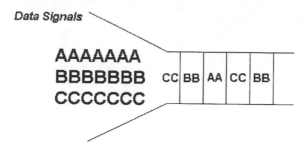

Figure 13.14   Time division multiplexing

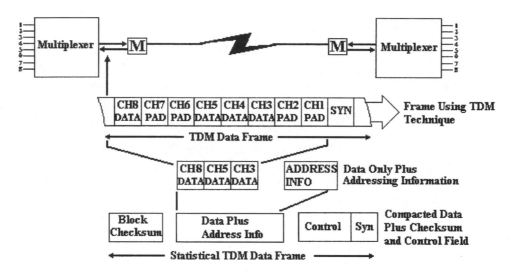

Figure 13.15   Simple time division multiplexing and statistical time division multiplexing compared

a PSTN where the volume of traffic is high, then this is not a problem. For use with asynchronous slow devices, however, statistical time division multiplexers (STDM) have been developed which insert characters into the high-speed channel as they are ready, along with some address bits to identify the subchannel. Since there is then the need for address decoding to decide where the character has come from, this type of multiplexer is based on a microprocessor. Simple time division multiplexing and statistical time division multiplexing are illustrated in Figure 13.15. In the figure, the box labelled 'M' represents a WAN access device of some kind, e.g., a modem or a DSU/CSU.

13.5.3   WAVELENGTH DIVISION MULTIPLEXING

Wavelength Division Multiplexing (WDM) is a technique in which prisms are used to send multiple colours of light down a single fibre. That is, each

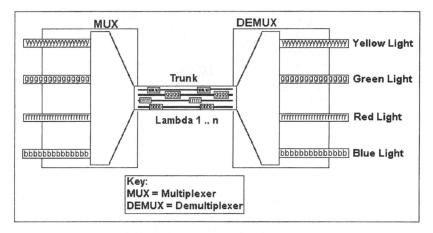

Figure 13.16 Wavelength division multiplexing

signal uses its own wavelength of light. Using this technique, many channels (*lambdas*) can be carried simultaneously at very high data rates over a single optical fibre. At the destination the channels are demultiplexed. Wavelength division multiplexing is illustrated in Figure 13.16.

An enhanced version of WDM is Dense Wavelength Division Multiplexing (DWDM). This spaces the colours closer together, resulting in even greater data rates.

13.6   TRANSMISSION MEDIA

Transmission of data in the form of an electrical signal requires the use of some sort of transmission medium, often referred to as a 'line'. Whilst this may take the form of some sort of copper cabling it could equally be a beam of light passing through glass fibre or even radio signals.

13.6.1   WIRE CABLING

The simplest form of cabling is a two-wire piece of cable with each wire insulated from the other. The signal (a voltage) is applied to one wire and the ground reference to the other. It may in fact take the form of a pair of wires, or could be a number of pairs moulded into one cable either as a flat ribbon cable or in a single protective sheath known as multicore cable (see Figure 13.19). The major problems with such cables are those of electrical interference from nearby electrical signal sources, and of crosstalk – the cross-coupling of electrical signals from one wire to another. Hence this type of cable is only used for short distances and with low bit rates.

An improvement on this in terms of immunity to noise is provided by the use of pairs of wires twisted together, known as unshielded twisted pair (UTP) cable. UTP cable is illustrated in Figure 13.18.

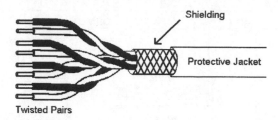

Figure 13.17 Shielded twisted pair cable

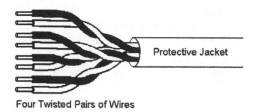

Figure 13.18 Unshielded twisted pair cable

The effect of twisting the wires together reduces the incidence of both crosstalk and susceptibility to extraneous noise. At higher frequencies (for faster transmission), however, the effect of noise gets more severe, so an improvement on UTP is given by the use of shielded twisted pair (STP) cable. Here there is a foil shield around the bundle of twisted pairs (see Figure 13.17). (In some forms of STP cable, e.g., 'Category 7', there is additional shielding around each pair of twisted wires). An older kind of copper cable, which is not now used for network installations as much as it once was, is coaxial cable (as used in the receipt of television transmission. It is also commonly used in hybrid fibre optic/coaxial systems to connect up cable modems for Internet access.) Here the signal and ground wires occur as a solid centre conductor concentrically (coaxially) inside a braided outer conductor separated with an insulating material (see Figure 13.19). With all this wire cabling, the bandwidth of the wire is limited and hence the transmission speed (or the number of lower speed channels which can be multiplexed) is limited. For improved rates, optical fibre or microwave links must be used.

13.6.2 OPTICAL FIBRE

Optical fibre cable carries the transmitted information in the form of a fluctuating beam of light in a tube of glass or plastic fibre. Each fibre is surrounded by material (cladding) that has a different refractive index from the fibre core. The phenomenon of *total internal reflection* prevents the light escaping, even when the fibre is bent. Fibre optic cable provides the high performance capabilities of very high bandwidth, high noise immunity and

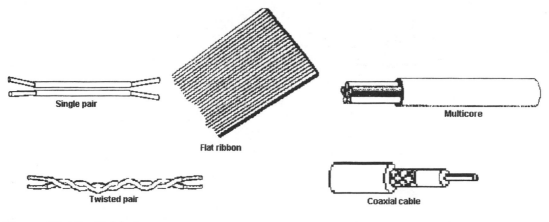

Figure 13.19 Cable types

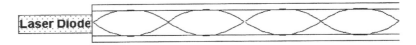

Figure 13.20 Single mode optical fibre

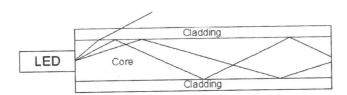

Figure 13.21 Multimode optical fibre

long distance spacing between signal amplifiers, whilst remaining cost competitive. Because of its high noise immunity it is particularly useful for transmission through electrically noisy environments such as industrial plants employing high voltage switching equipment. The bandwidth of such optical fibre cables is much greater than that of copper cables. Most trunk telephone lines and most local area network backbones consist of fibre optic cable. However, since fibre optic cabling is expensive to deploy compared with copper, it is relatively uncommon in the local loop and in 'horizontal' wiring in local area networks. Single mode fibre is employed for long distances and uses a laser to send the signal. The fibre has such a small diameter that there is room for only one wavelength of light, the light travelling in a straight line along it. Multimode fibre uses a light-emitting diode (LED) and is used over shorter distances. Multiple wavelengths of light bounce around inside the fibre. Single mode fibre is illustrated in Figure 13.20 and multimode fibre in Figure 13.21.

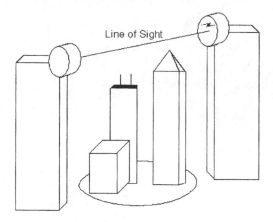

Figure 13.22   Microwave transmission

13.6.3   MICROWAVES

Microwave transmission carries the transmitted information in the form of radio waves through the atmosphere (or space) and hence requires no cabling. It has a very high bandwidth and therefore can provide many hundreds of high-speed links. Because it requires no cable it is very convenient where laying cables would be difficult or expensive. However, because the signals travel through the atmosphere they are affected by weather conditions and buildings and so require line-of-sight transmission between relay towers. Microwave transmission is commonly used for mobile communications (both phones and computers). (See Figures 13.22 and 16.2.)

For longer distances (intercontinental, for example) the microwave beam can be transmitted to a satellite, which then retransmits to a ground station many thousands of miles away.

13.7   ERROR DETECTION

As has been discussed earlier in this chapter, all transmission systems are subject to 'noise' and the effect of this is that bit patterns being transmitted may be corrupted. As a simple illustration consider the following:

Suppose only two messages are to be sent, and since both ends of the communication channel know what the messages are they can be coded. For example, send a binary 1 to indicate the occurrence of something and a binary 0 to indicate its absence. This communication system could be handled thus:

1   Simply transmit 0 or 1. However, if this bit is corrupted (so 0 becomes 1 or 1 becomes 0) the wrong message is sent but neither end knows.

2   Send 00 for one message and 11 for the other. If 01 or 10 is received the receiver knows that an error has occurred (it has *detected* an error) but does not know what the message should have been. If both bits are corrupted this remains undetected.

3 Use three bits 000 or 111 to represent the two messages. If 001 or 010 or 100 is received the receiver knows that an error has occurred and may assume that the message should have been 000 (assuming, of course, that only one bit has been corrupted). If 110 or 101 or 011 is received then it will assume that the message should have been 111.

Hence, technique 2 illustrates a method of detecting single bit errors, whereas 3 shows a method of detecting and correcting single errors. The conclusion reached from this simple example is that if the code is made more complicated the effect of noise can be reduced. In general, recovery from transmission errors may be achieved in one of two ways:

By including enough redundancy (extra bits) in the message to enable the receiver to reconstruct the message even when it is in error.

By using an error detection scheme and requesting retransmission when an error is detected.

Because of the great overhead involved in transmission if an error correction scheme is used (particularly if the error rate of the line being used is low), most systems will merely use an error detection scheme and ask for retransmission if an error occurs. Therefore, the techniques described below are error detection systems.

13.7.1 PARITY CHECKING

Parity checking is one technique that can be used for error detection. Just prior to transmission an additional bit is appended to a character such that the sum of binary 1s in the character is an odd number (odd parity) or an even number (even parity). For example, say that we want to transmit the character 'J' in an 8-bit word, using *odd* parity. The 7-bit ASCII code for 'J' is 1001010. There is an odd number of 1s in this code (three), so the parity bit must be set to a 0. The 8-bit code that is transmitted is therefore 01001010. On the other hand, we might want to use *even* parity to transmit the character 'J' in an 8-bit word. There is an odd number of 1s in this code (three), so the parity bit must be set to a 1. The 8-bit code transmitted is therefore 11001010.

The receiver will then re-compute the parity for the received characters and determine whether any transmission errors have occurred. *Note* that this simple mechanism will only detect errors that occur in a single bit (or 3 or 5, etc.). This mechanism is commonly used with asynchronous transmission and the generation and checking of the parity bit is often incorporated into the circuitry of the UART or USARTS.

13.7.2 BLOCK PARITY CHECK

With a block-oriented transmission system (blocks of characters are transmitted), in addition to the parity bit being appended to each individual character, an additional character is generated and transmitted, where each

								Parity bit
Character 1	0	1	1	0	1	1	0	1
2	1	0	1	0	1	1	1	0
3	0	1	1	1	0	1	0	1
4	1	1	1	0	0	0	1	1
5	0	0	0	1	0	1	1	0
Parity check character	1	0	1	1	1	1	0	0

Figure 13.23 Block parity check

of its bit positions is made up of a parity bit of that bit position down the block of characters (a column or longitudinal parity bit). Figure 13.23 illustrates this with a block of five characters to which has been appended a block check character.

Assume that character 1 is sent with bits 6 and 7 reversed (or both corrupted). The parity within the character is still odd and so that will not detect the error, but the parity check character would now be incorrect. This, of course, is true only if no 2-bit errors occur in the same column in the same block. Whilst this is unlikely in general, if the line is very error prone or more security is essential then the system will have to use a more effective method, such as that provided by cyclic redundancy check.

13.7.3 CYCLIC REDUNDANCY CHECK (CRC)

This method is based on treating a string of bits as the coefficients of a polynomial. That is, a k bit message is the coefficient list for a polynomial with k terms:

x^{k-1} to x^0

For example, 110001 represents the polynomial:

$x^5 + x^4 + x^0$

The mathematical theory of polynomial codes and their manipulation is beyond the scope of this book but is used in error checking as follows.

Both the sender and the receiver must agree on a *generator* polynomial, $G(x)$, in advance.

The idea is to append a checksum to the end of a message prior to transmission in such a way that the polynomial represented by the checksummed message is exactly divisible by $G(x)$.

When the receiver gets the transmission it tries dividing it by $G(x)$. If it has been transmitted correctly it should still be exactly divisible by $G(x)$ and hence the remainder will be zero. If the remainder is not zero there has been a transmission error.

All polynomial arithmetic is performed modulo 2. This means that there are no carries for additions or borrows for subtraction and hence plus and minus are the same as Exclusive OR (see section 2.1).

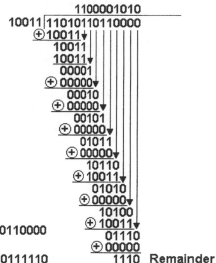

Message: 1101011011
With appended zeros: 11010110110000
Generator polynomial: 10011
Transmitted message: 11010110111110

Figure 13.24 Cyclic redundancy check

To compute the checksum:

1 Let r be the degree of the generator polynomial G(x). Append r zero bits to the low order end of the message so that it now contains $m + r$ bits, and corresponds to $x^rM(x)$ (where $M(x)$ is the message polynomial of order M). (In other words, the number of zeros to append to the number is one less than the number of bits in the divisor.)

2 Divide G(x) into the message with the zero bits appended ($x^rM(x)$) using modulo 2 division.

3 Subtract the remainder (modulo 2) from $x^rM(x)$. The result is a message to be transmitted. The principle of this is that in a division problem, if you diminish the dividend by the remainder what is left is divisible by the divisor, e.g., 35/6 leaves a remainder of 5 and $35 - 5 = 30$, which is divisible by 6.

Figure 13.24 illustrates the technique.

Clearly, if this method is to be effective the choice of generator polynomial is crucial. A lot of investigatory work has been done on possible generator polynomials and there are some, internationally agreed, that have been found to be particularly effective.

An example is the polynomial defined by the CCITT for use on the switched telephone network:

$$x^{16} + x^{12} + x^5 + x^0$$

This would have a 16-bit remainder appended to the message. It has been found that it will detect:

all single and double errors;

all errors with an odd number of bits;

all burst errors of length 16 bits or less;

99.998 per cent of 18-bit and longer bursts.

A burst error is when a string of bits is corrupted due to, for example, a burst of electrical interference, or to electrical noise caused within a switching exchange. Since the arithmetic which is carried out in this technique is done modulo 2, which is equivalent to Exclusive OR, the method is not difficult to implement in hardware and it is commonly found in data communication integrated circuit chips. The only circuitry that is necessary is a dividing circuit that consists of exclusive OR units and shift registers (see Chapter 3 for an explanation of the circuits themselves and section 6.1.2 for an explanation of how shift registers are used for division).

13.8 SUMMARY

This chapter has presented the basic physical characteristics of the transmission of information between two points. The material contained here corresponds to the physical layer 1 of the ISO OSI reference model (see Chapter 12).

The most important result is that the rate of transmission of information is limited by the bandwidth and noise of the communication channel.

13.9 EXERCISES

1 Draw a block diagram of a link between two microcomputers using a telephone network as a transmission medium. Describe how the data is transferred down the link, explaining all the technical terminology commonly used.

2 Explain the relationship between bandwidth and the rate of information transfer through a transmission medium. Describe two schemes for sharing the bandwidth of a single channel and indicate the advantages of using optical fibres as a transmission medium.

3 a In an attempt to reduce the effect of error on a certain link it has been decided to 'echo back' every character from the sender to the receiver. How would you detect and correct errors using such an arrangement? Under what circumstances would it be difficult or impossible to detect and correct errors using such arrangements? Outline the algorithms that might be used by the sender and the receiver.

   b Assuming:

     i a line speed of 9600 baud;

     ii asynchronous transmission with single start and stop bits and eight data bits;

     iii a receiver delay of 2ms between the receipt of a character and the start of the 'echo back';

     iv a transmitter delay of 1ms between the receipt of an echoed back character and the transmission of the next character;

     v instantaneous transmission, i.e., no delay between either end placing a bit on the link and the other end seeing it;

    vi there are no errors;

Calculate the effective data transmission speed for such an 'echo-back' arrangement.

   c In order to improve the speed of such an arrangement it is proposed to transmit blocks of 100 characters with a 0.3ms delay between each character and then wait for an 'echo-back' of the block. Estimate the effective data transmission speed of this arrangement and discuss its susceptibility to errors compared with the basic arrangement.

In each case calculate the effective data transmission speed in the presence of a 0.001 character error probability. You may ignore 'error-on-error' conditions (*note*: $0.999^{100} = .905$).

4 a Describe the factors that limit the channel capacity of a telephone line, illustrating your answer with any relevant equations.

   b Define the terms 'frequency shift keying' and 'differential phase shift keying' and show how the latter technique may be used to increase channel capacity.

5 A message 1011101 is to be transmitted with additional error detecting digits to enable cyclic redundancy coding to be used. The generator polynomial to be used is 11001.

   a Calculate the bits of the actual frame to be transmitted with the error bits added.

   b Check that no error results if the receiver receives this frame.

   c Assume that an error burst of three 1s is added to the least significant end of the transmitted frame.

Show how the error will be detected by the CRC.

6 Assuming a generator polynomial of $x^4 + x^3 + x + 1$ compute the checksum for the message 110010101.

14 Network types

The physical aspects of the transmission of data were explored in Chapter 13 and the concepts and techniques for the reliable transfer of data across a network will be discussed in Chapter 15.

This chapter will explore further the two basic types of networks introduced in Chapter 12 (section 12.3). For point-to-point networks it will discuss different types of switching and possible routing techniques whilst, for broadcast networks, it will study the different types, some of which have had significant impacts as local area networks.

14.1 POINT-TO-POINT NETWORK TYPES

Section 12.3.1 discussed a number of possible topologies for point-to-point networks (star, fully connected, irregular, hierarchical and loop). Particularly with wide area networks, the use of an irregular topology is most common since it has the considerable advantages of ease and cheapness of adding a new computer to the network. It may also be fairly resilient to a node or communication path failure, depending on the precise topology. However, because there is not a direct path between every pair of computers that may wish to communicate, some form of switching within the network is necessary. This raises a number of issues such as, what type of switching, how is the route worked out and what about congestion? These issues will now be examined.

There are essentially three forms of switching which can be used:

circuit switching;

message switching;

packet switching.

14.1.1 CIRCUIT SWITCHING

When you use the telephone network by dialling the number of another subscriber, there is usually a delay before the ringing tone is heard. This delay might be quite considerable if the call is over a long distance, international for example. The reason for this is that the intervening telephone network is searching for a continuous physical path between the two local exchanges. Although the concept of a 'physically continuous' circuit conjures up an image of a continuous copper path, it may be that part of that path is one channel on a multichannel fibre optic cable or even a microwave link. However, there does exist a physical communication channel from the calling to the called subscriber which remains in force for the whole duration of the call. The principle of forming a continuous circuit by appropriate switching at the intermediate switching centres is called *circuit switching*.

This is the principle on which public switched telephone networks (PSTNs) operate and which has often in the past been used for the transmission of data from one computer to another. However, when used for the transmission of data there are a number of disadvantages.

1 The time required to set up the call (for all the switching to be completed) is relatively long, though digital exchanges (computerised switching) and digital transmission between exchanges significantly reduce the set-up time (measured in milliseconds).

2 The two computers have to communicate at exactly the same speed (data rate).

3 There is no error or flow control provided by the network on the transmitted data. Such control has to be provided by the two users.

4 The line utilisation is often low. With most computer communications the network traffic often consists of short bursts of data separated by relatively long periods of inactivity, during which time the dedicated circuit is not being used. A possible alternative might be to place a separate call for each burst of data, but this is likely to be inefficient due to the relatively long call set-up time.

14.1.2 MESSAGE SWITCHING

Message switching is a technique that overcomes most of the disadvantages of circuit switching when a network is being used to carry data. Instead of switching the circuit, the circuits are permanently set up and the message is switched around the network. That is, for a network with an irregular topology the message is passed from node to node until it reaches its destination.

In particular, it operates as follows:

The message incorporates some sort of header that includes the address of the remote destination for which the message is intended. Clearly some sort of routing algorithm is necessary.

The message is transferred from node to node as a whole, i.e., the entire message is received at a node and stored before being sent on to the next node on its route. Error checks will be performed at each node to ensure the accurate receipt of the message. This mechanism is known as *store and forward*.

This technique overcomes the disadvantages of circuit switching in the following ways:

1 There is no call set-up delay, although there will be delays as the message may go via a circuitous route rather than by a direct connection and the various node to node protocols will introduce delays.

2 The two user computers do not have to communicate at the same speed because they do not communicate directly. A message may be received at a particular node at a different speed from the one used subsequently to transmit it to the next node. In this case the network is effectively acting as a buffer. In fact, the sender may send the message when it is ready, even if the receiver is not ready, since the network will store the message ready for delivery when the receiver is ready.

The disadvantage of this technique lies in the fact that the message is treated as a whole unit. For some applications the message may be quite short, such as a database query. In other applications the message may be very long, such as a complete file or even a whole database. Because of this, a long message being transmitted may monopolise a particular network link, preventing other (perhaps more urgent) messages being transmitted over that particular link. Since the store and forward concept requires *all* of the message to be stored at an intermediate node before being forwarded, it is possible for an intermediate node to have insufficient memory to store all the message, or, at least, prevent this node handling other messages until this one is sent.

14.1.3 PACKET SWITCHING

Because the transmission of long messages requires a large amount of buffer storage and a long transmission time leading to slower response times for other users, it would seem that the answer would be to insist on only very short messages. However, these short messages may lead to inefficient operation because of the overheads associated with such things as addressing, routing and acknowledgements. Thus, there must be some optimal length that provides an acceptable compromise between efficiency and response time.

Clearly, however, it is not convenient to force a user to limit all the messages to this optimal length and therefore organising this must be a function of the network. Variable length messages will be supplied by an application for transmission across the network to a remote destination. The source node will break that message down into a number of smaller messages each corresponding to that optimal length. The name of this smaller transmission unit is a *packet*. The packets can then be sent across the network separately, and, when they have all reached the destination, reassembled into the original message. Since these packets are being switched across the network the technique is known as *packet switching*.

Clearly the storage requirement and management at each intermediate node is easier than for message switching because of the small maximum packet size. Also, the small packets may be interleaved on the network links, thus reducing delays as seen by the host computers.

Because of these advantages most computer networks are packet switching networks (there are, however, a few circuit switched networks). Packet switching is the basis of the protocols known as TCP/IP (described in Chapter 15). Data networks based on packet switching are known as packet switched data networks (PSDNs).

14.1.4 CONNECTIONLESS AND CONNECTION-ORIENTED SERVICES

Chapter 12 (section 12.2) introduced the principle of a data communication network to which host computers can be attached. The purpose of such a data communications network is to provide a means of carrying data from one host computer to another. All the host computers have to do is become connected to the nearest node on the network and supply information to the network using the appropriate protocol (probably TCP/IP – see Figure 12.1). With a PSDN, two major types of service are offered: datagram and virtual circuits.

With a connectionless or datagram service, each packet is treated as a separate unit. Therefore, the packet must include a destination address to ensure that it is delivered to the correct destination. Because the packets are treated separately, each packet may travel across the network by a different route and hence they may arrive in a different order to that in which they were sent. Of course, they may not arrive at all! Any error and flow control necessary to detect lost or duplicate packets must be implemented by the users in the host machine (within OSI layer 4 – the transport layer). Clearly this service is advantageous to the network nodes since routing can be flexible and sequencing and flow control are not necessary, but it places more requirements on the user of the network. It is called a datagram service since it bears some resemblance to the service offered by the Post Office. You can send a series of letters but they may arrive in a different order (or not at all!). The IP protocol, the basis of the Internet, provides a datagram service. (IP is described in section 15.5.4.)

If it is accepted that the network itself should provide a higher level of service to the users, then a connection-oriented or virtual circuit service can be used. In this case the network service appears to the user very much like that provided by a telephone network. After establishing a logical connection between two users of the network, that logical connection remains open until the users disconnect it. Packets are routed across the network via the same route established when the virtual circuit was established. Because they go via the same route they will be delivered in the same sequence as they were sent and, hence, the network itself will provide end-to-end flow control. This logical connection, or virtual circuit, is identified by a virtual circuit number field contained within each packet transmitted. This is described in section 15.5.2. Note that this connection is only 'logical'. Actual physical transmission links are only allocated while a packet is being transmitted, hence the name *virtual* circuit. As is discussed in Chapter 15, whether the packet travels on exactly the same route depends on which layer of the system is guaranteeing a connection-oriented service. For example, the network layer may offer such a service but not the lower layers. In this case, the network layer may have to re-order packets before

presenting them to the user layer above it. The TCP protocol provides a virtual circuit between two nodes (computers) on a network. (Please see section 15.6.1 for an explanation of TCP.)

14.1.5 SIMPLE ROUTING TECHNIQUES

Most wide area, point-to-point networks are of the irregular topology type. The major characteristic of this topology is, of course, that there is not a direct path between every pair of computers that may wish to communicate. Because of this, the messages or, more commonly, the packets, are switched around the network. Hence there is a need for routing decisions to be made, to decide on the precise route the packet will take.

Consider the network illustrated in Figure 14.1. Suppose Host 1 wishes to communicate with Host 2. Packets could take the following routes.

1	2	3			
1	2	8	4		
1	7	4			
1	7	8	3		
6	5	4			
6	5	8	3		
6	5	7	2	3	
6	5	8	2	7	4

Some of these routes may appear preferable to others. For example, some involve only three links, whereas others involve four, five or six links. Of course, for a wide area network some of the links may be a very great distance so that a route involving four links may turn out to be shorter in distance than one involving three links. The routing decision may involve the fact that of two alternative links, the next node on one of the links is very busy, so it may be quicker to send the packet down the other link.

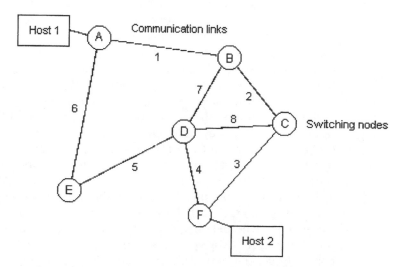

Figure 14.1 Routes through a network

Whatever method is chosen, it is important that the following situations do not arise:

Looping   where, for example, the message is sent along
                 1 7 8 2 7 8 2 7 8 2 . . .

Oscillating   e.g., 1 7 1 7 1 . . . ,
                 that is the message continually bounces back and forth
                 between two nodes.

Clearly, the routing algorithm used could have a significant effect on the performance of the network. Some alternative strategies will now be examined.

Fixed routing

Each node in the network will contain a *routing table* or route directory. This contains one entry for each node in the network, including itself, and that entry indicates which link a packet should be transmitted on if the packet is for that ultimate node address. Table 14.1 illustrates such a table for node D of the network shown in Figure 14.1. *Notice* that there is, in fact, more than one entry for some nodes. These are in case there is a failure at the next node on a particular link, or a failure in the link itself. Consider, for example, node D receiving a packet that is intended for node A. The routing table suggests that it should be transmitted on link 5. However, if it is unable to do this because link 5 or node E has failed, there is an alternative route via link 7 (or even link 4, though this would be a tortuous route to node A).

If on receipt of a packet, the node inspects the routing table to see which link to retransmit it on and discovers a * entry, then clearly that packet is intended for the host attached to that node.

The routing tables are organised manually, taking into account the lengths of the various links and the projected traffic on the links. The tables will then be loaded into each node just prior to the network being brought into operation. With the exception of alternative routes in case of failures, once the tables are loaded into each node the routing is fixed until there is some further manual intervention in the form of loading new routing tables at each (or some) nodes. New tables can be introduced as new nodes are added to the network, nodes are removed, or some significant change in the traffic patterns becomes apparent. It is a relatively simple mechanism and can give good performance if the topology and traffic patterns do not change

Table 14.1   Routing table for node D

Destination node	Link to transmit on	Alternatives	
A	5	7	4
B	7	8	5
C	8	7	4
D	*	*	*
E	5	7	8
F	4	8	—

very much. If the traffic is very dynamic, however, then clearly this fixed routing mechanism is unable to adapt.

Adaptive routing – centralised

In order for the network to adapt to changes in traffic fairly rapidly, a mechanism for updating the routing tables quickly is necessary. With a centralised system there will be one node somewhere in the network called the network control centre or the routing control centre (RCC). Each node in the network will periodically send some status information to this centre. The status information may include items such as a list of those adjacent nodes which appear to be working and to which its link is working, the size of queues of packets waiting to be transmitted on each link and the amount of traffic on each link since the last report. From all this information, the routing control centre will re-compute the appropriate routes and generate and transmit new routing tables to every node. Whilst this sounds as if it overcomes the problems inherent in fixed routing there are some significant disadvantages.

> To enable the network to adapt to changes in *topology* the process of updating the tables does not need to occur very often, in which case it may be an acceptable solution.

> However, to enable it to adapt to changes in *traffic* it will need to occur very often, particularly since overload conditions are likely to occur in bursts. For a large network, the time taken for all the information to reach the RCC, and for it to perform its calculations and return new routing tables, may be such that the overload condition has cleared, i.e., the traffic pattern has changed completely.

> The transfer of status information from all nodes and the new routing tables to all nodes is adding a considerable amount of extra traffic. Since the purpose of this mechanism is to reduce the effect of heavy traffic, the solution is, in fact, adding to the problems.

> If the RCC node fails then clearly the network is unable to adapt at all and will revert to a fixed route system with the existing routing tables. However, those tables will be as a result of the last update, satisfying a particular set of traffic conditions, which may be less appropriate generally than the tables created in a genuine fixed routing system.

Adaptive routing – distributed

The problem with a centralised system is the considerable extra traffic generated, particularly in the vicinity of the RCC, and the significant delay in the updated routing tables arriving back at each node, by which time the overload problems may have cleared.

A distributed system is one where a node updates its own table to reflect its own knowledge of its local traffic, queue sizes and failed links, and then sends a copy of this to each of its immediate neighbours, that is, those

Table 14.2 Route table for node E

Destination node	Number of links	Via link
A	3	5
B	3	4
C	2	4
D	1	4
E	*	*
F	1	5
G	2	5

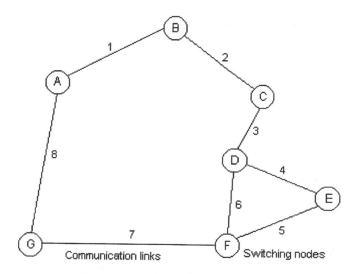

Figure 14.2 Routing through a network

that are only one link away. On receipt of a neighbour's table, a node will compare it with its own and, for every entry, retain the lower of the two values for each destination and update the transmit link entry. As this process is repeated by all the nodes in the network the current state of the network is propagated throughout.

As an example, consider the network in Figure 14.2, with the routing table for node E shown in Table 14.2. This routing table, in order to keep the example simple, is based on recording purely the number of links to a destination node. Assume that node G fails. This will mean that shortly after, node E will receive a routing table from node F as shown in Table 14.3(a) and from node D as shown in Table 14.3(b). Note that node D's table does not yet reflect the fact that G has failed. D is only just receiving the table from F that node E is also just receiving.

Node E can now compute an entry for each destination node. Considering just node A as an example, to go via link 5 (which is to node F) will now require a total of five links (one to F plus the four that F now says it

Table 14.3(a) From node F

Destination node	Number of links	Via link
A	4	6
B	3	6
C	2	6
D	1	6
E	1	5
F	*	*
G	∞	–

Table 14.3(b) From node D

Destination node	Number of links	Via link
A	3	3
B	2	3
C	1	3
D	*	*
E	1	4
F	1	6
G	2	6

requires to get to A). However, the table from node D indicates that from D to A will require only three links, so node E computes that it will require only four links from E to A via node D (link 4) and hence its entry for node A will now read:

Destination	No of links	Via
A	4	4

This same calculation would, of course, be performed for all the other destination nodes.

Compared with the other routing methods discussed, this is certainly advantageous in that it is responsive to network changes and yet each node only communicates with its immediate neighbours. However, as a network grows in size, the routing tables become bigger and hence require more local memory, more bandwidth is used in order to send them to each other and more CPU time is consumed in calculating new tables. Eventually, it will become too expensive for each node to have an entry for every other node and so the routing may be done in a hierarchical fashion as with the telephone network. Each group of nodes will only know the topology of that area. A routing table for a node in a particular area will have an entry for all nodes in that area but all nodes outside that area will be represented by one particular node so that all packets for the other areas are routed via that one node. For networks with a lot of communication within an area and occasional communication to other areas this is a very good compromise solution.

14.1.6 CONGESTION

Congestion is the situation where there is simply too much traffic for the network to cope. It may be caused for a variety of reasons, e.g., the buffer space may become full at a node, or packets arrive at a node much faster than it can transmit them on because an incoming line is faster than the outgoing line. Failures of nodes may also cause congestion. If a node goes down completely then this places a heavier burden on other parts of the network. However, it may fail in a not so obvious way. Imagine, for example, that as a result of some error condition, a node suddenly decides that it can communicate with all other nodes in the network over zero links because the links column in its routing table has become zeros. As this routing table propagates throughout the network all other nodes will begin to direct their packets towards this particular node that is not, in fact, working properly.

At first sight, it may appear that the techniques of flow control, particularly the sliding window mechanism (see section 15.3.3), will solve congestion. You will see that the window size is related to the amount of buffer storage available at a node. Although it has a contribution to make it does not solve the problem. Remember that a node in a network will be receiving packets from a number of other nodes. If the window size for each incoming link was such that there was always buffer space for a full window for every link then, although congestion could not occur, it would be at the expense of throughput because most of the time much of the buffer space would be empty. In order to give good performance most of the time, networks are designed for average traffic. This is analogous to the banking system, which will allow you to withdraw cash at any time but, if all customers went to the bank on the same day to withdraw all their cash, the bank would be unable to meet the demand.

There have been techniques suggested to handle the problem of congestion although they will not be discussed here. Suffice it to indicate that if congestion occurs the performance (throughput) of the network drops considerably until the congestion eases.

14.1.7 ASYNCHRONOUS TRANSFER MODE (ATM) LANs

Most local area networks are based on the broadcast principle (see sections 14.2.2 and 14.2.3). However, one kind of point-to-point network that has been successfully used in local area networks is *Asynchronous Transfer Mode* (ATM). ATM is fundamentally a WAN technology but it is sometimes used in LANs, particularly where multimedia information is being transmitted. Though commonly used in the wide area, ATM is much less popular in LANs, mainly because it tends to be more expensive than Ethernet.

ATM is a *cell-based* technology that uses switches. (Switches are described in section 16.1.2.) Instead of the data being packaged into variable-length packets, as is done in Ethernet or Token Ring, it is divided into cells that are always 53 bytes long. It is these cells that are switched through the ATM network. One advantage of ATM is its Classes of Service, which can be used to guarantee different kinds of traffic (voice, video or data, for example) the bandwidth that they need. A disadvantage of ATM is that it is so different from Ethernet and Token ring that using it in LANs is a fairly complicated exercise. The major problem is that there are no broadcasts in ATM.

14.2 BROADCAST NETWORKS

Chapter 12 (section 12.3.2) introduced the concept of broadcast networks and the most common topologies. Remember that broadcast networks use a channel to which all the users are connected, so all the users receive any transmission made on the channel. The only wide area broadcast networks all use radio broadcast, either relatively local up to a few hundred kilometres or over much further distances using satellite transmission. Section 14.2.1 will examine this further. The most common examples of broadcast networks are local area networks. These may use twisted pair cables, coaxial cable or optical fibre cable as their transmission medium (see section 13.6). Comparison between twisted pair and coaxial cable is not helpful because there are many variants of each to meet the different requirements of bandwidth, loss, noise immunity, etc. In general, coaxial cable has higher noise immunity and bandwidth, but the cable is stiffer (which may or may not be helpful depending on whether it is being surface mounted or pushed through ducts). Both types can adequately serve most LAN environments, but coaxial cable has been dropping out of use. Optical fibre is particularly suited to environments which have high levels of electromagnetic radiation, or to meet demands for very high speeds of transmission. However, it is more difficult to tap into, which makes it more difficult and expensive for the installation of a LAN.

LAN protocols have developed into the following layers:

physical layer identical to ISO layer 1

medium access control (MAC) layer to manage communications over the link

logical link control (LLC) layer, which provides a form of multiplexing to handle multiple-source data (a number of users attached to one host)

In addition, the LLC layer assembles the data into a frame complete with address and error checking bits and disassembles them on receipt.

For a particular LLC protocol there may be several different MAC options provided, since this is the protocol layer in which the differences in topology are involved.

The major standards activity for LAN networks has been by the US Institute of Electrical and Electronic Engineers (IEEE). Their work has been organised into a number of committees, of which some are as follows:

802.2   Logical link control (LLC)

802.3   CSMA/CD networks (Ethernet, etc.)

802.5   Token ring networks

14.2.1 RADIO AND SATELLITE BROADCASTING

Radio and satellite broadcast networks have one thing in common: a fairly high bandwidth communication channel that is shared between all the users.

This channel could be shared by using similar techniques for sharing a line (see section 13.5). Frequency division multiple access divides the bandwidth of the channel into non-overlapping subchannels. Each station is assigned a separate subchannel. Thus, each station uses a dedicated portion of the whole channel at all times. The difficulty with this is twofold. First the limit on the number of stations determined by the number of subchannels that the channel can be divided into and, secondly, the wasted bandwidth when some channel may not be transmitting. Time division multiple access permits each station to transmit in non-overlapping time slots. Each station is assigned a time slot, so that at any time only one station is transmitting. Again, if a station is not wishing to transmit, that bandwidth is wasted. In both these cases stations are penalised if there is only light loading on the network, because large parts of the bandwidth are unused.

A different approach would be to assume it is a single channel and allow any station to transmit at any time. However, if two or more stations transmit simultaneously their transmissions will interfere with each other, so some mechanism is necessary for handling this.

The simplest technique is called *pure aloha*. The name *aloha* is used because it is based on a technique first developed at the University of Hawaii for a broadcast network using local radio transmission. With this technique, if a node has a packet to transmit, it does so immediately. It is then required to wait for an acknowledgement. If such an acknowledgement is not received within a time-out period, the packet is assumed lost and the packet is retransmitted after a random time. The packet will probably have been lost due to a collision with transmission from another node and hence they must retransmit after a random time to prevent exactly the same thing happening again. The system is simple but as the volume of traffic increases, so does the number of collisions and hence the productive use of the bandwidth decreases.

Slotted aloha is where the transmission channel time is divided into time slots of equal length. Each node is only allowed to transmit a packet at the start of a time slot, so that, if a collision occurs only that time slot of the bandwidth is wasted. This will increase the usage of the overall bandwidth.

Clearly, the problem that the above schemes are trying to overcome is that of collisions. An improvement that avoids many (but not all) possible collisions is known as carrier sense multiple access (CSMA). Here, each node will listen to the channel and detect a carrier signal indicating that a transmission is taking place. A node is allowed to transmit only if nothing is being transmitted currently. This does not completely solve the problem since in the time between deciding that there is nothing being transmitted, and starting to transmit, another node may do exactly the same, so that these will then subsequently collide. Even so, it is a big improvement on the *aloha* techniques. The CSMA technique, however, can only be used with a radio network, not a satellite, because of the considerable delay with the latter between transmitting and receiving due to the very long transmission distances involved.

There are a number of mechanisms that have been proposed and used for satellite communication. The most successful of these are schemes that use an *aloha* mechanism for low channel utilisation (little traffic) and move gradually over to some kind of time division mechanism as the channel traffic increases.

14.2.2   BUS-BASED LANs

With a bus-based local area network the nodes are attached to a continuous bus and some mechanism is necessary to allow the nodes to share this bus to transfer messages. This mechanism can take two basic forms: in one case the nodes can literally compete or contend with each other for access, whereas the alternative allows access as required in an orderly sequential fashion.

CSMA/CD – Ethernet

Ethernet is the best-known example of such a network and was originally developed jointly by DEC, Intel and Xerox. There are some differences between the original Ethernet specification and the IEEE 802.3 specification but the term Ethernet is now a generic term for all contention bus systems.

Figure 14.3 shows the classical form of Ethernet network, in which coaxial cable is used for the bus. A computer is attached to the bus by a device known as a transceiver, which is responsible for transmitting and receiving to and from the bus. (These days, the transceiver is an integral part of the network interface card.) As a message is transmitted onto the bus it

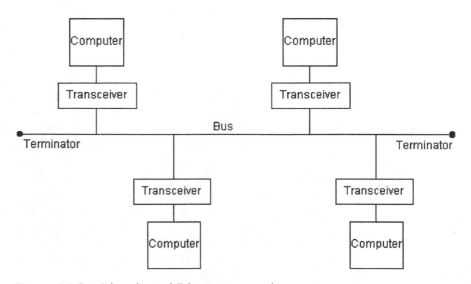

Figure 14.3   A bus-based Ethernet network

will propagate in both directions along the bus and all other nodes will receive it. By examining the contents of a header included within the message the transceiver can either pass the message to the attached computer or ignore it, depending on the destination address. Both ends of the bus are terminated by a special terminator, which prevents the signals being reflected back down the cable, causing interference.

Because any computer can transmit to any other at any time there needs to be a mechanism to control the contention for the line. This mechanism is known as CSMA/CD – carrier sense multiple access with collision detection – and is carried out by the transceiver. Basically, this means that, before a node can begin to transmit, it has to 'listen' to the bus to see if anything is already being transmitted. It can detect this by the presence of a carrier signal (hence the name carrier sense – multiple access simply means that there are a number of nodes attached to this bus). If there is something already being transmitted it will wait for a period of time and try again. If, however, nothing is currently being transmitted, the transceiver will send its message onto the bus. However, there may be a pair (or more) of nodes that, at more or less the same time, decide that nothing is being transmitted and so begin to transmit. Clearly these simultaneous transmissions will corrupt each other, and a 'collision' is said to have occurred. In order to recover from such a situation the transceivers operate as follows. As a transceiver is transmitting a message onto the bus, it will also receive what is propagating along the bus. If it is the same as it is transmitting there is no problem. If, however, it is not the same then it has detected a collision. In this case it will stop transmitting (it is said to 'back off') and will try again after a random time period. This time period is random so that the colliding stations do not simply try again at the same time.

Figure 14.4 illustrates the layout of a message in Ethernet. The preamble consists of seven bytes of alternating bits, 010101 . . ., which allow the receiver to synchronise. The start frame delimiter indicates the start of a frame. The destination and source addresses indicate the node for which the message is intended and the node from which the message has come, respectively. In Ethernet these address fields may be either 16 or 48 bits long, but must be the same for all nodes in a particular network. One particular address, say all 1s, may be used to indicate that the message is intended for *all* nodes, so that a message can be truly broadcast to all nodes. The length field identifies the length of the following data field, since this is allowed to be of variable length. However, if this value is less than the minimum

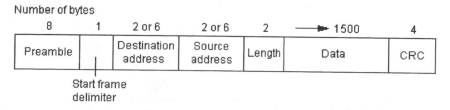

Figure 14.4   Ethernet IEEE 802.3 frame format

number required for a valid frame (minimum frame size is 64 bytes) a sequence of bytes is added to pad it out. The checksum is a 32-bit CRC check value based on all fields including the addresses. (CRC checks are explained in section 13.7.3.)

Although the CRC check allows a receiver to check receipt of a valid message there is no confirmation to the sender (acknowledgement) of receipt and so this and other protocol features must be built into a higher-level protocol. These higher-level software protocols will be implemented in the nodes and will use the data portion of the Ethernet message or packet for fields appropriate to these protocols. The appropriate protocols are those defined by IEEE 802.2.

Note that the data field of a message may be up to 1500 bytes long. This would make Ethernet well suited to the transmission of long files between nodes. With long messages, the utilisation of the bus can be quite high because there will be few collisions (remember that the carrier sense mechanism avoids many collisions which might otherwise occur). However, long messages prevent other communication between nodes taking place (it is therefore difficult to guarantee any sort of message delivery time, or response to message time) and also require large buffers for sending and receiving.

A number of variants of Ethernet exist. 10Base-5 Ethernet used thick yellow coaxial cable with a transmission speed of 10 Mbits per second. Each network could have 1024 nodes, on a number of segments of cable each up to 500 m long and linked by *repeaters*, the total network length being 2.5 km. (A repeater simply boosts a signal and allows it to travel further.) 10Base-2 Ethernet uses a thinner, more flexible and cheaper coaxial cable than 10Base-5, but the permitted segment lengths are shorter. Coaxial-cabled Ethernet networks are now uncommon.

10Base-T networks use twisted pair cable. The transmission speed is, once again, 10 Mbits per second. However, instead of a bus topology star wiring is used, with all nodes on the network being plugged into a *hub*. (This arrangement is shown in Figure 14.5.) One of the main advantages of such a

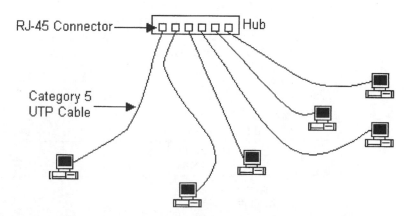

Figure 14.5 Use of a hub in a 10Base-T LAN

wiring scheme is flexibility: moves, additions and changes to the network are facilitated. 100Base-T Ethernet networks are very similar to 10Base-T networks, but the transmission speed is 100 Mbits per second.

In Gigabit Ethernet networks the data rate increases to 1000 Mbits per second. In the 1000Base-T variant of Gigabit Ethernet, signals can be sent over twisted pair wiring for a distance of 100 metres. The fibre optic variants of Gigabit Ethernet permit much greater distances. The CSMA/CD access mechanism is retained, but only for half duplex operation. Gigabit Ethernet also supports full duplex transmission, where devices can send and receive at the same time. In full duplex mode there is no need for CSMA/CD, as listening to the network until no transmissions can be detected is pointless. The minimum and maximum frame sizes for Gigabit Ethernet were changed from the sizes that had been used for 100Base-T. The minimum frame size was increased from 64 bytes to 512 bytes and the maximum frame size was increased from 1,514 bytes to 9,000 bytes. These larger frame sizes gave transceivers more time to receive collision notifications.

10 Gigabit Ethernet (10GbE) networks have a data rate of 10,000 Mbits per second. This technology is full duplex only and is used with fibre optic cable only. For this reason, CSMA/CD is no longer needed, though the frame format remains the same as in earlier forms of Ethernet. In a radical departure from previous forms of Ethernet, one variant of 10GbE is deliberately intended for use over metropolitan area networks (MANs) as well as LANs. (A metropolitan area network falls somewhere between a LAN and a WAN in size. It is big enough to connect up a whole city but not to connect two cities together.)

Since its inception, Ethernet has been continually evolving. As a result of the subtle changes made with every new Ethernet standard through the years, 10GbE has almost nothing in common with Ethernet in its original form. A summary of Ethernet variants can be found in Table 14.4. The 'x' in the final row represents a range of 10GB standards. There are too many of these to include in this table. Space does not permit the inclusion of all variants but one that is particularly interesting is 802.11b, which permits a data rate of up to 11 Mbits/sec over a wireless LAN (WLAN). (WLANs are described in section 16.1.1.)

14.2.3   RING BASED LANs

A ring based LAN consists of a number of nodes, each connected to its own repeater. The repeaters are then linked by the communication medium (typically twisted pair cables, although fibre optics have also been developed) in the form of a complete ring. The repeaters pass on serial data from one link to the next and also allow the attached node to read the information as it passes. The repeaters take their power from the ring itself so that they are independent of whether a particular node is powered up or not. Figure 14.6 illustrates the general layout.

There are two main strategies for managing the access to this ring network: *token ring* and *slotted ring*, though the token ring has become the more widely used.

Table 14.4 Ethernet variants

Name	Data rate	Medium	Maximum segment length	Chief advantage
10BASE-5	10 Mbits/sec	Thick coaxial	500 m	Longer cable runs than 10BASE-2
10BASE-2	10 Mbits/sec	Thin coaxial	200 m	Cheaper than 10BASE-5
10BASE-T	10 Mbits/sec	UTP	100 m	Allows structured cabling
10BASE-F	10 Mbits/sec	Fibre optic	2000 m	Longer cable runs than 10BASE-2
802.11b	Up to 11 Mbits/sec	Wireless microwave	Up to 46 m indoors	No cables needed
100BASE-T4	100 Mbits/sec	UTP Cat 3 and above	100 m	Can use Cat 3 cable
100BASE-TX	100 Mbits/sec	UTP Cat 5	100 m	Full duplex
100BASE-F	100 Mbits/sec	Fibre optic	2000 m	Full duplex, long cable runs
1000BASE-SX	1000 Mbits/sec	Multimode fibre	550 m	Cheaper than LX
1000BASE-LX	1000 Mbits/sec	Single-mode fibre	5 Km	Long cable runs
1000BASE-T	1000 Mbits/sec	UTP Cat 5e	100 m	Cheaper than SX and LX
10GBASE-x	10,000 Mbits/sec	Single-mode and multi-mode fibre	Up to 40 Km	Very high data rate

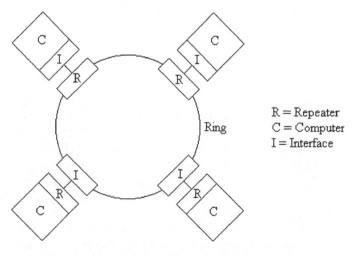

R = Repeater
C = Computer
I = Interface

Figure 14.6 Layout of a ring-based LAN

Token ring

This was originally developed by IBM as its strategic offering for LAN networks. It was then adopted by IEEE and ISO and is defined by the IEEE 802.5 standard. A unique bit pattern called the token continuously circulates the ring while no station needs to send a message. When a repeater station is instructed by its attached node to transmit a message to another node on the ring, the station must wait for the token to pass through its repeater. When the token is recognised the station alters one of its bits, say from 1 to 0, so that the token is no longer available to any other station. The station then sends its message, which may be of variable length, onto the ring. The message or packet format includes the destination node's address and as the packet passes through each repeater on the ring, that station will examine this destination address to see if the packet is for it. If so it will read the message. If not it will ignore it. When the packet arrives back at the sending station, the sender is required to reinstate the token onto the ring so that the next station downstream may use the ring.

There is a token holding time, which limits the length of time a node can hold the token before passing it on. Hence, if there is a limit to the size of the packet then a guaranteed response time can be given to communication over the ring, based on the worst-case condition of every node using its right to send a maximum sized packet in turn. This may be important in control situations, such as process control.

Figure 14.7 illustrates the layout of the frame. The starting delimiter is a unique pattern indicating the start of the frame or token. The access control byte contains various control bits including the token bit. Frame control indicates whether the frame is a data frame or one of a number of control frames. There is no limit to the number of information bytes but the frame transmission is limited by the token holding time. The frame status byte is used to acknowledge receipt of the frame (remember that on a ring the frame will return to the sender after it has gone round the ring once).

Clearly, the system is dependent on the token not being corrupted. If it were (a bit changed, for example) then the ring simply would not operate. To counteract this, there is the concept of an *active monitor* station. This is one of the nodes, determined at start-up time, and is responsible for generating the token, and checking for its presence. It does this by employing a timer that is started whenever the token passes its repeater. The

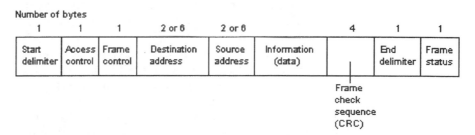

Figure 14.7 Token ring frame format

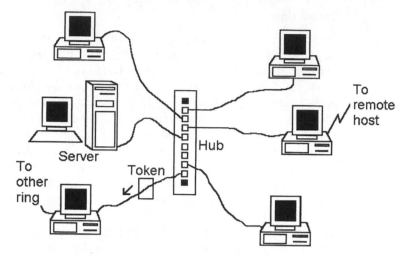

Figure 14.8 Token ring LAN

initial value of the timer is chosen to correspond to the expected maximum time between consecutive tokens, whether free or busy. Should a time-out occur, an error is assumed to have occurred. The monitor station will then reinstate the token, and perform an error logging function.

In addition to the activities of the active monitor station, all other nodes can take part in control procedures by the use of control frames. Each node on the ring can act as a standby monitor and is able to take on the role of the active monitor should that become necessary due to failure. When a new node wishes to join the ring it can go through a procedure that involves exchanging control frames to ensure that there is no duplication of node address.

Token ring networks are laid out in a *physical* star topology, with all the stations plugging into a hub as shown in Figure 14.8. However, the *logical* topology is a ring. In other words, information flow is controlled in a ring. (Twisted pair Ethernet networks are 'physical star, logical bus': information flow is on a linear bus but the network is wired as a star.)

The data rate of Token ring networks evolved from 4 Mbits per second to 16 Mbits per second and then to 100 Mbits per second. However, this technology, though sophisticated and versatile, was unable to compete with Ethernet on price. As a result, the use of Token ring has been declining for some time.

The *FDDI* (Fiber Distributed Data Interface) system uses token passing to connect up to 500 nodes via a 100 Mbits per second ring network. A distance of up to two kilometres between stations is possible using multimode fibre and, if single-mode fibre is used, the distance can be much greater. Fault tolerance is built into the system. However, FDDI has proved expensive compared with 100Base-T Ethernet and has become relatively uncommon.

14.3 SUMMARY

The issues concerned in the network layer of the ISO reference model have been introduced. With point-to-point networks, these include the principle of switching and the subsequent problems of routing and congestion.

Local area networks, most of which are of the broadcast type, present different problems and the most common types have been described.

14.4 EXERCISES

1 In a multiple node communications network describe how a packet is routed from source to destination. What is the difference between flow control and congestion?

2 Explain the need for a routing strategy and discuss the advantages and disadvantages of:
fixed routing
centralised adaptive routing
distributed adaptive routing.

3 Explain to which layer(s) of the ISO reference model you would relate LANs, summarising the functions of your chosen layers.
Compare and contrast Ethernet and Token ring LANs, indicating the strengths and weaknesses of each.

4 Explain the principle of packet switching and distinguish between the two major types of service provided on a PSDN, namely datagrams and virtual circuits.

5 Refer to the network shown in Figure 14.2 and assume that node G has just failed. Show how this information propagates through the network and generates the new routing table for every node.

6 Ten thousand airline booking offices are competing for the use of a single slotted aloha channel. Each office makes on average 20 requests per hour. A slot is 90 microseconds. What is the average channel load?

7 Full-screen (640 × 480 pixels) video is being transmitted in full colour at 20 frames per second. Each pixel uses 32 bits. What is the data rate, assuming that compression is not being used?

8 Critically compare CSMA/CD and Token ring local area networks. For each identify strengths and weaknesses and hence recommend operational circumstances in which each is most appropriate.

9 Find the effective data rate for the information in packets of the following Ethernet:

network length	1.5 km
propagation speed	200 m/μs
transmission rate	10 Mbps

packet length	512 bits	
packet overhead	32 bits	
acknowledge packet	32 bits	sent after data packet received.

10 Investigate your local LAN to discover what principle of operation it uses, and the details of its data transfer rate, its error detection mechanisms and the protocols it uses.

Communication protocols

When two parties wish to exchange information it is clearly necessary to establish some rules by which that exchange can sensibly take place and ensure that it is received correctly. With a telephone conversation, for example, the principal requirement is that both parties do not speak at the same time, otherwise the transmissions interfere with each other and neither party knows what the other was saying. Also, before the messages are exchanged, some initial information is exchanged to establish that the correct parties are in fact present and in a position to receive the messages. If the receiving party is writing down the message it could be that the information is being spoken too quickly so that the caller (transmitter) will have to stop for a while and then continue. All of these 'rules' are essentially a communications protocol. With human communication the 'rules' are often imprecise, with the result that misunderstandings or even gross errors are commonplace. With computer communication it is obviously important to try to establish more precise protocols to reduce the effect of errors.

A communications protocol, then, is a set of rules, adhered to by the communicating parties in order to ensure that the information being exchanged is received correctly. Section 13.7 described some error detection techniques and, clearly, the detection of errors is of prime importance in a protocol. However, there are many other potential problems to be solved by the protocol. These will be introduced in section 15.1 and the major ones explored further in some detail in section 15.3.

Having laid the basic groundwork of communication protocols section 15.5 studies examples of real protocols which relate to levels 1, 2, 3 of the OSI reference model (see section 12.5) while section 15.6 studies the higher-level protocols.

15.1 FUNCTIONAL TASKS OF A PROTOCOL

There are many different types of protocol, some concerned with a simple exchange of messages between two parties connected by a single link, and others concerned with communicating computers connected in a network.

Clearly there will be different requirements of these differing protocols, but all of them will incorporate the following protocol elements in some way or other.

15.1.1   ERROR CONTROL

Section 13.7 described some error detection mechanisms to allow a receiver to discover if any transmission errors have occurred. Clearly, if an error is detected, some action is necessary so that the receiver obtains a correct copy of the transmitted information. This action is termed 'error control'. A very simple example is that of a user at a terminal that is connected to the computer using asynchronous transmission. When the computer receives a character it will echo back the bit stream to be displayed on the screen of the terminal. If that is not in fact the character the user intended, the user can then send a special character (a delete, for example) to inform the computer to ignore the last character received. However, most communication systems require this mechanism to be built in rather than provided by an 'intelligent user'.

15.1.2   SEQUENCE CONTROL

Most communication systems do not involve the exchange of just a single message, but a whole series of messages, usually in a particular sequence. In addition, the message may be split into a number of smaller blocks or packets (see section 14.1.3) and these packets need to be in a particular sequence to make up the required message. If a particular message or packet gets 'lost' or is sent on a 'long route' over a network it could be that it will be received out of sequence. Therefore, the protocol must include some sort of sequence identification that designates the order in which the message or packets should be processed at the destination, as the order in which they were received might be different.

15.1.3   FLOW CONTROL

If, in a communication system, the source generates information faster than the receiver can accept it then some means of controlling the production or flow of the information is necessary. Flow control is the management of the flow of information from the source to the destination. This can be particularly important when two computers are communicating over an intermediary communications network. The network will only buffer a limited amount of information (see section 14.1.2) and so it becomes necessary to control the output of the faster computer to prevent the network becoming congested.

15.1.4   TIME-OUT CONTROL

Time-out control is essentially concerned with the action to be taken if the flow of messages stops. Some protocols, for example, require that after sending a message, the sender receives an acknowledgement that the message was apparently received correctly or not before sending the next message. If that acknowledgement does not come (e.g., the line has been disconnected or the receiving node has failed), the sender may wait for ever and hence be deadlocked. A time-out is a mechanism whereby, on transmission of a message that requires a reply, a clock is started. If no reply is received within a certain period the communication is 'timed-out'. The message could either be retransmitted or the communication abandoned.

Clearly the time-out time must be appropriate for the communication system. In a simple point-to-point system connecting two computers the time-out time could be quite small. On a large communications network, however, if particular nodes become congested the reply might simply be delayed. If the time-out were too small the sender could be re-transmitting unnecessarily, adding to the congestion of the network.

15.1.5 START-UP CONTROL

Start-up control is responsible for getting transmission started in a system that has been idle. As with a telephone conversation it is necessary first to establish the physical link and then to exchange control information to verify that the correct parties are at each end.

With a very short link between, say a terminal and a computer, these functions can be achieved by an exchange of signals on control lines, known as a *handshake* (see section 15.2.1).

When the communicating devices are computers the start-up control is achieved by the exchange of a set of control or supervisory messages or packets of information. With a half duplex link this process will also establish which is the sender and which is the receiver, and there must then be an additional mechanism to reverse their roles during the communication process.

15.2 LEVELS OF PROTOCOL

Chapter 12 introduced the concept of structuring the communication software and hardware into a series of levels in order to provide a reliable communication system independent of any particular manufacturer's equipment. This is typified by the ISO reference model, which is discussed in section 12.5. Each of these levels or layers is concerned with a protocol defining a set of rules that is used by that layer in order to communicate with a similar layer in the remote system. Most of this chapter is concerned with protocols in the lower three layers, that is the network-dependent layers, though the physical layer will only be briefly described. We have already met some physical protocols in use in the hardware of the computer and these examples will be re-examined first.

15.2.1 INPUT/OUTPUT BUS HANDSHAKING

A typical I/O bus consists of three sets of lines: data lines, address lines and control lines (see section 10.1). Some of the control lines are used to

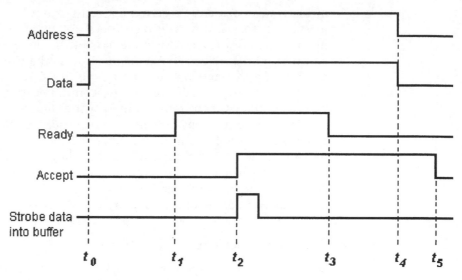

Figure 15.1 I/O bus handshaking

coordinate data transfers over the bus and these are discussed here. With asynchronous transmission, the fact that there is no common clock to which activities can be related means that there needs to be an exchange of signals which is referred to as a handshake. There are two timing control lines named 'Ready' and 'Accept'. The handshake protocol proceeds as follows.

The CPU places the address and mode (input or output) information on the appropriate lines. It then indicates that it has done so by a signal on the Ready line. When the addressed device receives the ready signal, it performs the required operation and indicates the completion of this by a signal on the Accept line. On receipt of the Accept signal the CPU will remove the address, mode and ready signals and, in the case of an input operation, strobe the data into its input buffer. The timing of these operations for an output transfer is illustrated in Figure 15.1.

Because this is an output operation, the CPU places the output data on the data lines at the same time as the address and mode information. The addressed device strobes the data into its buffer when it receives the Ready signal. The delay t_1–t_0 is to allow for both the possibility of skew (see section 10.2.1) and for the devices to perform address decoding. It also sets the Accept signal to indicate its acceptance of the data. On receipt of the Accept signal the CPU drops the Ready signal. After that the CPU will remove the data, address and mode signals from the bus and when the device interface detects the transmission of the Ready signal it will then remove the Accept signal. An error detection scheme is provided by the interlocking of the Ready and Accept signals. If the Accept signal is not received within a specified time after setting the Ready signal, the CPU assumes that an error has occurred. This could cause an interrupt to an error routine.

15.2.2 EIA/TIA-232 INTERFACE PROTOCOL

As was discussed earlier in section 10.2.4 the EIA/TIA-232 (or V.24) interface (formerly known as RS232-C) can be used very simply as an interface for connecting a terminal to a computer using just three of its pins. However, it was intended as a standard, completely specifying the interface between data communication equipment (DCE), such as modems, and data terminal equipment (DTE), that is, computers or terminals. It involves a comprehensive protocol to establish connections before data transmission takes place. As an example of this, consider the link illustrated in Figure 15.2.

Figure 15.3 indicates the interface pins required in this example. The sequence of signals required to establish a connection, transmit data and terminate the connection is now described.

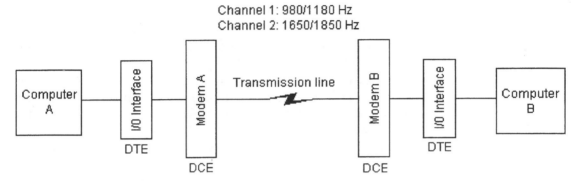

Figure 15.2 DCE and DTE

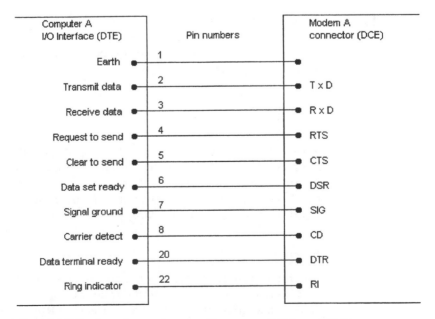

Figure 15.3 Interface pins used between DCE and DTE

When computer B is ready to accept a call it sets the data terminal ready signal (DTR) to 1.

Modem B monitors the telephone line and when it detects the ringing current, indicating an incoming call, it signals computer B by setting the ring indicator (RI) to 1. If DTR is 1 at the time the ringing current is detected. The modem automatically answers the call by going 'off-hook'. Then it sets the data ready (DSR) signal to 1.

Computer B directs modem B to start transmitting the frequency 1850 Hz by setting request to send (RTS) to 1. Then modem B will set clear to send (CTS) to 1. The detection of the 1850 Hz frequency at Modem A causes it to set the carrier detect (CD) signal to 1, and turn on a front panel indicator light.

Computer A sets request to send (RTS) to 1, causing transmission of a 1180 Hz signal. Modem A then sets CTS and DSR to 1. When Modem B detects the 1180 Hz frequency it sets CD to 1.

A full duplex link is now established between two computers. Computer B can now transfer data to and from computer A using the Transmit Data (T×D) and Receive Data (R×D) pins.

When the user finishes, computer B sets the RTS and DTR signals to 0, causing modem B to disconnect from the line. Signals CTS, DSR and CD are also set to 0. When modem A senses the disappearance of the 1850 Hz frequency it sets the CD signal to 0.

Modem A then removes its 1180 Hz frequency from the line and sets CTS and DSR to 0.

Computer B sets DTR to 1 to prepare for a new call.

15.3 PRINCIPLES OF DATA LINK PROTOCOLS

Section 15.1 introduced the major functional tasks of a protocol. These will now be examined in more detail.

15.3.1 ERROR CONTROL

The various error detection schemes discussed in section 13.7 allow a receiver to detect when an error has occurred but do not provide any mechanism for correcting the error. The combination of an error detection mechanism and some means of correcting such errors is known as error control. There are two basic mechanisms in common use for handling the correction of errors: echo checking and automatic repeat request (ARQ).

Echo checking

Echo checking simply involves the receiver in sending back (echoing) the data it received to the transmitter. If the transmitter receives the same data as it sent, it assumes it was received correctly. Although a simple concept, it is very expensive in bandwidth since everything is transmitted twice. The major use of such a system is in an asynchronous terminal-computer time-sharing system. When the user types a character at the terminal that character is not displayed by the terminal. Instead it is transmitted to the computer, which then echoes it back for it to be displayed to the user. If the displayed character is not the one it was intended to send, a special character can be sent to the computer by the user indicating that it should ignore the last character sent.

Clearly this mechanism is simple as far as the computer is concerned. All the error checking and error correcting is, in fact, being done by an intelligent user at the terminal. If the correcting mechanism needs to be automatic then another system, such as ARQ, should be used.

Automatic repeat request – ARQ

As has just been discussed, echo checking depends on the intelligent user checking the received character against the transmitted character and re-transmitting it if in error. Clearly, this same function could be programmed into the transmitter in computer–computer communication, but the method is still very wasteful of bandwidth since everything is transmitted twice.

Section 13.7 introduced techniques whereby the receiver could detect the occurrence of an error, and an obvious improvement on transmitting everything twice is for the receiver to inform the transmitter when an error has been detected and ask it to retransmit that data, hence the name – automatic repeat request. Because the block of data in error is being discarded and retransmitted it would seem to work best with as small a block as possible. However, in order to utilise the transmission channel efficiently a high ratio of data to check bits is required, indicating a large block size. Hence, the solution is always a compromise although the amount of storage available at the receiver can also play a significant part.

There are two ARQ mechanisms in common use: idle RQ and continuous RQ. Figure 15.4 illustrates their principles.

Idle RQ

The transmitter will send a single block of data (including appropriate check bits) and then wait for an acknowledgement (hence the name idle RQ, because the transmitter is idle whilst the receiver is checking the data received and sending back an acknowledgement).

The receiver will check the block of data on receipt and, if there are no errors, return a positive acknowledgement (e.g. an ACK character from the ASCII character set – see section 15.4.1). If an error is detected the receiver will ignore that block and return a negative acknowledgement. If the block never arrives (or its format is corrupted so the receiver does not recognise it) no acknowledgement is returned.

If the transmitter receives a positive acknowledgement it will then transmit the next data block. If it receives a negative acknowledgement it will retransmit the same data block. If it receives no acknowledgement within a specified time-out period (see section 15.1.4) it will also retransmit

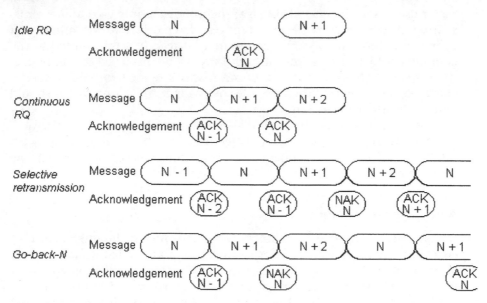

Figure 15.4 Automatic repeat request mechanisms

the same block. After a specified number of consecutive time-outs for the same block the transmitter will assume the receiver is unable to continue and will abort the communication. There may be occasions when the transmitter will time-out before the receiver has had a chance to return an acknowledgement, in which case a duplicate copy of the same data block is transmitted. In order to allow the receiver to detect such duplicate data, a data block will usually contain some sort of sequence number.

The advantage of idle RQ is that both the transmitter and the receiver only need sufficient storage for one block, so storage requirements at each end are minimised. The system is also relatively simple. Its disadvantage is the wasting of bandwidth, since the transmitter is idle for the following time:

propagation delay for one block;

+ time for receiver to process block;

+ time for receiver to send acknowledgement;

+ time for transmitter to process acknowledgement.

If this idle time is small compared with the transmission time of a block, then its efficiency is increased and the simplicity of the system may make it attractive. In many cases, however, its inherent waste of time (idleness) renders it very inefficient.

Continuous RQ

The problem with idle RQ is that of the transmitter wasting time waiting for receipt of an acknowledgement from the receiver. An obvious improvement is for the transmitter to send data blocks continuously without waiting for an acknowledgement. As the receiver receives blocks it will perform appropriate error checks and acknowledge their receipt as in the idle RQ scheme. The essential difference is that by the time the transmitter receives an acknowledgement for a block, it will already have transmitted a number of others. This has two implications for the sender:

Each block clearly needs a sequence number and each acknowledgement needs to include the sequence number of the block that is being acknowledged, so that if it does need retransmission the transmitter knows which one to send.

The transmitter needs to store a copy of every block it transmits in case it needs retransmitting. The receipt of a positive acknowledgement (with its sequence number) can be used to remove that particular data block from this storage area.

From the receiver's point of view the occurrence of an error, resulting in the retransmission of a data block, means that blocks are going to be received out of sequence, since the transmitter will have continued to send more blocks up to the time a negative acknowledgement was received.

There are two ways of handling this situation, again illustrated in Figure 15.4. The first of these is *selective retransmission*. With this procedure only the single block that was corrupted is retransmitted. Its operation can be described as follows:

1 Assume block with sequence number N is corrupted.

2 The receiver returns an acknowledgement block (an ACK + sequence number) for each correctly received block.

3 Hence the transmitter receives acknowledgement blocks for blocks N − 2, N − 1, N + 1, N + 2 . . .

4 On receipt of the acknowledgement block for block N + 1, the transmitter will detect that this is not the correct sequence and that therefore block N has not been acknowledged. It will therefore retransmit block N before transmitting the next block in the original sequence. (*Note* that we have already identified the need for the transmitter to store each block sent until it receives an acknowledgement.)

Note that there is no need for a negative acknowledgement. The transmitter knows that a block was not received correctly by detecting an out of sequence acknowledgement. It will still be necessary to have a time-out mechanism in case the flow of acknowledgements stops altogether, or in case the transmitter has no further blocks to send at this time so there will be no acknowledgements coming back.

The receiver does need to store the received blocks for two reasons:

1 In order to be able to pass a complete message (which may have been broken down into blocks or packets) in the correct sequence, since some blocks may be out of sequence.

2 If the acknowledgement block gets corrupted and hence not recognised, the effect is that the transmitter will retransmit that block. As the receiver can detect that this is a duplicate (from the sequence number) it will discard it (but it does need to return an acknowledgement to satisfy the transmitter).

The major problem associated with selective retransmission is the receipt of out of sequence blocks. The number of blocks the receiver has to buffer is not known and, if the receiver is doing this for a number of messages, the store requirement might be quite large. For this reason, if messages do have to be passed on with their blocks in sequence, the other method, *Go-back-N*, is more common.

With this mechanism, when the transmitter is informed of a block being received incorrectly, it retransmits it and continues transmission from that point even though it may already have transmitted some of the blocks.

Its operation is as follows:

1 Assume block with sequence number N is corrupted.

2 The receiver returns an acknowledgement block for each correctly received block.

3 On receipt of a block in error, the receiver will return a negative acknowledgement (NACK), plus the sequence number of the last block received correctly (N − 1). It will also ignore all blocks it has received since block N − 1.

4 The transmitter, on receipt of a NACK, will retransmit from block N and continue.

Note that if acknowledgement (ACK) blocks are corrupted, the effect is that the transmitter suddenly receives an ACK block out of sequence. Since it is an ACK block, it assumes that those acknowledgements which did not arrive were simply corrupted and so will use this acknowledgement block to acknowledge the others also.

In contrast with selective retransmission, this mechanism does not require a lot of buffer store at the receiver but does occasionally cause the retransmission of blocks which had, in fact, been received correctly. That is, it occasionally wastes bandwidth. However, because of the minimum storage requirements it is a common method where it is essential that the blocks are passed on in sequence.

15.3.2 SEQUENCE CONTROL

As has just been discussed, blocks being transmitted need sequence numbers in order to ensure both the correct sequence of received blocks and, in some cases, detect corrupted or 'lost' blocks. It has been assumed that the sequence numbers are integers starting at, say, 0. However, if a large number of messages, consisting of a large number of blocks is to be transmitted these sequence numbers could potentially get very large and hence require a large number of bits in the blocks being transmitted. Therefore, in order to limit the size of such sequence numbers they could be computed (incremented) using modulo *n* arithmetic, so that they cycle round a limited number of integers. For example, HDLC uses modulo 8 arithmetic for incrementing the sequence number so that they cycle round the digits 0 to 7. However, it is important to make sure that a new block is not given the same sequence number as a previous block which has not been acknowledged. Since this also implies a limit on the storage requirement for blocks (it means the receiver cannot store more than eight blocks), this restriction is handled by an appropriate flow control mechanism (see section 15.3.3).

In addition to the sequence number sent with a block or an acknowledgement, both the transmitter and receiver need to maintain an integer variable which in the case of the transmitter is the sequence number of the next block to be transmitted and, in the case of the receiver, is the sequence number of the next block that it should receive.

In order to introduce the principles simply, all the above discussion about ARQ mechanisms has assumed that blocks flow in one direction only, and that, therefore, the acknowledgements flow in the reverse direction. Typically, however, messages are being transmitted in both directions across a link, hence both ends are both receivers and transmitters. Therefore, each end of a link needs to maintain both of these sequence number variables, one for receiving and one for transmitting.

Also, if messages are being transmitted in both directions, then rather than sending a special acknowledge block, the appropriate acknowledge sequence number could be included in a block being transmitted in that direction. In this case, a block contains two sequence numbers. One is that of the block of data being transmitted and one is that of a previously transmitted block that is being acknowledged. This technique is known as *piggy-backing* and is intended to improve the efficiency of use of the link. The protocol HDLC uses such a technique (see section 15.5.1).

15.3.3   FLOW CONTROL

When two parties are communicating, the receiver clearly has to do something with the data blocks it is receiving. There may be occasions when it has not completed its tasks before the next data block arrives. For example, a printer receiving records into its print buffer will not be able to print the records as fast as they are arriving. Once its buffer is full it cannot accept any more. With the selective retransmission scheme described in section 15.3.1 the receiver has a fixed number of blocks which might become full before the out of sequence block is received. In both these cases the receiver will have to inform the transmitter that it cannot cope with more blocks and that it should therefore temporarily stop sending them. There are two common ways in which this can be achieved.

X-on/X-off

Consider the example of a printer, printing records sent to it by a computer. Clearly the computer may be able to supply records faster than the printer can print them even if the printer has a print buffer capable of storing a number of records. When the print buffer becomes full the printer will return a special character, X-off, to the computer indicating that the computer should stop transmission of records. When the buffer is emptied, the printer will then return another special character, X-on, indicating that the computer should recommence sending records.

The window mechanism

With the ARQ mechanisms described, there was a requirement for the receiver to store the received data blocks in order to allow the forwarding of the correct sequence of blocks, if a block has been transmitted in error. Assuming that there is a fixed amount of buffer storage at the receiver for this purpose, this imposes a limit on the number of blocks the transmitter can transmit without receiving an acknowledgement for any of them. This limit is also associated with the range of sequence numbers allowed (see section 15.3.2). The name given to this group of blocks is a *window* and the number of blocks is the *window size*. Figure 15.5 represents a window and how the window progresses along the blocks being transmitted as blocks are acknowledged.

The mechanism is implemented as follows:

1 The transmitter and receiver must agree on the window size for the link.

2 As the transmitter sends blocks it monitors the number of blocks it is storing in case they need retransmitting. (Remember that acknowledged blocks are removed from this store.)

3 When the number of blocks builds up to the window size the transmitter will cease to transmit blocks.

4 As acknowledgements are received and the blocks stored are reduced the transmitter can recommence transmission.

Note that if the window size is 1, the mechanism then becomes identical to the idle RQ method, since each block needs to be acknowledged before the next one is sent.

As mentioned above the window size is associated with the range of sequence numbers allowed.

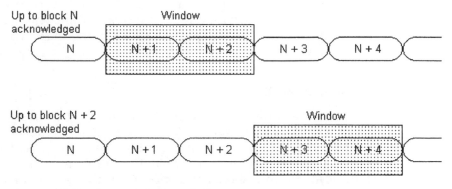

Figure 15.5 A transmission window

If the protocol uses the go-back-N mechanism and a window size of W, then the number of identifiers should be W + 1. To confirm this, imagine a link with a window size of 4. The transmitter sends blocks 0, 1, 2 and 3. They are received correctly and the receiver returns acknowledgements for all four. If the range of sequence numbers allowed was also 4 then the next sequence number that the receiver is expecting is 0 (using modulo 4 arithmetic). Unfortunately, all the four acknowledgements are 'lost' (corrupted) and so, on the occurrence of the time-out, the transmitter retransmits the original block 0. The receiver, on receipt of block 0, has no way of distinguishing between this repeated block 0 and the next block it was expecting (with sequence number 0). If, however, the range of sequence numbers was 5 (one more than the window size) it would be expecting sequence number 4 and so would know that block 0 was a repeat of the previous block 0.

If the protocol uses the selective retransmission mechanism and a window size of W, then the range identifiers should be 2W. This can be seen by a similar situation to the last example. Suppose the window size is 4 and all four blocks are sent but their acknowledgements are corrupted. All four blocks will then be retransmitted but the only way the receiver has of distinguishing these from the next four in sequence is if the next four in sequence have a completely different set of sequence numbers. Hence the sequence numbers must be 0, 1, 2, 3, 4, 5, 6, 7.

15.4 PROTOCOL TYPES

As has been discussed, data link protocols must be capable of detecting errors in strings of bits the contents of which, or meaning of which, is unknown. No method can be devised which can detect errors in a continuous arbitrary bit stream. In order to be able to detect errors the data is broken up into blocks and, typically, the block of data is transmitted together with some error control character(s) (for example, a CRC checksum). Another common term for such data blocks is a *frame*.

A number of schemes have been devised for separating data into frames ready for transmission. The aim of all of them is to preserve the transparency of user data. This means that if special characters or bit patterns are used to convey protocol meaning, some other mechanism is incorporated to allow that same bit pattern to be transmitted as part of the user data without causing confusion.

Three types of protocol, that is, three types of frame format, are now described and illustrated in Figure 15.6.

15.4.1 CHARACTER ORIENTED

This type of frame format assumes that the data being sent is a sequence of characters (groups of 8 bits) and it uses special characters to indicate the start of frame, the end of frame and other protocol information. Transparency is achieved as follows: the start of frame sequence is the pair of characters DLE and STX (see ASCII character set) and the end of frame is indicated by DLE ETX. To avoid the possible occurrence of this bit pattern in the user data

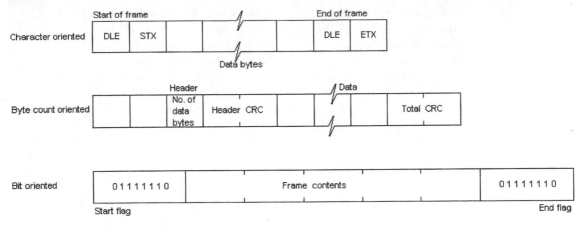

Figure 15.6 Three types of frame format

the transmitter will insert another DLE character after every occurrence of DLE in the user data. The receiver will recognise the end of frame by the occurrence of DLE ETX. Every other occurrence of a DLE (after the start of the frame) will be followed by another DLE, which the receiver will remove.

15.4.2 BYTE COUNT ORIENTED

This frame format precedes the data bytes with a header containing, amongst other information, a count of how many characters (bytes) are in the data field of the frame. The receiver then merely has to count the number of data bytes, continually comparing the count with this header field in order to determine the end of the frame. Because the header information has to be used correctly before the end of the frame is found, the header is usually terminated by its own CRC checksum, which is validated by the receiver before beginning to read the rest of the frame.

15.4.3 BIT ORIENTED (BIT STUFFING)

With a bit oriented frame format the data field does not have to be an integral number of bytes (although it often is). The start and end of the frame are delineated by a special 8-bit flag, consisting of the following bit pattern.

01111110

Transparency (making sure that this bit pattern cannot occur in the data) is achieved by the transmitter inserting a zero bit after any contiguous group of five one bits (apart from the final flag which it transmits after all the data bits have been transmitted). The receiver will remove any zero occurring after five contiguous ones. This technique is known as bit stuffing.

15.5 EXAMPLE LOWER LEVEL PROTOCOLS

15.5.1 HIGH-LEVEL DATA LINK CONTROL – HDLC

HDLC is a protocol which has been defined by the International Standards Organisation (ISO) for use on both point-to-point and multi-point data links. Historically, it was developed for links having one master station controlling one slave or a number of slaves. The master station is responsible for initiating all data transfers and for initialising and controlling the link. The master station in HDLC is called a *primary* and the slave a *secondary*. Figure 15.7 shows examples of such links. In a distributed network each node is of equal status to all other nodes and hence a balanced configuration with a combined station at each end of the link is possible. The combined station has the capabilities of both primary and secondary stations.

HDLC uses bit stuffing techniques for delimiting frames (see section 15.4.3). Many types of frames can be sent and received by stations and these are divided into *commands* and *responses*. Commands are sent by primary stations to secondary stations and responses are replies to commands returned by a secondary to a primary station. Figure 15.8 illustrates the frame format and the control byte layout for the three kinds of frame. The address field is used for addressing on multi-point lines (links connecting more than two devices). The control field is different for each of the three kinds of frame.

In *information* frames (the actual data being sent) the sequence and next fields contain the sequence number of the current frame and of the next frame expected respectively. In other words the *next* field is an acknowledge being piggy-backed on a data frame (see section 15.3.2). *Note* also that the sequence number is 3 bits long, indicating that HDLC uses modulo 8 sequence numbers. The window size depends on whether Go-back-N or selective retransmission is being used (it will support either depending on the supervisory frame). The checksum is a 16-bit CRC for the complete

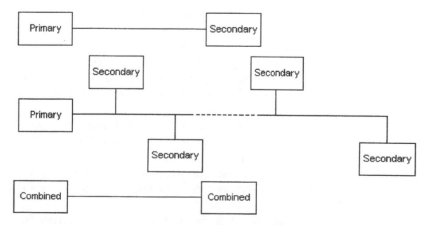

Figure 15.7 Primary and secondary stations in HDLC

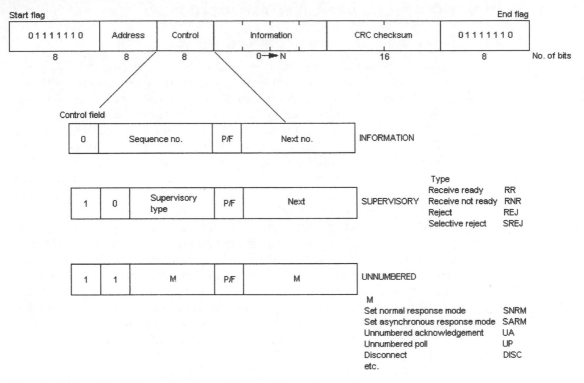

Figure 15.8 HDLC frame format and control byte layout

frame contents enclosed between the two flag delimiters. It uses the CCITT polynomial defined in section 13.7.3.

Supervisory frames are used for error and flow control purposes. When no reverse traffic is present on which to piggy-back acknowledgements, a Receive Ready (RR) supervisory frame is used (as an acknowledgement). The Receive Not Ready (RNR) frame is used to indicate that the transmitter should not send any more frames for the time being (flow control). Whether the receiver has just accepted the last one or not will depend on the sequence number returned with the RNR. REJect (REJ) and Selective REJect (SREJ) are used as negative acknowledgements with Go-back-N and selective retransmission error control mechanisms respectively.

The *unnumbered* frames (so called because they do not contain any sequence numbers) are used for such functions as link setup and disconnection.

The P/F bit in the control field is known as the *poll/final* bit. If a frame is sent by a primary station (a command frame) and the P/F bit is set to 1, it is called the poll bit and indicates that the receiver must acknowledge this frame at its earliest opportunity. The secondary station will respond by returning an appropriate response frame with the *final* bit (the P/F bit) set to 1.

As was indicated, the origins of HDLC are with protocols for multi-point configurations. Thus, what is referred to as the *Normal Response Mode* (NRM) of operation is that the secondary only transmits in response to a poll from the primary. A secondary gets permission to transmit frames when it receives a command from its primary with the poll bit set. It will then transmit a series of frames and indicate completion of this by setting the final bit to 1 in the last frame. The secondary must wait for another poll before it can transmit again. If the secondary has no data to transmit it returns an acknowledgement (RR – Receive Ready) with the final bit set to 1.

There also exists an *Asynchronous Response Mode* (ARM). In this mode a secondary can transmit at will without having to wait for a poll.

As an example of the operation of HDLC, consider a multi-point link operating using NRM and with a Go-back-N mechanism for error control. A logical connection between the two communicating parties needs to be set up first, then the data transferred and, finally, the link closed down. It would operate as follows:

1   The primary station sends a Set Normal Response Mode (SNRM) frame with the poll bit set to 1 and an appropriate secondary address in the address field.

2   The secondary station will respond with a UA frame (an unnumbered acknowledgement) with the final bit set and its own address in the address field.

3   This exchange also causes both the primary and the secondary station to initialise to zero their sequence variables.

4   The primary station then sends a UP frame (unnumbered poll) with the poll bit set to 1.

5   If the secondary has no data to transmit, it returns an RNR frame with the P/F-bit set.

6   If it has data waiting, it transmits the data as a sequence of Information frames with the P/F-bit set to 1 in the last frame of the sequence.

7   Each frame is eventually acknowledged and the sequence number can be used for detection of errors, with subsequent Go-back-N request (REJ) as described in sections 15.3.1 and 15.3.2.

8   When the primary receives the last frame (with P/F set to 1) the link is cleared by the primary sending a disconnect frame (DISC) and the secondary acknowledging that with a UA.

Whilst the above mechanism may be satisfactory for a terminal network, in a network of communicating computers each station has equal status and needs to act in combined mode. This is known in HDLC as *asynchronous balanced mode* (ABM). In this case, information frames can be flowing in both directions and so the acknowledgement information can be piggy-backed onto information frames which are going in the opposite direction.

15.5.2   X.25

The X.25 protocol was developed in the 1970s by the CCITT, as the ITU-T was formerly known. It is used to connect devices with DTE and DCE interfaces to packet switched data networks. Data is broken up into packets

Figure 15.9   An X.25 network

Figure 15.10   Electronic point of sale application using X.25

and sent over virtual circuits. It is in fact a set of three protocols which correspond to the first three layers of the ISO OSI reference model. The data link layer protocol of X.25, LAP-B (Link Access Protocol B), is very similar to HDLC. An X.25 network is shown in Figure 15.9.

There are two kinds of virtual circuit. A *switched virtual circuit* (SVC) is a temporary connection between two DTEs. The call is set up by sending a call request to the destination address. Then a call accept returns with a virtual circuit number. The data is transferred and finally the call is cleared. Each virtual circuit (VC) number has 12 bits. This allows up to 4095 simultaneous VCs from one DTE (VC 0 is reserved). *Permanent virtual circuits* (PVCs) are much longer lasting than SVCs. They are set up by the X.25 network provider between two DTEs and provided on fixed VC numbers. No call setup or call clearing are required for PVCs. PVCs are useful when the network configuration is relatively static.

X.25 is useful for low-bandwidth applications requiring no guarantees in terms of latency (delay) and jitter (variation in delay). X.25 is not suitable for voice or video because it suffers from latency and jitter. It is used for terminal access. An example is credit card checking in Electronic Point of Sale (EPOS) applications. This is illustrated in Figure 15.10. In the United Kingdom X.25 is used to connect National Lottery terminals in shops to the central computer centres.

15.5.3   FRAME RELAY

Frame relay is a high-speed communications technology that is widely used to connect LAN, Internet and even voice applications. X.25 was designed for use with unreliable analogue networks, and so checks for errors are done link by link throughout a packet's route. When frame relay was developed there was no longer any need to do this because error-checking could be done by higher-layer protocols (such as TCP) instead. Also, since networks are mainly

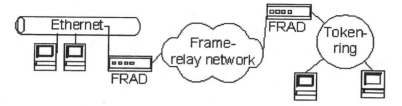

Figure 15.11 The use of frame relay access devices

digital there are few errors in the first place. Frame relay data is sent in frames (packets). An HDLC-derived protocol, LAP-F, is used to perform a similar function in frame relay to that performed by LAP-B in X.25.

In similar fashion to X.25, data is sent on virtual circuits (SVCs or PVCs). PVCs are commonly used to construct virtual private networks (VPNs), which provide the equivalent of a private network but actually run over a public network. Much higher data rates are possible than with X.25. Frame relay service agreements define what is expected of the network. If the agreement is breached then this can be seen as a breach of contract and monetary compensation is required. Frame Relay Access Devices (FRADs) are used to connect to the network. These can often do TCP/IP routing in addition to their basic function. Frame relay is suitable for high speed traffic which occurs in bursts. This makes it useful for LAN interconnection and FRADs can be used as is shown in Figure 15.11.

15.5.4 INTERNET PROTOCOL – IP

The most widely used protocol is the Internet Protocol (IP). It was developed originally in the mid 1970s for the US Department of Defense, in order to provide wide area host-to-host communications in a heterogeneous environment (that is, using computers from different manufacturers). It was designed to be fault tolerant in case of war. Originally, it was heavily based on UNIX systems. In conjunction with other related protocols, first and foremost the Transport Control Protocol (TCP), it provides a framework for interconnection and interoperation regardless of the platform or the physical network medium. IP is the underlying protocol of the Internet but is also widely used in other contexts, for example in LANs. In terms of the OSI seven-layer model, it is a layer 3 protocol. IP provides a connectionless service across a mixture of potentially diverse networks.

The service provided by the IP protocol is responsible for moving packets from source to destination across the network. Sometimes a packet may be too big for a particular section of network that it has to traverse, and so the packet has to be *fragmented*, that is chopped up into smaller pieces. The packet later has to be *re-assembled* (put back together again). The IP service is responsible for dealing with fragmentation and re-assembly of packets across small packet subnets (groups of addresses). Fragmentation and re-assembly are illustrated in Figure 15.12.

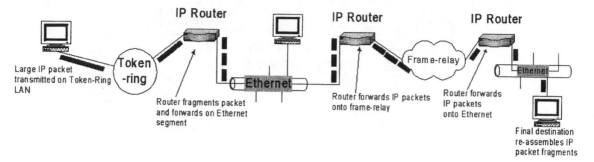

Figure 15.12   IP packet fragmentation and re-assembly across an internet

IP is a datagram protocol; it does not guarantee delivery, guarantee sequence of delivery or control the flow of packets into the network. The IP protocol is not dependent on any particular hardware and is ideally suited to integrate LANs and WANs into one network.

IPv4 addressing

The IP addresses are independent of the hardware addresses (for example, Ethernet addresses) contained within a packet. The version of IP that is currently the most widely used is IP Version 4 (IPv4). Four decimal numbers (one for each byte) separated by dots are used to represent IPv4 addresses, for example 192.0.64.111. Since each number is a byte its range is 0–255. So far as computers are concerned, of course, the IP address is simply a 32-bit binary number. The dotted decimal version is used in an attempt to make the addresses more comprehensible to humans. The address is split into two parts: network identifier and host identifier. Routers (computers used for connecting networks together) use the network identifier to route a packet, that is to decide on which of the router's interfaces the packet should be sent out.

The addresses can be split up into network and host part in a number of standard ways. In a class A address, the first byte is the network identifier and the other three bytes are the host identifier. This means that only a small number of class A networks is available. These were all assigned a number of years ago to large organisations such as the US government. With a class B address, the split between network and host comes in the middle of the 32 bits. In a class C address, the first three bytes are used to identify the network and the last byte to identify the host. Table 15.1 contains details of the IPv4 address classes.

IPv6

A huge number of class C networks is available, but, even so, this number is not great enough to satisfy the demand. This is one reason why IP Version 6 (IPv6) has been developed. Among other features designed to make IP more suitable for modern requirements, IPv6 has 128-bit addressing,

Table 15.1 IPv4 address classes

Class	Network IDs	Host IDs	Address range
A	126 0 & 127 reserved	16,777,214 0 & 16,777,215 reserved	1.0.0.0 to 126.255.255.254
B	16,382 0 & 16,383 reserved	65,534 0 & 65,535 reserved	128.0.0.0 to 191.255.255.255
C	2,097,152 0 & 2,097,153 reserved	254 0 and 255 reserved	192.0.0.0 to 223.255.255.255
D		268,435,456 multicast addresses	224.0.0.0 to 239.255.255.255
E			240.0.0.0 to 247.255.255.255

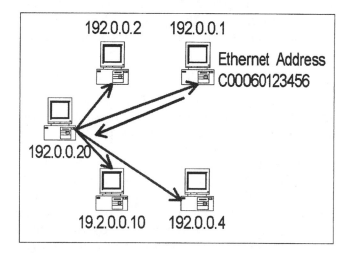

Figure 15.13 ARP request to station 192.0.0.1

which permits approximately 3.4×10^{38} addresses, a vastly greater number than IPv4.

15.5.5 ADDRESS RESOLUTION PROTOCOL – ARP

When IP packets are sent over a network, they are encapsulated in data link LAN or WAN frames such as Ethernet, Token ring or ATM. Somehow, the sending computer has to find out the correct data link layer destination address (for example, Ethernet address) to put in the frame. It does this by using the Address Resolution Protocol (ARP) to map from the IP destination address to the Ethernet destination address. The host broadcasts an ARP request packet that contains the IP address of the required station. The station that has that IP address replies directly (unicast) returning the correct IP address. Now the IP packet can be sent directly to the correct Ethernet address. An ARP request is shown in Figure 15.13.

15.5.6 REVERSE ADDRESS RESOLUTION PROTOCOL – RARP

RARP allows a station to determine its IP address from its hardware address.

A server can be configured to respond to RARP requests automatically, allocating IP addresses across the network. Usually, however, more powerful auto-configuration protocols such as the Dynamic Host Configuration Protocol, which is discussed in section 15.6.4, are used instead.

15.6 HIGHER LEVEL PROTOCOLS

Section 12.5 described the ISO reference model as having three lower level layers which are network dependent, three upper level layers which are end-user orientated, with a linking layer, the transport layer, which provides the link between the communications network and the end user. The TCP/IP suite of protocols predated the OSI 7-layer model and its hierarchy of layers is somewhat simpler. There are no direct equivalents of the session or presentation layers. The TCP/IP protocol stack is illustrated in Figure 15.14.

15.6.1 TRANSMISSION CONTROL PROTOCOL – TCP

Transmission control protocol (TCP) establishes sessions between end user processes and provides a reliable, connection-oriented transfer of data. It approximates to OSI layer 4, the transport layer.

The service that the Transmission Control Protocol (TCP) provides guarantees end-to-end delivery of packets. It controls the flow of data from host to host and from the host into the network. It also provides multiplexing: the TCP header has a port number which is used to determine which application should receive the packet. If several applications, say, an e-mail package and two web browsers (Netscape and Internet Explorer) are running on a computer, when a TCP/IP packet arrives, which application should receive the packet? The answer is that each application sets up its connection using a different port number. When the replies come back from the server the port number is used to send the packet to the correct connection. A client knows which server port to send its request to because 'well-known port numbers' are assigned to particular services. Examples of well-known port numbers are 23 (Telnet – for remote terminal sessions), 21/20 (FTP – for file transfer) and 25/110 (SMTP/POP – for electronic mail). Well-known port numbers are illustrated in Figure 15.15. Each application is allocated a different port number by the TCP software.

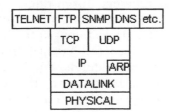

Figure 15.14 TCP/IP protocol stack

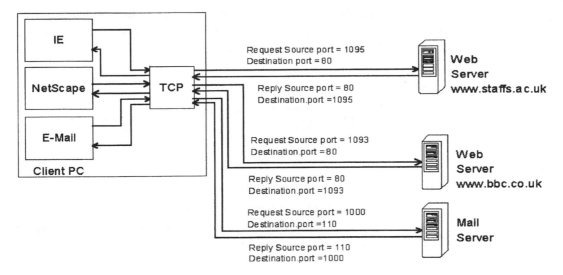

Figure 15.15 Well-known port numbers

TCP also provides error control. The acknowledgement and sequence number fields are used to guarantee delivery of packets to the destination. For each packet sent out, an acknowledgement must be sent back. If no acknowledgement is sent back within a certain time the packet is sent again. By default, TCP uses a selective retransmission policy. (Selective retransmission was explained in section 15.3.1.) Each new packet to be transmitted is allocated a new sequence number. The returning acknowledgement number informs the sender of the next expected sequence number. The sequence number is used to keep the packets in order.

TCP provides flow control. A window size field is used by the receiver to control the flow of packets from the sender. If the receiver sets the window size to 400 the sender is only allowed to send 400 bytes before stopping. The receiver can stop the sender by setting the window size to 0. (Window size was explained in section 15.3.3.)

15.6.2 USER DATAGRAM PROTOCOL – UDP

The User Datagram Protocol (UDP) is an alternative to TCP that provides a much simpler service. It provides port allocations, just as TCP does, but it guarantees neither delivery nor sequencing. TCP is more commonly used than UDP, but UDP comes in useful when speed is more important than reliability. Internet telephony is a good example of an application where UDP is used rather than TCP.

15.6.3 DOMAIN NAME SYSTEM – DNS

It is rather difficult for humans to remember IP addresses. The purpose of the Domain Name System (DNS) is to translate easier-to-remember text names, for example www.soc.staffs.ac.uk, into IP addresses, for example, 128.10.20.30. When a host requires a domain name translation it makes the request to its local Domain Name Server.

Domain naming

Each name in the DNS can be split up into a series of domains. For example, the address www.soc.staffs.ac.uk is made up of the following components:

uk = domain of the UK;

ac.uk = academic domain within the UK;

staffs.ac.uk = Staffordshire University domain within UK academic;

soc.staffs.ac.uk = School of Computing domain within Staffordshire University within UK academic.

Domain name servers

Each domain name server is responsible for a different domain. The first request for the translation of an address will go to the server in the local machine's domain. The DNS server can react in one of three different ways: directly, recursively or indirectly. If the local DNS server knows the correct IP address, it can simply return it *directly* to the requesting host. If the DNS server does not know the IP address, it has to make a request to another DNS server for the address. One possibility is that when the local server has discovered the IP address from the other server, the local server then sends the address back to the host. This is a *recursive* query. Alternatively, the local DNS server could send back the IP address of another DNS server which knows the answer. The host then sends the address translation request to this server. This is an *indirect* query. The three types of DNS query are illustrated in Figures 15.16–15.18.

15.6.4 DYNAMIC HOST CONFIGURATION PROTOCOL – DHCP

DHCP allows a client's IP address to be configured automatically over the network. This means that machines do not have to have been configured by hand. The advantages of this are that new machines can be added to the IP network more easily and there is less chance of error (for example, duplicate IP addresses being configured). A DHCP server is used to do this.

15.6.5 HYPERTEXT TRANSFER PROTOCOL – HTTP

HTTP is used to transfer pages of WorldWide Web information. In an HTTP transfer, a TCP/IP connection is first set up from the client to the server. The GET command (format: get <filename>) is then used to retrieve data from the server. At this point the TCP/IP connection is broken. Alternatively, the HTTP POST command can be used to transfer data from browser to server.

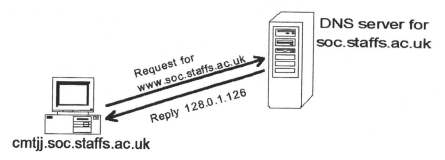

Figure 15.16 Direct DNS query

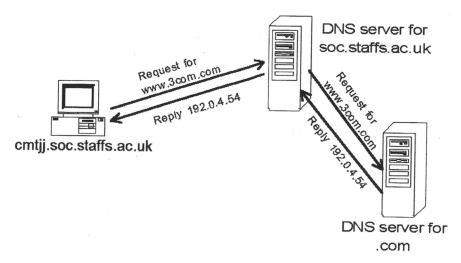

Figure 15.17 Recursive DNS query

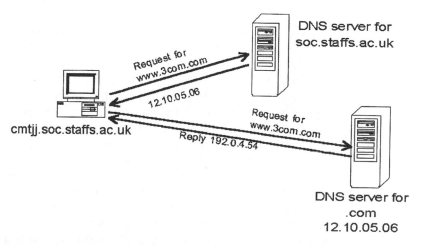

Figure 15.18 Indirect DNS query

Table 15.2   FTP commands

FTP Command	Purpose
open <remote_machine_name>	opens connection to remote machine
dir or **ls**	lists the contents of a directory
cd <directory_name>	changes the current directory on the remote machine
close	closes the connection
get <filename>	copies a file from the remote machine to the local machine
put <filename>	copies a file from the local machine to the remote machine
lcd <directory_name>	changes the current directory on the local machine

15.6.6   FILE TRANSFER PROTOCOL – FTP

The File Transfer Protocol (FTP) allows the user to download files from, or upload files to, an FTP server. The interface can be command-line, WIMP-based or Web browser-based. Users must log in, allowing the server to control file access via user permissions. An anonymous FTP service, where the user does not need an account on the host, is widely offered on the Internet. Files can be of any format, text or binary. Most host machines are UNIX based and accept UNIX shell commands. Table 15.2 shows some FTP commands.

15.6.7   NETWORK FILE SYSTEM – NFS

NFS is a distributed file system protocol developed by Sun Microsystems for use in a Unix environment. Some network systems provide a very simple method for exchanging files, where one needs special commands to access remote files and where a transfer operation involves taking a copy of the file, leading to multiple copies with all the attendant problems of different versions. Other systems may have a distributed operating system allowing easy access to files wherever they are but all the nodes need to run the same operating system. NFS is designed to allow *transparent* access to files from any node on the network even if they are different computers running different operating systems. Transparent access means that they appear to the user just as if they are local files. Indeed the user does not need to have any knowledge as to where the files are actually stored. NFS was designed independently of the operating system and underlying network and hence is not a network operating system but a network service.

In order to enable this transparency Sun developed an interface which consists of a virtual file system (VFS) interface, which defines the operations on the file system and a virtual node interface, which defines the operations on a file or directory within the file system. They also developed an external data representation (XDR) which defines the size, byte order and other data representation functions in order to make the system machine independent and encourage heterogeneous networks.

A typical network using NFS would consist of a number of workstations all running Unix and a number of personal computers running Microsoft® Windows®.

15.7 ELECTRONIC MAIL

The components of an electronic mail (e-mail) system are user agents and message transfer agents. The *user agent* allows users to compose, send and transmit mail messages. The *message transfer agent* moves mail messages from the source to the destination. E-mail transfer is done on a store-and-forward basis. Each MTA stores the message before forwarding it on to its destination. Figure 15.19 illustrates user agents and message transfer agents.

When forwarding the message, a new TCP connection is set up for each MTA to MTA hop. E-mail addressing is usually done using the Internet standard, for example J.Smith@soc.staffs.ac.uk. However, other standards exist, for example, X.400. An example of an e-mail envelope and message can be seen in Figure 15.20.

15.7.1 SIMPLE MAIL TRANSFER PROTOCOL – SMTP

The Simple Mail Transfer Protocol (SMTP) is the standard protocol for sending electronic mail over the Internet. Potentially, it could also be used to retrieve mail from a server, but normally other protocols, such as the *Post Office Protocol (POP)* or the *Internet Message Access Protocol (IMAP)*, are used to do this. The SMTP header contains forward and reverse paths. To route a packet to the destination the forward path is defined (SMTP command TO: <forward_path>. An SMTP hub delivers a message to an address by doing a DNS lookup (see section 15.6.3) to find out which machine handles mail for that address. Then a TCP call is made to that machine.

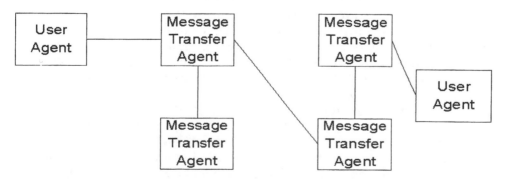

Figure 15.19 User agents and message transfer agents

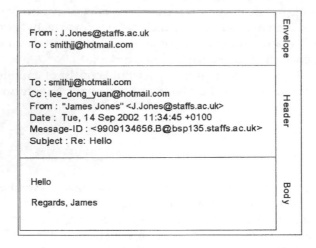

Figure 15.20 An e-mail envelope and message

15.7.2 MULTI-PURPOSE INTERNET MAIL EXTENSIONS – MIME

Standard e-mail messages are expected to be delivered in ASCII plain text format. This may be a problem for some messages, so the Multi-purpose Internet Mail Extensions (MIME) are commonly used. MIME allows messages in different languages (with added accents or different character sets such as Chinese or Japanese). It also allows binary messages, audio or video for example, to be encoded.

15.8 SUMMARY

This chapter has introduced the need for protocols, their various functional tasks and the concepts of protocol levels. It has then looked in detail at some major protocol functions. A number of examples of real protocols from various levels of the OSI model have been studied, although it must be recognised that since protocols tend to be very complex only the major features of the examples have been introduced.

Hardware is available which performs all the framing functions of link level protocols including insertion and removal of characters or bits for transparency and calculation of the CRC. In packet switched networks where the information is transported in discrete units, the use of these link level protocols does not require any additional processing to divide the data into blocks for transmission.

As has been indicated, various standards bodies are continuously working on developing and enhancing their standards and vendors are continuing to develop their products, increasingly in line with international standards. Hence, any text such as this cannot be absolutely up to date so it is essential to check on the latest position of both the standards bodies and the vendors.

15.9   EXERCISES

1   Explain the difference between data terminating equipment (DTE) and data communications equipment (DCE).

A DTE computer is to be connected to a public switched telephone network via an EIA/TIA-232 modem which provides the following interface circuits: GND, TXD, RXD, DSR, DTR, CD, RI.

Explain the functions of the circuits, indicating whether they are from the DCE to the DTE or from the DTE to the DCE. Outline the software you would write to enable the computer to detect an incoming call and respond suitably.

How would you detect and respond to call termination by:

a   the remote party hanging up?

b   the computer terminating the call?

What problems might arise if the incoming call was a wrong number? How would your software cope?

2   a   Indicate why protocols are necessary in data communications and name the main functions a protocol must embody, giving a brief definition of each.

b   Explain why transparency may be a problem within a protocol and give two examples of how this problem may be overcome.

3   In the HDLC communications protocol explain:

a   the difference between the normal response mode (NRM), asynchronous response mode (ARM) and asynchronous balanced mode (ABM) of operation. When might they be used?

b   how software would distinguish between the I, S and U classes of frame.

c   how data transparency is achieved.

d   how the SREJ mechanism may be used to improve the efficiency of flow control error recovery.

4   Using available computers which have a serial I/O port and a suitable programming language (e.g., 'C') develop the software for a file transfer utility to transfer files from one machine to another over the serial link. Incorporate a robust protocol which exhibits all the major features described in this chapter. Investigate methods of introducing burst errors into the transmission in order that its robustness can be demonstrated.

5   a   Describe the sliding window technique.

b   For a data link the parameter x can be defined as

$$x = \frac{\text{signal propagation delay}}{\text{frame transmission time}}$$

Draw two sets of diagrams:

   one set for the case $W > 1 + 2x$,

   one set for the case $W < 1 + 2x$,

   where W is the window size,

to show the following events during frame transmission on a data link which uses a sliding window protocol:

(1)   Start of transmission of frame 1 by the sending station.

(2)   Arrival of leading bit of frame 1 at the receiving station.

(3)   Complete absorption of frame 1 and acknowledgement of frame 1 by the receiving station.

(4)   Arrival of the acknowledgement at the sending station.

Indicate on your diagrams the times, relative to the time T_0 of the first event, at which the subsequent events occur.

c   From these diagrams, derive expressions for the utilisation of an error free data link which uses a sliding window protocol.

If P is the probability that a frame will be in error show that the utilisation U for selective retransmission ARQ is given by:

$$U = 1 - P \text{ when } W > 1 + 2x$$

or

$$U = \frac{W(1 - P)}{1 + 2x} \text{ when } W < 1 + 2x$$

d   A series of frames with a mean length of 1000 bits is to be transmitted across a data link of length 100 km at a data rate of 10Mbps. If the velocity of propagation of the link is 2×10^8 m/s and the bit error rate is 1×10^{-4}, determine the link efficiency for a sliding window protocol with a window size of 3 and using selective retransmit ARQ.

6   Locate copies of the IETF's RFCs – a likely source is the Internet – and study the way in which the TCP/IP protocols are specified.

7   If you have access to a UNIX system, find out about the following commands (by consulting the appropriate manual pages) and then try out the commands. If you have access to a Microsoft® Windows® system, then try out the alternative commands given in parentheses.

nslookup (Windows equivalent: nslookup (not available on Win 9x or Mc));
ifconfig – a (Windows equivalent: ipconfig /all or winipcfg, depending on the version of Windows);
ping (Windows equivalent: ping);
traceroute (Windows equivalent: tracert).

8   Find out how to use the following ways of invoking FTP interactively, and then try them out if possible:

by pointing a Web browser (e.g., Netscape, Internet Explorer) at an FTP server;
by entering a command at the system prompt;
via a GUI-based FTP application (for example, WS-FTP).

Try out both anonymous and non-anonymous file transfer with the last two options.

16 Installing and managing a local area network

This chapter builds upon preceding chapters in considering what is involved in installing a simple local area network (LAN). Just as Chapter 11 made use of concepts introduced in Chapters 1 to 8, this chapter also builds on ideas covered in previous chapters. For example, the coverage of interrupts (Chapter 9), cabling (13.6.1), microwave transmission (13.6.3) and broadcast networks (14.2) are all relevant to this chapter. The current chapter also refers to some of the topics covered in Chapter 11, for example, the installation of adaptor cards in a PC and uninterruptible power supplies. A fresh topic, network management, is also covered.

Firstly, overall LAN design decisions are discussed and then detailed decisions are suggested/outlined. Next, preparing the site for the installation is covered, followed by cable installation. Workstation and server installation, customising the server operating system and installing the applications are also discussed.

Managing the network is also considered. Functional areas of network management are described, followed by Simple Network Management Protocol. Finally, there is a brief section on network security.

16.1 INSTALLING A LAN

A local area network (LAN) is a network that is often restricted to a small geographical area, such as an office, a building or a university campus. Normally, the whole of a LAN is owned and controlled by one organisation. A LAN connects computers and peripherals so that the users can share them. Users can also share programs and data from other users on the network and are often able to share connections to other networks.

The essential parts of a LAN are:

a network interface card – installed in a server;

a network interface card – installed in workstations (desktop computers);

a communication path or network medium such as copper and/or fibre;

a network operating system (NOS);

data and services to share.

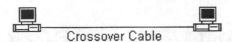

Figure 16.1 Connecting two computers with a crossover cable

Note the term *workstation* is sometimes given a more specialised meaning than in this text. It is also used to refer to a UNIX desktop machine in particular.

16.1.1 OVERALL DESIGN DECISIONS

In designing a network, there are fundamental decisions to be made. Type of network, cabling media, topology and network operating system must all be decided upon. Different types of network (for example, varieties of Ethernet) were discussed in Chapter 14. Ethernet is the most common choice for a LAN, with several nominal data rates on offer (e.g., 10 Mbps, 100 Mbps, 1000 Mbps). Cabling media were discussed in Chapter 13.6. UTP cabling is the default choice here.

Cabling

The standard way of connecting up a LAN is to use Cat 5 UTP cable and RJ-45 connectors. The various devices are then linked together via a *hub*. (This is illustrated in Chapter 14, Figure 14.5.) However, if there are only two devices to be connected, the simplest way is to use a *crossover cable*. If a crossover cable is used, then there is no need for a hub at all. This is shown in Figure 16.1. The ends of a crossover cable are different from each other, but the normal *straight through* cable that is used with a hub has identical ends. When using a hub the transmit and receive wires are crossed over inside the hub, but if there is no hub, this crossing over has to be done by the cable.

Wireless LANs

One way of dealing with the problem of cabling is to do away with the need for cables altogether. WLANs are a particularly attractive way for portable computers to communicate. A portable machine can be carried round a building and still be connected to the LAN, instead of having to be attached to a cable via an adaptor. WLANs allow temporary networks to be set up and dismantled very rapidly. If a WLAN is used, an architecturally important (listed) building does not need to be disfigured by cables. WLANs are commonly used in airports, hotels and conference centres.

Either infrared or radio transmission can be used in WLANs although radio is the more popular by far. In infrared transmission, the technology is that which is used for remote controls for TVs. A great advantage of infrared

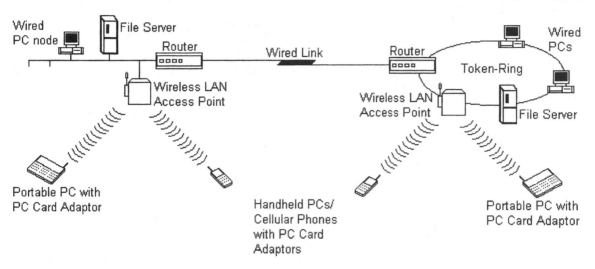

Figure 16.2 802.11b WLAN access

is that its use is not regulated as is radio. However, its disadvantages are that it needs line-of-sight transmission/reception and that it can be used only within a room.

Radio WLANs are the most promising form of WLAN, but there is a serious potential security problem from eavesdroppers. To alleviate the security problem two techniques are used: direct sequence spread spectrum (DSSS) and frequency hopping spread spectrum (FHSS). In DSSS each bit is represented as an encoded group of bits that are simultaneously transmitted on a number of different frequencies. The power level is so low that each individual transmission is lost in the normal background noise. A popular standard for WLANs is IEEE 802.11b, which provides Ethernet at up to 11 Mbps over a wireless network. IEEE 802.11b uses DSSS transmission in the 2.4 GHz microwave band, which does not need a licence. 802.11b WLAN access is illustrated in Figure 16.2.

FHSS uses stronger signals transmitted in a pseudo random sequence on a range of frequencies. The receiver has to keep exactly in step with the transmitter and be on the same frequency as the transmitter at a given time. Bluetooth wireless technology uses FHSS transmission in the 2.4 GHz band. Bluetooth provides very short-range links between mobile computers, mobile phones and other portable handheld devices, as well as connectivity to the Internet.

Topology

The topology (layout) of the network must be considered. Various network topologies were discussed in Chapter 12. If Ethernet is chosen, star wiring is the usual choice.

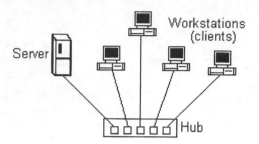

Figure 16.3 Server-based LAN

Network operating system (NOS)

In addition to hardware, a LAN needs software to make it complete. LAN software falls into three categories: computer operating system, network operating system and applications. The network operating system (NOS) is software that controls the interaction of the LAN workstations with the server and with each other. It interprets data from the network and presents it to the local operating system as if it were local. The dominant NOS for PC LANs is Microsoft® Windows®. Novell NetWare® is another example of a NOS.

Peer-to-peer and server-based networks

In a server-based network, each workstation relies on a dedicated computer to provide such functions as printing or file storage. A typical server-based network is shown in Figure 16.3. The computers that use network resources are sometimes called 'clients'; the devices that service the clients are called 'servers'. (The terms *client* and *server* are also used to refer to programs. Here, a client is any program that needs the services of a server.) Not all LANs have a dedicated server, however. Peer-to-peer networks make do without one. (The term *peer-to-peer* is also used to refer to a system that allows users to share files over the Internet without a central server.)

In a peer-to-peer LAN, each computer shares data and resources with other computers on an equal footing. The client/server computer relationship is not fixed, as it is in the case of a server-based LAN. A given workstation may be acting as a client, say, at a certain time, and may then switch over to act as a server. Indeed, a machine may act as client and server at the same time. For example, it may simultaneously be using a printer that is attached to another machine, while that machine is accessing the first machine's hard disk. A typical peer-to-peer network is shown in Figure 16.4.

Peer-to-peer PC LANs are often of a lower specification and slower than server-based LANs, as well as being easier to set up and cheaper to purchase. They are used for smaller workgroups than server-based LANs. Peer-to-peer networks usually consist of no more than ten machines. Microsoft® Windows® is often used to set up peer-to-peer LANs (as well as server-based

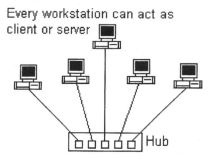

Figure 16.4   Peer-to-peer LAN

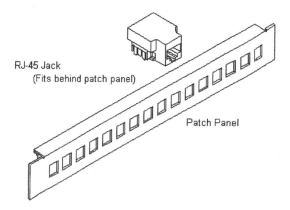

Figure 16.5   Patch panel

LANs). In this case it is unnecessary to purchase a server version of Windows®. Incidentally, UNIX/LINUX-based systems are peer-to-peer.

16.1.2   DETAILED DESIGN DECISIONS

Once the overall decisions have been taken, the details need to be considered. If a server-based network has been chosen, the number of servers and their location must be decided on. Irrespective of whether the LAN is peer-to-peer or client/server, a decision is needed on how many workstations and where they are to be located. The same goes for network printers.

A network diagram should be drawn up. This will show the locations of wiring closets, assuming that the network is of sufficient size to need these. A *wiring closet* is a special room where racks of equipment such as patch panels, hubs and routers are kept out of harm's way. A *patch panel* acts as a miniature switchboard that is used to organise the wiring in the closet. RJ-45 jacks (sockets) are mounted on the patch panel. RJ-45 plugs and UTP cable are then used to connect pieces of equipment together. A patch panel is illustrated in Figure 16.5.

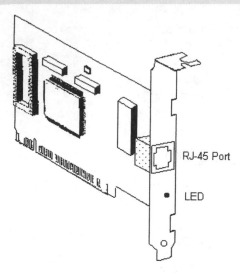

Figure 16.6 Network interface card

Network interface cards

Decisions need to be made about the network interface cards that will be used for the network. NICs, sometimes called *adaptors*, or *controller cards*, are circuit boards that plug into each LAN workstation. They enable a connection to be made via a cable or some other medium. The NIC performs three important functions. Firstly, it encodes the data according to the rules that have been defined for the physical medium (i.e. the cable system or other medium). Secondly, it makes sure that only one computer transmits at a time. Thirdly, it detects transmission errors.

There are several kinds of NIC. Firstly, the NIC varies according to which kind of media access (usually Ethernet) is used. Secondly, there are different kinds of NIC for the various types of PC bus (for example, ISA (Industry Standard Architecture – an older bus than PCI) or PCI (Peripheral Component Interface – a vastly superior bus to ISA). Thus, there is a choice of 8-, 16-, 32- or 64-bit cards. Thirdly, the cabling used will determine what kind of connectors the NIC has. With Ethernet, for example, there is a choice of twisted pair or fibre optic cabling. Most cards come complete with drivers for the most popular NOSs and networking software. NICs are usually configured by software. A typical NIC is shown in Figure 16.6.

Hubs, switches and routers

Decisions need to be taken about the installation of hubs and routers. (These devices were described in Chapters 12, 14 and 15.) It may also be necessary or desirable to install one or more layer-2 *switches* in the network. The switches function at OSI Layer-2 and are used to connect LAN segments. They build up tables of MAC addresses and can thus determine on which segment a frame should be transmitted. They allow several users to

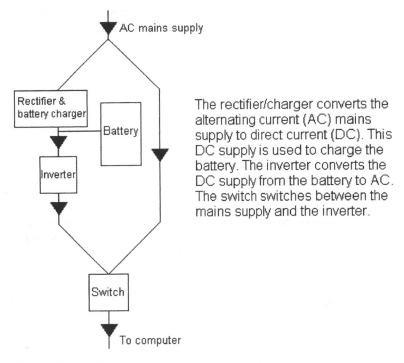

The rectifier/charger converts the alternating current (AC) mains supply to direct current (DC). This DC supply is used to charge the battery. The inverter converts the DC supply from the battery to AC. The switch switches between the mains supply and the inverter.

Figure 16.7 Uninterruptible power supply

communicate in parallel, with no collisions. In the case of Ethernet, a switch will usually have the effect of increasing the available bandwidth in the network.

16.1.3 PREPARING THE SITE

Computer equipment needs an electricity supply, so it is important to check that a sufficient number of electrical power sockets is available. Each circuit should be able to handle the load to which it will be subjected. Network printers, hubs, switches and routers all need power as well as the computers. Servers should be on a separate circuit. If it is important that the network remains working all the time, it is desirable to fit an *Uninterruptible Power Supply (UPS)*. A UPS is designed to provide an uninterrupted power source in the event of a power failure. If there is a power cut, the UPS will keep the server running from its battery. A UPS is illustrated in Figure 16.7. Finally, it is important to check that there is enough room for the LAN cables in the available conduit and that building regulations permit cables in open ceilings.

16.1.4 CABLE INSTALLATION

The first decision to make about installing the cable is who is going to do the job. It is often possible to do it in-house but it may be better to use a specialist cabling installer. If the installation is done on a do-it-yourself basis, it is important to be aware of possible sources of interference and crosstalk, especially with UTP cable. The cables must be fastened securely and both ends must be labelled. A clear and detailed record of cable runs and patch panel connections should be made.

16.1.5   WORKSTATION AND SERVER INSTALLATION

The LAN workstation

The LAN workstation might be a PC, an Apple Macintosh or a high-performance UNIX machine. Here we will concentrate on PC LANs, however, since these are by far the most commonly encountered kind of computer. The LAN workstation will normally be of a lower specification than the server computer, if there is a dedicated server. The workstation may have a network capability built in or it may need a NIC added to it.

Each workstation on the LAN will be running its own operating system. In the case of PC networks, Microsoft® Windows® is the most common workstation operating system. However, other operating systems are also used.

Installing network software

Irrespective of whether the LAN is peer-to-peer or client/server, every workstation has to have network client software installed on it. Usually, this software is part of the operating system. It lets the system use the NIC to communicate with other machines.

The LAN server

As we saw in section 16.1.1, in a server-based network, each workstation relies on a dedicated computer to provide such functions as printing or file storage. There are many different types of server computer but the file server is the most common. The server holds the bulk of the operating system and shares its resources with the workstations. A server has a big, fast hard disk, which is used by many workstations. The disk has to be relatively fast because of the work it has to do. In any computer system, the disk tends to be a bottleneck because it has mechanical components that cannot keep up with the processor, which is a purely electronic device. In a server-based LAN, this problem can be magnified if the disk is inadequate.

In many LANs an ordinary high-specification PC is used as the server but there are also machines that have been deliberately designed to function as servers. These may have more than one processor. If there are multiple processors the operating system may handle them by using *symmetric multiprocessing*. In symmetric multiprocessing the operating system's scheduler assigns tasks to available processors on a first come, first served basis. Any processor can run any task. Symmetric multiprocessing is contrasted with

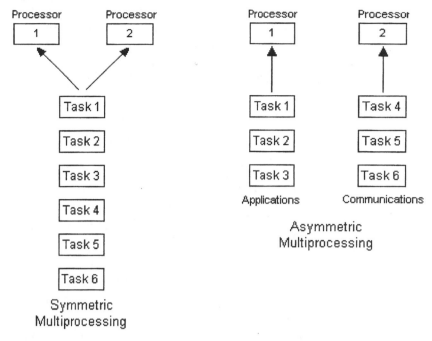

Figure 16.8 Symmetric and asymmetric multiprocessing

asymmetric multiprocessing in Figure 16.8. In asymmetric multiprocessing the tasks are not shared out equally between processors.

Installing the NIC

Before attempting to install a NIC in a computer, one should first find out what cards are already installed. The computer may already have a network card on board. If there are other cards, there may be possible conflicts in I/O addresses, DMA channel, shared RAM address and so on and the NIC will have to be configured to avoid these.

The NIC must be mounted in an appropriate expansion slot inside the PC. If it is a PCI card, for example, then it must go in a PCI slot. The computer's case must be opened and then the cover must be removed from the chosen expansion slot. The card must be inserted in the slot and then screwed up securely. If the card is a Plug and Play (PnP) card, the computer and the operating system will often be able to configure the card automatically. The hardware configuration settings that the NIC uses are an Interrupt Request (IRQ) and an I/O port address range. Most other expansion cards use the same system. The NIC needs the IRQ to get the operating system's attention when it wants to deliver data. (Interrupts were discussed in Chapter 9.) A few IRQs are available for use with add-on devices such as a network card. The card can be configured to use one of these IRQs. The NIC needs the range of I/O port addresses to send information about where the data will be.

When the server(s) and workstations have had NICs installed and have been connected to the LAN, the NICs need to be tested. Usually, the NICs will have with them a disk containing diagnostic software that can be used for testing purposes. The network operating system (NOS) will need to be configured to correspond to the NIC settings.

16.1.6   CUSTOMISING THE SERVER NOS

A directory structure will have to be decided upon. User and group accounts will have to be created. Access rights for users and groups to resources (such as files) can then be set. Login scripts, which set the user environments, must be created. When a user logs in, the login script will run, executing whatever commands are contained in it. Network printers must be configured. Various other custom features, such as password expiry periods, accounting and intruder detection must be set.

16.1.7   INSTALLING THE APPLICATIONS

A variety of applications software is available for use on LANs. After an application has been installed, it needs to be added to the network menu. Access rights to the application have to be set. If a software metering system is in use, the permitted number of simultaneous users has to be set.

16.2   NETWORK MANAGEMENT

The network may be just as important to a business as its electricity supply or its telephone network. Unfortunately, such a complex arrangement of hardware and software is bound to fail sooner or later. A business cannot function properly if its network is down, so network management that can help keep the network up and running is vital. Among the benefits that network management systems offer are measuring traffic levels, keeping a record of the locations of all hardware and software components and allowing the impact on the network of adding new users and applications to be assessed.

16.2.1   FUNCTIONAL AREAS OF NETWORK MANAGEMENT

The ISO management model offers a useful way of classifying network management, dividing it into five functional areas.

Fault management

Fault management is concerned with the detection, isolation and diagnosis of network faults. Various fault-testing devices are available. Examples of such devices include the time domain reflectometer and the protocol analyser. A *protocol analyser* is a monitoring device that provides statistical information on the network and attached devices. A *time domain reflectomete*r *(TDR)* can send signals through a cable to check continuity, length and other attributes. TDRs are used to find problems in the physical layer of a network.

Configuration management

Configuration management deals with administering and configuring network elements. Up-to-date records must be kept of wiring, workstations and NOS configuration. Some automated software tools are available to help with this.

Performance management

Performance management covers monitoring and evaluating the perform-ance of the network. Disk usage, CPU usage and traffic load must all be monitored. System logs have to be checked for errors and the server has to be tuned periodically.

Accounting management

The function of accounting management is to analyse the composition of traffic so as to be able to apportion the cost of the network infrastructure. Items to be looked after include addition and deletion of users and groups of users, assignment of home directories and creation and modification of access rights.

Security management

Security management deals with access control, authentication and encryption. Virus control also comes under this heading.

Aspects of managing a LAN that are not covered by the ISO model include applications management, backup of data and user support. Applications need managing in the sense that new network applications need to be installed and existing applications need to be upgraded. A sensible backup strategy is crucial to safeguard the company's data. Backups must be tested to make sure that they are usable. The network manager also has to provide the first line of support for users.

16.2.2 SIMPLE NETWORK MANAGEMENT PROTOCOL (SNMP)

The OSI management system itself is not used to any great extent. Instead, the Simple Network Management Protocol (SNMP) is commonly employed. There are also proprietary network management systems but these are beyond the scope of this book. SNMP was originally developed to manage TCP/IP-based networks but it has been extended to include other kinds of network.

Every SNMP-manageable device has an embedded SNMP agent that responds to SNMP requests. There is a network management station that can monitor and control network devices by issuing SNMP commands. The

SNMP commands access the Management Information Base (MIB) in the SNMP agent.

Management information base (MIB)

The MIB is a database that describes the status of the network device being managed. It consists of a large number of pieces of data, called *MIB objects*. For example, the MIB object bandwidthUsageCurrent displays the bandwidth currently consumed by a device. The MIB objects are organised in a hierarchy called the MIB tree. Some of them are read-only, while others are read-write. There is a standard way for manufacturers to add their own MIB extensions to the basic set of MIB objects.

SNMP protocol

SNMP frames are delivered via UDP. There are three major commands. The manager generates the *get* command to read a MIB object and the *Set* command to modify a MIB object. The agent generates the *Trap* command in order to report an event (for example, that a communication link has failed) to the manager.

Remote monitor (RMON) MIB

The RMON MIB is a special form of MIB that allows the RMON agent to provide information on a whole segment of a network. For example, objects from the History monitoring group can record periodic statistical samples from a network and store them for later retrieval. Using RMON, a network manager can see the traffic on a LAN segment even if it is on the other side of the world. RMON data comes mainly from the data-link layer. RMON II, a further development, adds support for layers 3 to 7. Figure 16.9 shows RMON probes being used to send network management information back to a central point.

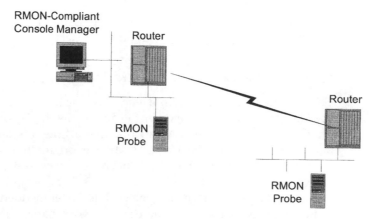

Figure 16.9 Use of RMON in a network

16.2.3 NETWORK MANAGEMENT SYSTEM

A network management system maintains a network map that displays the status of network devices. There is a graphical user interface with colour-coded status information. When network devices fail, alarms are generated. Such systems allow the user to utilise SNMP to query MIB objects. SNMP is used in the background continuously to query network device status.

16.2.4 NETWORK SECURITY

Network security is a major issue in this day and age. It is such a large topic that it can be treated only cursorily here. (Some aspects of security were touched on briefly in section 16.1.6.) However, it is important to point out that a network security policy is vital for an organisation, particularly if it is connected to the Internet. There are many facets to a successful security policy but one important means of enforcing it is the use of a firewall.

Firewalls

A firewall consists of software (and possibly hardware too) that can be configured to keep ill-intentioned intruders out of an organisation's network. Firewall designs may be classified into four types.

Most routers can be configured to perform *packet filtering*. (The main use of routers – routing packets – was described in sections 14.1.5 and 15.5.4.) Particular IP addresses, subnets or TCP or UDP port numbers can be blocked by using the filtering facilities offered by routers. Sadly, intruders can defeat packet filtering by constructing packets that appear to originate from a legitimate address but actually come from elsewhere ('packet spoofing').

Stateful inspection is the second kind of firewall design. Here, in addition to packet filtering, whole series of packets are checked. As well as working at the Network Layer like packet filtering, stateful inspection also works at the Transport Layer. For example, a TCP acknowledgement packet that was not preceded by a synchronisation packet with the right sequence number is suspicious and can be prevented from passing.

Application proxy firewalls operate at the Application Layer. This allows great flexibility in applying rules to network traffic. For example, FTP Puts can be prevented while Gets are permitted. An application proxy does Network Address Translation (NAT). NAT means that nobody outside the organisation's internal network ever sees the addresses or structure of the internal network. *Circuit-Level Gateways* are very similar to application proxies except that they do not operate at the Application Layer.

16.3 SUMMARY

This chapter has discussed the factors that need to be considered when installing a simple local area network (LAN) and when managing an existing network. Overall LAN design decisions were discussed and then detailed design decisions. Preparing the site for the installation, cable installation, workstation and server installation, customising the server operating system and installing the applications were also discussed.

Managing the network was also considered. Functional areas of network management were described, followed by Simple Network Management Protocol. Finally, there was a brief section on network security.

16.4 EXERCISES

1 What is the difference between the wiring of a crossover cable and a normal 'straight through' cable? For what purposes would these two kinds of cable be used?

2 Find out what tools are needed for do-it-yourself UTP cabling and, if possible, practise fixing RJ-45 plugs to a piece of cable. Try wiring a straight through cable and a crossover. If an electronic tester is available to you, test your work with it.

3 Explore the range of backup hardware that is commercially available. Which would be the most suitable device in the following situations (and why)? Consider ease of use, speed of recovery, capacity, duty cycle and cost.
   a a peer-to-peer LAN consisting of five PCs
   b a LAN consisting of 250 PC workstations and three servers that carry 'mission-critical' data

4 Explain the differences between a hub, a switch and a router.

5 Find out how to install the TCP/IP protocol for an operating system that is available to you.

6 Find out what the standard SNMP commands are and how they are used.

7 Find out what the standard RMON MIB objects are and what their purpose is. Then find out how one manufacturer has added to them and why.

Conclusion

This book has traced the structure of a computer system from basic logic concepts, from which fundamental circuits can be constructed, right through the many details of typical structures and on to sets of connected, communicating computers.

However, do not think that you now know all about computer architecture and communications. Many of the topics included here have only been introduced and in some cases are considerably more complex than appears. You can also be sure that it will not be long before some new ideas and techniques are introduced in order to improve the service a computer system might provide.

Index